the wild table

the wild table
SEASONAL FORAGED FOOD AND RECIPES

Connie Green
Recipes by Sarah Scott

Photography by Sara Remington
Foreword by Thomas Keller

VIKING STUDIO

OPPOSITE: *Black trumpet mushroom*

VIKING STUDIO

Published by the Penguin Group

Penguin Group (USA) Inc., 375 Hudson Street, New York, New York 10014, U.S.A.

Penguin Group (Canada), 90 Eglinton Avenue East, Suite 700, Toronto, Ontario, Canada M4P 2Y3 (a division of Pearson Penguin Canada Inc.)

Penguin Books Ltd, 80 Strand, London WC2R 0RL, England

Penguin Ireland, 25 St. Stephen's Green, Dublin 2, Ireland (a division of Penguin Books Ltd)w

Penguin Books Australia Ltd, 250 Camberwell Road, Camberwell, Victoria 3124, Australia (a division of Pearson Australia Group Pty Ltd)

Penguin Books India Pvt Ltd, 11 Community Centre, Panchsheel Park, New Delhi – 110 017, India

Penguin Group (NZ), 67 Apollo Drive, Rosedale, North Shore 0632, New Zealand (a division of Pearson New Zealand Ltd)

Penguin Books (South Africa) (Pty) Ltd, 24 Sturdee Avenue, Rosebank, Johannesburg 2196, South Africa

Penguin Books Ltd, Registered Offices: 80 Strand, London WC2R 0RL, England

First published in 2010 by Viking Studio, a member of Penguin Group (USA) Inc.

10 9 8 7 6 5 4 3 2 1

Copyright © Connie Green and Sarah Scott, 2010
Photographs copyright © Sara Remington, 2010
All rights reserved

Prop stylist: Ethel Brennan
Food stylist: Erin Quon
Food stylist assistant: Victoria Wollard
Camera assistant: Stacy Ventura

Publisher's Note

It is important to use caution when gathering and preparing wild edibles. Use reliable guidebooks and/or consult with a professional before partaking of any unfamiliar wild ingredients. The recipes contained in this book are to be followed exactly as written. The publisher is not responsible for your specific health or allergy needs that may require medical supervision. The publisher is not responsible for any adverse reactions to the recipes or ingredients contained in this book. Anyone participating in the activities that this book discusses or suggests assumes responsibility for his or her own actions and safety. The information contained in this book cannot replace professional advice, or sound judgment and good decision making.

ISBN 978-0-670-02226-7

Printed in the United States of America
Set in The Serif, Helvetica Neue
Designed by i4 Design, Sausalito, CA

LYNX! CONSORTIUM
BOISE MAIN LIBRARY

Items that you checked out

Title: Shroud of Eternity
ID: 31150015877463
Due: Sunday, October 30, 2022
Messages:
Item checkout ok.

Title: Siege of stone : sister of darkness
ID: 31150016596278
Due: Sunday, October 30, 2022
Messages:
Item checkout ok.

Title: The wild table : seasonal foraged food and
       recipes
ID: 31150012231847
Due: Sunday, October 30, 2022
Messages:
Item checkout ok.

Total items: 3
Account balance: $0.00
Sunday, October 2, 2022 11:27 AM
Ready for pickup: 0
Messages:
Patron status is ok.

For library hours call 208-972-8200
To Renew any items
Phone 208-384-4450 or visit
http://www.boisepubliclibrary.org

For my ancestors, whose communion with nature was no abstraction but a reality planted deep in their heart and gut. | **CONNIE GREEN**

For Ben Patterson—a wild and beautiful soul. | **SARAH SCOTT**

Contents

Foreword

As a child in the 1950s, I had my first encounter with mushrooms through a can. I have vivid memories of my mother's using Campbell's cream of mushroom soup whenever she cooked her beef stroganoff. While it was a humble and simple recipe, it remains one of my most beloved childhood memories and a favorite dish to this day. Later, working as a young chef in Rhode Island, I started adding dried mushrooms to my repertoire. But it was during my apprenticeship in France that I was exposed to their fresh counterparts and became skilled in their preparation. Morels, chanterelles, cèpes, the prized black truffles of Périgord, and the white truffles of Alba were some of the incredible varieties that I learned to cook well and appreciate. Mushrooms have an earthy quality that tends to add flavor, dimension, and a sense of luxury to almost any ingredient with which they are paired.

Opening the French Laundry in 1994 was the realization of a lifelong dream, and Connie was one of our very first purveyors at the restaurant. The quality of her mushrooms was so exceptional that she quickly earned the nickname the "Mushroom Lady." But while mushrooms were what she was known for, she has also brought in other outstanding wild foods for us to discover and enjoy, such as ramps, huckleberries, and sea beans. My philosophy is simple: to use the very best ingredients available in order to establish a memorable dining experience for our guests. Though they might never meet Connie face-to-face, her contributions help us with our success as a restaurant each and every day. She is an integral part of the process.

Connie continues to live up to her nickname by providing us with a wonderful array of mushrooms that are often the highlight of our menus at the French Laundry. They represent a simple, fundamental ingredient that, with the application of skill and patience, is capable of elevating any dish in which they are introduced. The mushrooms that she and her foragers discover throughout the year help us mark the passage of the seasons—from the first delicate morels of spring to the rich, luxurious porcinis of winter. As she steps into our kitchen to make a delivery, basket of mushrooms in hand, our chefs eagerly await to glimpse what new treasures they have unearthed for us that day. It is a ritual we look forward to each and every time.

—Thomas Keller, *The French Laundry*

Introduction

The call of wild foods was a gentle murmur when I first started gathering food. It was the sound of my grandmother's voice as we dug sassafras and picked scuppernong grapes. Delights like poke salad and mayhaws weren't just funny words in old country songs; they were hunted, put on the table, and eaten with great relish.

As the years passed, wild food retreated to the fringes of public interest, but it never lost its hold on me. I was probably standing at the low-tide mark in the late seventies, when I visited numerous San Francisco restaurants trying to sell my baskets of wild mushrooms. I found only two chefs who'd ever seen a chanterelle before—and both were French. One refused even to believe my mushrooms were chanterelles because "they do not grow in this country." The other chef recognized the fresh chanterelles but thought they were far too large. He informed me that the ones he was using from a *tin can* were superior because they were small and French. These were the two best-known chefs in San Francisco's two finest restaurants. Five years later, both restaurants' doors were closed and in had swept the dawn of fresh, local, seasonal California cuisine.

Now, more than three decades later, I find myself sitting squarely at the curious crossroads of the Stone Age and haute cuisine. I can't count the times over the years I've crawled out of the woods quite oblivious to the leaves and twigs in my hair and marched directly to a chef in a crisp white uniform. Thirty years ago the late, great chef Masataka was thrilled to parade me and my chanterelles past diners whose private jets were parked just a few miles from the woods I hunted. One minute I'm worried about how we can get our mushrooms across a raging creek and eight hours later I'm putting the fresh cèpes into the hands of a delighted sous-chef at the French Laundry.

At the "picker" forager camp you sit with muddy knees, hoping there's enough dry firewood or that the mother bear and cubs don't come back. Meanwhile, the chef in the immaculate whites prays his line cook isn't impossibly hungover. The camp crew has just enough water to rinse the black trumpets to put on the hot dogs (quite good!), while the chef wonders whether to cook them in *sous-vide*. Muddy jeans and glistening stemware, old pickup trucks and limousines, campfires and Viking ranges, a roll of bills and a wallet full of plastic: The contrasts may seem huge from a distance, but there isn't a hairbreadth of difference between the foragers' and the chefs' passion for their work. I know; I cross these worlds every day.

about foraged wild foods

This crossroads is a very interesting and increasingly busy place. The glamorous mushroom varieties like morels, porcini, or chanterelles are well known for very good reason. Gary Danko's roasted lobster with chanterelles or the classic combination of morels with asparagus are justly famous dishes. Yet there are more great treasures from the wild world waiting to be found or even remembered. A few are forgotten but hiding in plain sight, like the richest of all nuts, our native black walnuts. Others are little known, like the candy cap mushroom, which confounds and thrills taste buds with its maple mushroom flavor. More and more of America's chefs and home cooks are heading to the off-road world of untamed foods. Where they go, others will and do follow.

Pioneering chefs like my friend Daniel Patterson are born to experiment. I snipped off the chartreuse spring tips from a fir tree by my barn and gave some to Daniel. I pluck them for my salads because that particular fir has a unique flavor. Daniel fell in love. Now diners in his San Francisco restaurant, Coi, might be lucky enough to experience a heavenly green-hued oil tasting a bit like bitter orange peel, yet made from this fir. Even my chanterelle-infused vodka, a fixture at nearly twenty years of my annual chefs' mushroom forays, might be made by a boutique vodka maker. The flavor of the wild is sneaking back into our modern world.

While the food world is awash in celebrations of artisanal producers, organic growers, farmers' markets, and pioneering restaurants, more and more wild food is appearing and gaining star status. This is causing confusion for even experienced food folk. I'm often asked, for instance, if my chanterelles or some other wild food are organic. I have to say, "No, it's beyond organic." When the San Francisco farmers' market was first forming many years ago, I was approached to be a part of it. It was assumed that wild mushrooms, huckleberries, sea beans, and so on were organically certified. They aren't. They grow wildly where they want to grow, not where a governing body says they're allowed to grow. While an organic farmer is planting his or her crop in rows from atop a tractor, I'm out with baskets, making the rounds of my favorite chanterelle-bearing trees scattered over miles in the forest.

Another frequent question I get is "Where do you grow your wild mushrooms and wild foods?" I don't. I can't. They're *wild*! Most people can't wrap their minds around the reality that some of our most magnificent foods simply defy the taming of human cultivation. I, and other wild crafters, have to hike and search with great perceptiveness in our quest for the treasures scattered throughout a wild world. People are challenged to think of circumstances beyond human control, beyond agriculture. The foods in this book make "heirloom" varieties seem as if they were born yesterday. In the unfortunate wars of purity, wild foods—nature unvarnished—win. Once people remember and make the leap back to just what the word *wild* means, there's always a little glimmer of wonder.

This is a very romantic, mysterious, and inviting world. The story of wild foods—the gathering, the foragers, and the chefs who make art with these foods—is a compelling one. The chefs who receive the mushrooms and the diners cooing over the cuisine often haven't the foggiest notion of where the foods came from. Yet on that particular day morels have been picked by Rolly, Clint, and Russ in the Blue Mountains. Their closest neighbors are an elk herd. The nearest structure is a disintegrating gold mine. What looks like a lake is actually a field of blooming blue camas, the bulbs of which were once a staple in the diet of the natives there. The nearest pay phone is sixty miles away, but no matter. The men drive what they picked all the way to Pendleton to put them on a small plane. The next day I pick the mushrooms up at the airport, box them, and bring them in the door to this particular chef. These morels and sweetbreads will haunt his diners' taste buds that night.

As romantic as morel hunting in far-off mountains really is, the instinct for and love of foraging is much closer to home for most all of us. It can be as close as a nearby vacant lot or roadside. I lived in Chicago for two years and picked mulberries for weeks on my walk to work down

North Webster Avenue. At the heart of it all is the hunger to play a part or have a hand in what we put on our tables. Even when I see people at farmers' markets with bags and baskets in hand, I see the foraging spirit at work. These are not Walmart shoppers. Yet there's a step beyond the farmers' market, beyond farming, where our ancestors' culinary treasures have always awaited. The only genetic engineer there is nature herself.

wine forest

When asked "How did you get into this business?" I have to think back over thirty years of selling wild foods and the founding of Wine Forest. It does seem an odd path for someone with a degree from a fine college and a previous job in Chicago television. In Chicago I met my late husband, an Estonian whose very life was saved by his family's foraging skills during the starvation days as refugees in World War II Europe. He showed me my first chanterelle. After we moved to the hills above Napa Valley, where I still live, I was as surprised as anyone to find that what made me truly happy was crawling around the woods finding absurd quantities of chanterelles. Although I began with a passion and talent for putting wild foods on my own table, by 1980 this passion was spilling over and into restaurant kitchens.

In the beginning there was no clientele for wild foods. It took years of educating chefs and creating my own customers. I was a purveyor during the birth of the California food scene. Jeremiah Tower, Patty Unterman, and Judy Rodgers were in the early wave of customers. Bradley Ogden, Julian Serrano, Mark Franz, Cindy Pawlcyn, Hiro Sone, and many others joined my customer list later. Thomas Keller, Traci Des Jardins, Gary Danko, and too many more to name came in the 1990s.

As one of the earliest pioneers in the wild mushroom business in North America, it is so gratifying for me to hear the average Joe on the street say, "Nice chanterelles," as boxes are carried into a restaurant. It seems like yesterday when no one even knew what chanterelles were. Now, all these years later I still sustainably harvest the same mushroom patches on the same forested mountainside above Napa Valley. Looking down on *Michelin*-star-cluttered little Yountville while I hunt mushrooms, my love for this "work" just flows over me.

My relationship with chefs is unique. Almost all stop what they're doing and come with delight to see what I've brought. No fruit, vegetable, or protein holds a candle to the charge they get out of porcini buttons or whatever wild treat I've found. It took awhile to realize that I was bringing more to the kitchen than an exquisite ingredient. I was bringing clear proof of a wild, vibrant, and beautiful natural world far away from the hot, windowless kitchens from which most of our great cuisine flows. I'm the lucky one. The wild foods I carry in have an aura no other food has.

When I am leaving the kitchen, there's not a chef who doesn't ask, "Can I go with you sometime?" This sweet question led to my organizing chefs' forays. Chefs often work until 1:00 A.M. yet they'll still get up at 6:00 A.M. and drive the three hours north to meet me for a bouncy day of mushroom hunting. After a morning shot or two of frozen chanterelle vodka, we're off into the woods. These are magical weekends. The actual experience of foraging has been an enchanting influence on many chefs.

Whether it be kitchen-bound chefs or city slickers, these foraging experiences deeply touch people. People who forage for wild foods, even rarely, have a deeper appreciation of nature and a profound interest in preserving the habitats that are too often destroyed by those with no knowledge of or intimacy with wild country. Too much of our modern attitude toward nature implies that we look at it from a distance—that we look but not touch—that the purity of nature should remain "uncontaminated" by perverse human contact. This is not as it should be. We are, in fact, all animals. Whether we are Queen Elizabeth, a New York publisher, or a Navajo, we are all the descendants of successful hunter-gatherers who wandered in this natural garden.

When people find out what I do for a living, I'm inevitably deluged with curiosity and questions. How did you learn how to do this? Where do you find those? How do you cook that? Can I go with you?

Some might find this foraging passion all a bit far afield. In fact, I once thought that most sophisticated urban people found nature to be a dangerous stranger and wild food to be scary. How wrong I was. Everywhere people are besotted with the idea of foraging for food. People are insatiably curious about this. They want to join me on a foray or pour out their own experiences. These encounters have proven to me that there is a hunger for a perennial Easter egg hunt living secretly in the hearts of most all of us.

People simply fall in love with wild foods. Lord knows these wild things swept me away. Folks want to be seduced by their mystery, their freedom from the bonds of agriculture. Our human civilization, based on agriculture, has struggled for millennia to no longer depend on foraging in the wild. But here at the start of the twenty-first century, the old hunter-gatherer lurking in all of us just won't let go.

about the book

Unlike other cookbooks, *The Wild Table* calls on you to put on your jeans, grab a basket, and go outside. Although the list of foods in this book could go on for miles and miles over the river and through the trees, not every beloved wild food could find a place here at *The Wild Table*. I feel as if I've betrayed old pals like sassafras and shaggy manes by not inviting them. Yet the plants and mushrooms chosen here have not only great culinary merit, but can be found in widespread areas of the continent and are not at all endangered. Most, like huckleberries or nopales, are indigenous to North America, but I could not be a purist about this. Some tasty, now feral, foreign species like fennel and dandelions are included, as well as one former domesticate that wandered away from the farm.

the recipes

These recipes are born from coauthor Sarah Scott's genius for making everything delicious. Hours of our joyful brainstorming were followed by more than a year in Sarah's kitchen, where she turned a passionate tumble of wild foods into these utterly scrumptious and beautiful recipes. During that time you might have found a mountain of elderflowers piled on her picnic table while smelly ramp leaves covered the counters. She also chased some of my favorite chefs around their kitchens with measuring cups and translated their dishes into things even I can make.

After cooking with and for most of the world's greatest chefs during her years as executive chef at Robert Mondavi Winery, she found that her trips to the market for this book required hiking boots and bug repellent. She's a sport.

All of these delicious recipes preserve the essential character of these beautiful, wild ingredients, which have little parallel in the tamed world. Nature's elegance is reflected in recipes whose comfortable flavors belie ingredients that are strangers to many people. Although many of these wild ingredients can be found at some market somewhere, there is absolutely no better way to search for them than with your own feet, eyes, and heart.

Foraging Fundamentals and Etiquette

These aren't the Ten Commandments, but they are some well-learned guidelines for safety and mindfulness in the wild:

one

Be 100 percent positive of identification. Use at least two field guides and, ideally, find the company of a knowledgeable club or person (see Guidebooks and Sources, page 336). Don't depend upon common names; they vary wildly and imaginatively from region to region. Scientific names are not as daunting as you may think.

I gather a new wild food multiple times to study it well before I am actually comfortable eating it. Don't rush into identification with wishful anticipation. Slowly, you'll get to know the plant or mushroom at different stages of its growth. Distinguishing between a cucumber and a zucchini, or a lettuce and a cabbage, is far harder than identifying the wild foods in this book, so we can all do it. It's also important to be familiar with plants like elderberries that may have delicious and poisonous parts on the same plant, something they share with tomatoes and rhubarb.

two

Eat small amounts to start. Everyone seems to be allergic to something. If you haven't eaten the food, give your body a gentle introduction to it.

three

Have the right equipment, the most important of which is a good sense of direction, a compass, or a GPS, if you're going far. It's easy to become engrossed in hunting and forget your path. Rain gear, a knife, baskets, bags to separate your treasures, and good boots are all wise choices that are ultimately personal and specific to the plant or mushroom you seek. Something as simple as dry socks, a towel, or a stocked ice chest waiting at your car can be a beautiful thing.

four

Obviously, avoid gathering wild foods in polluted or sprayed areas. Roadsides can be excellent gathering areas, but I'd suggest gathering on the uphill side to avoid road effluent runoff.

five

Each plant in this book has slightly different gathering parameters. Some invading species like chickweed can and perhaps should be plundered wantonly. Others, like ramps or fiddleheads, must be conservatively harvested. The mushrooms in this book are saprophytic—meaning they grow on decaying matter—or mycorrhizal—those in long-term symbiosis with a tree. In both cases, you can harvest the mushroom without harming the remaining fungal body.

six

Don't trespass on private land and be aware of gathering policies on public land. Where you do hunt, leave it looking like you were never there. Not only is this polite, but it keeps your spot secret.

seven

We share these wild foods with wild creatures. Leave some for them and other people, for that matter. The natural abundance of many of these foods can be seductive, but do resist the urge to gather more than you can use. Wasting wild treasures because you couldn't eat, cook, or process them is a sad thing.

eight

Fight to preserve the wildlands you gather in. Loss of habitat is the main concern of many of us who forage. Loss of wild resources is invariably loss of habitat. Gathering wild foods will make you passionate about preserving and expanding the habitat that feeds you and the creatures within it.

nine

Take children with you. Pass on this love of nature and the tradition of foraging to them. Be forewarned: The little monsters are inevitably better at this than we are.

In the tangled labyrinth of our food system, nature ultimately feeds us all. Yet with these wild foods, the food transportation distance is just the length of our arms. The sheer joy and immediacy of finding our own wild foods are an intoxicating contrast to the convoluted channels that most food flows through on its path into our homes. This is more than just another expensive gourmet adventure. A fat wallet won't help you here.

The intimacy we have with wild foraging places goes beyond just the solace of nature. These places can fill your belly as well as your heart, just as they did our ancestors'. The beautiful wild foods here can all be gathered sustainably, but they can offer us even more than this. The homelands of these foods give us and, most important, our children a direct kinship with nature. As these places feed us, we foragers return the favor and become good stewards of our gathering lands. The person in a distant office calculating board feet of timber can be quite surprised at the passion of those of us who treasure that special creek with the fine elderberry trees, that stand of firs loaded with great chanterelle patches, or the onion-perfumed glade filled with ramps.

spring

Morels

MORCHELLA ESCULENTA; M. ELATA; M. CONICA,
AND OTHER MORCHELLA SPECIES COMPLEX

Morels can't be trusted. They'll be nowhere in sight when conditions are just perfect. You'll hunt in all the ideal places and end up scorned with nothing but an empty basket. Then another day they'll throw themselves at your feet, carpeting the ground before you. They are fickle, wily tricksters. But, God help us, we're totally shameless in our passionate pursuit of these little dimpled darlings.

I know it's ludicrous to ascribe such traits to a fungus. Yet I've scouted for hours at a time and returned to my truck empty-handed, only to find perky morels speckling the ground within twenty feet of the opposite side of the truck. You can almost hear the faint chuckling of the morel "divinity" as he tosses you these crumbs. Every serious morel hunter has had experiences like this. My fellow morel pickers and I often act out a silly superstition. After failing to spot any morels despite lengthy scouting, we declare to the woods or whomever is near, "I give up. There's none here." Quite often, the odd morel will pop into sight just as we surrender and turn to head back.

Now these troubles make me sound like an inept wooer of morels, but this isn't so. I'm actually a superb morel hunter. You must get what we call a hunting eye honed to the visual image of a morel. At the beginning of every season you could begin a fool's morel museum from the morel-mimicking assortment of misshapen pinecones, cone-shaped rocks, odd hunks of bark, and so on. Morel populations clearly fire up their decoy factory early in the season.

Describing a morel habitat is a challenge. Morels grow wherever they want to, but there are some generalizations possible. They *love* the sites of fires from the previous summer. They relish dying elm trees, diseased or dying white firs, sick ash trees, decrepit apple orchards, logged areas, poplars and cottonwoods along floodable creeks, bulldozed areas, raked campsites, and occasional concrete pours. In short, disaster makes them feel like fruiting. Although this predilection fits nicely into the personification of them as tricky, chances are that the morel fruiting body (the mushroom) appears spreading its spores for pure survival.

In this hemisphere, I've found morels from outside Toluca, Mexico, to the extremes of the Far North. The morels of the Midwest may not have the flashy glamour or abundance of the postfire morel carpets of the West, but they've proven to be as reliable as morels are able to be. A spring stomp through the hardwoods is traditional in much of the Midwest. The slick East and West Coast food crowd forget that Midwesterners have been smothering their steaks in morels for generations now.

Morels are so popular that most people know what they look like. They're almost always referred to as looking like a sponge or an unfortunate brain or, I think, like a honeycomb made by the world's sloppiest bees. Decades ago my parents, aunt, and uncle went morel hunting successfully with no more than a bad picture cut from the local paper. This was very, very dumb. Although the consequences are rarely dire, there are very vaguely "morelish" mushrooms that can confuse or even sicken some. Give your field guide a good cruise through and avoid the "false morel" gang of verpas and gyromitras.

Morels can be roughly grouped into three unruly piles. Because morels are notoriously difficult to identify to species for even morel scientists, we sort them into "naturals," "burn" morels, and gray morels. (The magnificent gray morels get their own place in the summer chapter. See page 87.)

The naturals are the best-known group. They include the beloved blond morels, *Morchella esculenta*, and the black morel complex. As a general rule, these morels have thick or double walls, visible by looking at the cut stem. This gang is fleshier and unfortunately at times houses wormy critters. The naturals are common in the Midwest and in disturbed ground habitats, like raked campgrounds, elsewhere.

Most burn morels are regarded in the professional picker world as *Morchella conica*. These can erupt after forest fires, making normally sane people crawl through sad charcoal landscapes with big smiles on blackened faces. *Conicas* are on the small side, are very thin walled, and are generally worm free.

I've put chefs through blind tastings of various morel types. Inevitably, gray morels win, followed by burn morels, and then naturals. Morel tastings must be on the activities list in heaven.

kitchen notes

CLEANING AND PREPARATION: Cut most of the stem off and look carefully for worms. Rinse each morel and give a swirl of water on the inside too (they're hollow), then place on a towel. *Don't* soak in water. You can cook the smaller ones whole, but cut larger ones in half like little boats, or even slice them across to make morel rings. Since morels are totally hollow, stuffing them is always a great idea (see pages 90–97). If worms are present, there is no secret method to banish them. Placing morels in a sealable container and gassing with CO_2 (a CO_2 bath) does not work. The best of imperfect options is to put the mushrooms on a tray in the freezer for fifteen minutes, then remove them before frozen. The worms often crawl out of their hiding places.

STORAGE: Don't dawdle, but, then, who can wait to eat these? After cleaning, refrigerate and use morels within a couple of days. The burn morels can easily last for five days.

IDEAL MORELS: An ideal morel is about the size of your thumb. If it is smaller than this, the morel usually hasn't had chance enough to spread its spores. The spores should be free of dirt, and the cut end should be short in length, worm free, and show no yellowing. Tap the morel over a surface and make sure no worms fall out.

ALERT: *Never eat uncooked morels!* I'm serious; uncooked morels will make you quite ill. They contain a nasty compound that volatilizes in the cooking process. You really *do* want your morels to be well cooked.

Morel and Toasted Rye Bread Soup

Stuart Brioza, a great chef and fine man to roam the woods with, cooked his way to a *Food & Wine* best new chef award while he was chef in the tiny town of Ellsworth, Michigan. Ellsworth is in the heart of the territory used for the annual Morel Hunting World Championship. Through the spring Stuart could hunt morels by day and cook them by night. Stuart's fluency with morels shows in this great yet simple soup, which distills the very essence of morels' rich flavor with the surprisingly harmonious touch of rye. Stuart recommends washing your morels hours ahead in lukewarm water. If it isn't a hot day, leave them out to dry out a bit.

Have all the ingredients ready before starting the soup as it comes together quickly once you begin.

[SERVES 4 TO 6]

1½ pounds fresh morels, washed,
   stems trimmed to ¼ inch
½ pound artisanal-style rye bread loaf, unsliced
8 tablespoons (1 stick) unsalted butter,
   at room temperature, cut into 8 pieces
2 teaspoons caraway seeds
5½ cups homemade chicken broth
1½ teaspoons molasses
4 teaspoons kosher salt
3 tablespoons extra virgin olive oil

Preheat the oven to 375°F. Position one rack in the top third of the oven and a second one in the bottom third.

Set aside ½ pound morels for garnish.

Closely trim the crust from the rye bread, ending up with just the brown outer pieces. Place the crusts on a baking sheet and set aside. Cut enough of the remaining bread into ¼-inch cubes to measure 1½ cups. Use any leftover bread for another dish.

Melt 1 tablespoon of the butter and toss with the cubed bread. Place on a separate baking sheet and bake for 6 to 8 minutes, or until golden brown. Set aside.

Heat a small sauté pan over medium-high wheat. Add the caraway seeds and toast, stirring frequently, until they are fragrant and just starting to smoke, about 1 minute. Immediately turn out onto a clean baking sheet to cool. When cool, place the caraway seeds in the center of a 4-inch-square piece of cheesecloth. Fold in the sides and roll up tightly, making a compact package. Tie securely with kitchen string.

Have ready a blender and a fine-mesh strainer set over a medium saucepan.

Place the chicken broth, molasses, 2½ teaspoons of the salt, and the caraway bundle in a large stockpot over high heat. Place the remaining 1 pound morels in a large bowl and splash with 2 tablespoons of the oil and 1 teaspoon of the salt. Toss or stir quickly to coat the morels evenly with the oil. Arrange in a single layer on a baking sheet.

When the broth reaches a simmer, place the morels and rye bread crusts in the oven and bake for 8 to 10 minutes, or until the morels are wilted and the crusts are dried out and fragrant.

Meanwhile, when the broth reaches a full boil, cover the pot, turn down the heat, and hold at a simmer. When the morels and bread crusts are almost done, after about 6 minutes, turn the heat back up on the broth so that it is at a full boil when they come out of the oven.

Remove the morels and bread crusts from the oven. Add the morels, along with any pan juices, to the boiling broth. When the broth returns to a boil, add the bread crusts, pushing them down into the soup to submerge them completely. Cook for 1 to 2 minutes, pushing and stirring the bread crusts into the broth. When the broth returns to a full boil, cover the pot and turn off the heat. Let sit for 2 minutes. Remove the caraway bundle, set it in a small bowl, and set aside.

Place half the soup in a blender. Start at the lowest speed and blend for 1 minute. Increase the speed by one level and continue blending until the soup is smooth, 2 to 3 minutes. Do not blend on high—the mixture will become too thick. Pour the mixture through the strainer into the saucepan, pushing down with the bottom of a ladle to extract all the liquid. Discard the solids. Repeat with the remaining soup. Squeeze the caraway bundle into the soup, extracting all the liquid, then discard.

Add the remaining 7 tablespoons butter to the soup all at once, whisking continuously until the butter is melted and blended into the soup. Hold in a warm place.

Toss the reserved ½ pound morels with the remaining 1 tablespoon oil and the remaining ½ teaspoon salt. Place in a single layer on a baking sheet and cook for 8 to 10 minutes, or until the morels are wilted and fragrant.

While the morels are cooking bring the soup just to a boil, whisking frequently, then hold at a simmer.

Divide the soup among 4 to 6 bowls and top with the morels and the reserved croutons.

TIPS AND TECHNIQUES

The soup and croutons can be made a day ahead. Cook the final morel garnish just before serving the soup. Store the croutons in an airtight container at room temperature. Store the soup in a closed container in the refrigerator.

SUBSTITUTIONS AND VARIATIONS

Dried morels can be substituted for fresh. They must be thoroughly rinsed to remove any sand or grit before using. Place 3 ounces dried morels into the broth, bring to a boil, then turn off the heat and let sit for 30 minutes. Strain out the morels. Reserve some for the final garnish. Skip the step of cooking the morels in the oven, adding them directly to the broth with the toasted bread crusts. For the garnish, sauté the reserved morels in a little butter or olive oil and season with salt and pepper.

Canned chicken or vegetable broth can be used instead of the homemade chicken broth. Use half the salt called for in the broth, then taste for seasoning when the soup is finished, adjusting as needed.

Ramp greens, slivered and sautéed or deep-fried, can be used as a garnish. For a heartier garnish, add slivered smoked duck breast along with the morels and croutons.

Basket-Grilled Morels

This is it. This is simply the best way to cook morels. Whether you're at a campfire cooking the day's pickings or at your backyard BBQ, get out a grill basket and cook until the accordion pleats of each morel have a touch of crispy about them. Pile the morels on grilled bread, pour a big glass of zinfandel, then eat, drink, and pity the fools who aren't eating this tonight.

[SERVES 4 TO 6]

1½ pounds large fresh morels (more than 3 inches), cleaned and cut in half vertically

8 tablespoons (1 stick) unsalted butter, melted

3 garlic cloves, finely minced

1 teaspoon kosher salt

¼ teaspoon freshly ground black pepper

Prepare a grill to medium heat.

Toss the morels with the butter, garlic, salt, and pepper in a large bowl. Place the morels in a grill basket and grill, tossing the morels occasionally, until they are golden brown and crisped around the edges, 10 to 15 minutes, depending on the fire.

Taste for seasoning, adjust as needed, and serve immediately.

Pan-Roasted Wild Salmon with Morels and Fava Beans

Quintessential flavors of spring come together in this simple but elegant dish. Salmon, morels, and fava beans have a natural affinity for one another, showing up around the same time each spring as they do. The "meaty" morels are a great match with the richness of the wild salmon, and the fava beans bring the fresh green taste of early spring to the mix. Everything for the dish can be prepared ahead and finished at the last minute, making this a great dish for entertaining.

[SERVES 4 TO 6]

---

1 pound fava beans, shelled

½ pound fresh morels, cleaned

4 tablespoons pure olive oil

1 teaspoon kosher salt, or more to taste

¼ teaspoon freshly ground black pepper,
    or more to taste

2 medium shallots, finely minced (about ¼ cup)

1 teaspoon finely minced garlic
    (1 large or 2 small cloves)

1½ cups chicken broth

Four 6-ounce wild salmon fillets, skin on,
    pin bones removed

½ cup crème fraîche

1 tablespoon fresh lemon juice

1 tablespoon finely minced fresh chives,
    plus more for garnish

1 tablespoon finely minced flat-leaf parsley

Bring a medium pot of salted water to a boil. Have ready a bowl of water and ice nearby. Add the fava beans to the pot and cook for 3 minutes. Drain and place immediately in the ice water. When cool, peel and set aside the beans.

Trim the stems on the morels to ¼ inch, saving the trimmings. Heat 2 tablespoons of the oil in a large sauté pan over medium-high heat. When the oil is hot, add the morels, tossing to coat evenly with the oil. Add ½ teaspoon of the salt and ⅛ teaspoon of the pepper. Cook until the morels have released their liquid, then continue cooking until the liquid has evaporated. Add 1 teaspoon of the shallots and the garlic to the pan and cook for 1 minute. Remove the morels from the pan and hold in a warm place. Set aside the sauté pan to use for finishing the sauce.

Place the chicken broth, morel trimmings, and the remaining shallots in a small saucepan over medium-high heat. Cook until the mixture is reduced to ½ cup. Strain through a fine-mesh strainer into a bowl and set aside.

Place the remaining 2 tablespoons oil in a large sauté pan over medium-high heat. Have a lid nearby that fits the sauté pan. Season the salmon fillets with salt and pepper.

When the oil is hot, place the fillets in the pan, skin side up. Make sure they are not touching. Cook until the bottoms of the fillets are golden brown and the flesh is just starting to turn color as it cooks. You will see this by looking or gently lifting the fillets with a spatula. Do not turn over the fillets. Cover the sauté pan and turn down the heat to low. This technique is called unilaterale and creates the contrast of a golden, crispy crust with tender, steamed flesh. Do not remove the lid while the fillets are cooking. Cook for 6 to 8 more minutes, depending on the thickness of the fillets. Finish the sauce while the salmon is cooking.

Place the reserved sauté pan over medium heat. Add the strained chicken broth and bring to a boil. Cook for 1 to 2 minutes to reduce the broth slightly, then whisk in the crème fraîche, lemon juice, the remaining ½ teaspoon salt, and the remaining ⅛ teaspoon pepper. Bring the mixture to a boil, then turn down to a brisk simmer and cook until the sauce is just starting to thicken, 2 to 3 minutes. Add the reserved fava beans and morels and heat them through. Add the chives and parsley. Taste for seasoning and adjust as needed. Hold in a warm place until the salmon is cooked.

to serve

Peel the skin off the salmon fillets in the pan. Using a flat spatula, gently remove the fillets from the pan, turning them over to serve them seared side up. Place on serving plates and spoon the fava bean and morel sauce around or over the top of each fillet. Sprinkle with chives.

TIPS AND TECHNIQUES

If using canned chicken broth, use half the salt called for in the recipe, then taste for seasoning just before serving. Vegetable or mushroom broth can also be substituted.

SUBSTITUTIONS AND VARIATIONS

Dried morels can be substituted for the fresh. They must be thoroughly rinsed to remove any sand or grit before using. Soak 1½ ounces dried morels in a bowl of hot water for 10 minutes to rehydrate, then proceed as for fresh in the recipe.

Heavy cream can be substituted for the crème fraîche. It will need a few more minutes of cooking time to reduce and thicken.

Fresh or frozen peas can be substituted for the fava beans. Cook briefly, just until tender, before using in the recipe.

This recipe can also be made with halibut or other firm-fleshed fish. Adjust cooking times for thinner fillets.

OPPOSITE: *Mateo's Roasted Veal Chop with Morel and Cacao Sauce* [PAGE 16]

Mateo's Roasted Veal Chop with Morel and Cacao Sauce

Many talented chefs have flowed from the kitchen of chef Julian Serrano. When he left San Francisco to open Picasso (launching the food explosion in Las Vegas), a diaspora of his talented protégés occurred in the West. Mateo Granitas was one of that tribe. Many years ago I marched into Mateo's new kitchen. He thrust a sauce-filled spoon at me. "Taste," he ordered. I did. It was the best morel sauce I'd ever had. Like a diabolical teacher, he grinned and asked, "What is it?"

"Could it possibly be chocolate? Where are you from, Mateo?" I asked.

Mateo turned his head, displaying his magnificent nose-rich profile, and retorted, "Where do you think?"

This gifted Yucateco could finally add his Mayan roots to his French training. The straight sugar-free cacao he used was grown by his mother in a cenote ("sinkhole") near Uxmal. With this sauce he had welded natural savory cacao to intense beef stock. I truly love it. Through the years I haven't been able to eat a morel without tasting a shadow of the cacao flavor that Mateo rightly targeted as a flavor component of morels. This dish tastes regal and reminds me that chocolate was once reserved for Mayan royalty. The triangle of morels, savory cacao, and meat in this dish is luxuriousness itself.

[SERVES 4]

Four 10- to 12-ounce veal rib chops
1 tablespoon cocoa nibs
2 tablespoons unsalted butter
1 shallot, finely minced
½ pound fresh morels, cleaned,
    stems trimmed to ¼ inch
2 tablespoons Madeira
3 ounces veal demi-glace
3 tablespoons beef broth
1 cup heavy cream
2 tablespoons finely grated high-quality
    unsweetened chocolate
1 tablespoon finely grated high-quality
    70% bittersweet chocolate
⅛ teaspoon ground cinnamon
Pinch of ground cloves
2 tablespoons pure olive oil
Fleur de sel

Position a rack in the center of the oven.

Preheat the oven to 400°F.

Place the veal rib chops on a baking sheet.

Place the cocoa nibs on a cutting board and, using a sharp knife, chop through them until they are the texture of coarse-ground pepper. Reserve ½ teaspoon of the chopped nibs. Sprinkle the remaining nibs evenly over the surface of the veal chops. If you will be cooking the chops within an hour, leave them at room temperature. If not, refrigerate them and bring them out 1 hour before cooking.

Place the butter in a medium saucepan over medium-high heat. When the butter is just starting to turn golden brown, add the shallot. Cook, stirring frequently, until the shallot is slightly caramelized and tender, 3 to 4 minutes.

Add the morels to the pan and stir to coat them evenly with the butter and shallot. Continue cooking until the morels are tender and starting to caramelize, 4 to 5 more minutes. (If you are using fresh morels, remove them from the pan at this point and set aside. If using dried morels, leave them in the pan and continue.) Add the Madeira and cook, stirring, until it has almost evaporated. Add the demi-glace and beef broth to the pan. Turn up the heat and bring to a boil. Cook for 1 to 2 minutes, or until the veal stock has reduced a bit, then stir in the cream. Bring back to a boil, then turn down the heat to a vigorous simmer.

Stir in the unsweetened chocolate, the 70 percent chocolate, the cinnamon, and the cloves. Stir briskly until the chocolates are melted into the cream. Stir in the reserved cocoa nibs. (Add the fresh morels back to the sauce at this point.) Cook until the sauce is thick and evenly colored, 3 to 4 more minutes. Remove the sauce from the heat and hold in a warm place while you cook the rib chops.

Place the oil in a large sauté pan over medium heat. Have a large baking sheet or shallow roasting pan lined with a rack nearby. When the oil is hot, add the veal chops to the sauté pan, being careful not to crowd the pan. You may have to cook them in batches. Brown on each side, 2 to 3 minutes per side. Remove to the baking sheet or roasting pan after they are browned.

Place the chops in the oven and roast until the internal temperature is 125°F for rare, about 15 minutes, or 135°F for medium rare, 5 to 6 more minutes. Remove from the oven and let rest for 10 minutes before serving.

Reheat the sauce over low heat. Spoon the sauce over and around the veal chops and top with a sprinkling of fleur de sel.

TIPS AND TECHNIQUES

Use a Microplane to grate the chocolates. The fine texture will melt into the sauce more evenly.

Veal demi-glace can be found in the freezer section of grocery stores. Its richness adds to the velvety texture of this sauce. Thaw before using.

SUBSTITUTIONS AND VARIATIONS

Dried morels can be substituted for the fresh. They must be thoroughly rinsed to remove any sand or grit before using. Soak 1½ ounces dried morels in a bowl of hot water for 10 minutes. Lift out of the water, leaving any dirt behind, squeeze dry, and proceed as for the fresh morels.

This sauce would also work with pork chops or chicken breasts.

Ramps

ALLIUM TRICOCCUM

Ah, eau de ramp! Let others daub themselves with attar of roses. A real food person's head is spun by ramp cologne. Looking as they do like sweet lilies of the valley, ramps could not be more surprising. They are a notoriously smelly wild onion. These, our native wild leeks, are treasured by diners at the grandest of restaurants as well as by self-proclaimed hillbillies in the "rampuncious" ramp festivals that spread across West Virginia, ramp mecca, in April and May.

These small-town festivals touch my heart . . . and nose as well. That so many communities gather in a rite of spring to celebrate the ramp speaks highly of these hill folk. While strong onion essence and smoky bacon fill the air, an old medicinal tradition lies beneath the party. Ramps have long been regarded as a spring tonic in rural areas. With all the health virtues of onions and a nice blast of vitamin C, all medicine should be this delicious.

There is a stigma attached to "hillbilly" ramp eating. Schoolteachers of a more modern tradition were known to exile children who smelled of ramps. One of my customers, Tim Wheatley, now in the glamorous Las Vegas food world, grew up with his North Carolina family feasting madly on ramps on Saturdays only. They couldn't eat them Monday through Friday because of school, or on Sunday because of church. In those recent but more rigid times, the restrictions must have been very frustrating, because the season is a brief four to six weeks.

Wild onions or garlic of one species or another grow all over the world. They are linked by the distinct "oniony" aroma signature that also advertises their safety.

The luxurious place in which ramps find themselves situated in the culinary world is similar to their natural environment. They grow in rich, moist glades with fertile soils. Most in the culinary world place ramps at the top of the wild onion world. Other types of wild onions range far and wide, however. Once, after an epic day of morel gathering at Devils Gap with my pal Patrick, we sat bone tired on an old lava flow, looking over a magnificent stretch of the Sierras. Just below us, veins of small pink flowers filled cracks in the old lava. As we leaned over to look, the smell was adequate introduction. All the dainty pink posies were wild onions emerging from a hardscrabble life among the rocks. We pried out a few bulbs and cooked them on the fire with some of the morels from our mighty haul that day.

Whether they are the rugged little pink onions or the lush hollows of ramps, they are not limitless, however. The carpets of ramps that line the sides of creeks in much of the central United States do not go on forever. Experienced gatherers know to remove only part of the ramp clumps with their ramp hoes or shovels and to leave the rest of the cluster to fill in the gap the following season.

In traditional American cooking, ramps have eggs, bacon, and potatoes as favorite dance partners. One classic hill country recipe calls for local trout, split and stuffed with whole ramps, to be wrapped in foil and tossed on the grill. The chefs in my world have embraced pickled ramps as a classic creation of spring.

kitchen notes

CLEANING AND PREPARATION: Clean the dirt from the ramp base by blasting the dirt off with a hose. Leave the root tendrils on. Gently mist the leaves. Put the ramps upright in a small amount of water like smelly flowers.

COOKING METHODS: Grilling lightly oiled whole ramps or pickling (see page 311) are classic ways to prepare ramps.

STORAGE: Keep them far from the chocolate cake in your refrigerator. They will keep for five days this way after harvest.

IDEAL RAMPS: They will have fresh leaves with no trace of wilting or slime. The stalk will be larger than a pencil and smaller than a cigar. Whether to choose a stalk that is straight or beginning to form a bulbous shape, as it does later in the season, is personal preference.

Ramp and Shrimp Grits [PAGE 22]

Ramp and Shrimp Grits

This plate is prettier than an Easter egg. Perhaps the only enhancement is for the friends around your table to be drinking champagne while attired in pink or purple to complete the lovely colors of the dish.

Ramps have a reputation for furious "onioniness," and yet they have a warm and gentle side too. That's just what you'll find in this ramp pesto. The intense green of these ramp pesto grits comes from the subtle-flavored ramp leaves. The jaunty pink shrimp's taste is not at all swamped by the bed of rampy green grits.

Consider making extra ramp pesto and squirreling it away for tasty and vibrant pastas, potatoes, or rice. This dish just isn't complete without a hunk of great bread to chase the grits around the plate.

[SERVES 4 TO 6]

1 pound medium or large shrimp, shells on
¼ cup dry white wine
1 shallot, thinly sliced
1½ teaspoons kosher salt
1 cup quick-cooking grits
4 tablespoons (½ stick) unsalted butter
¼ teaspoon freshly ground black pepper
4 garlic cloves, finely minced
2 teaspoons fresh lemon juice
½ cup Ramp Pesto (page 308)
2 tablespoons crème fraîche
2 tablespoons fresh chive pieces (½ inch)

Peel and devein the shrimp, saving the shells.

Place the shrimp shells in a medium saucepan. Add the white wine, shallot, and 4 cups cold water. Bring to a boil, then turn down the heat to a bubbling simmer and cook for 20 minutes. Turn off the heat and let the shells steep in the liquid for 10 minutes.

Strain the liquid into a 4-cup measuring cup and discard the shells. Add enough cold water to make 4 cups. Place in a medium saucepan over medium-high heat, add 1 teaspoon of the salt, and bring to a boil. Whisk in the grits, bring to a boil, then cover and cook over very low heat, stirring occasionally, for 8 to 10 minutes, or until creamy. Hold in a warm place while you cook the shrimp.

to finish

Place the butter in a large sauté pan over medium-high heat. When the butter is melted and bubbling, add the shrimp, the remaining ½ teaspoon salt, and the pepper. Toss the shrimp in the butter and cook, stirring occasionally, until the shrimp are just pink. Add the garlic and finish cooking, another 2 to 3 minutes. Stir in the lemon juice.

Stir the ramp pesto into the grits, then stir in the crème fraîche.

Divide the grits among 4 to 6 bowls and top with the shrimp. Garnish with the chives.

TIPS AND TECHNIQUES

This dish can be served in individual bowls for a more elegant presentation or on a deep platter for a buffet.

Make a version of garlic toast using Ramp Butter (page 319) and grated Parmesan to serve on the side.

SUBSTITUTIONS AND VARIATIONS

Artisanal grits or polenta can be substituted for the quick-cooking grits.

Equal parts of clam juice or chicken broth and water, or simply water alone, can be substituted for the shrimp stock when cooking the grits.

Basil pesto can be substituted for the ramp pesto.

The crème fraîche can be eliminated from the recipe, if desired.

Twice-Baked Ramp and Goat Cheese Soufflés

The pungent, heady reputation of the ramp is tamed in these light-as-air soufflés. Gently stewed in butter, the ramp bulbs and greens release their natural sweetness. When they are combined with the tangy fresh goat cheese in this make-ahead soufflé, the result is a light, savory, and elegant dish that is perfect for brunch, for lunch, or as part of a multicourse dinner.

[MAKES 8]

for the ramps

¼ pound ramps with greens, washed
    and root ends trimmed
2 tablespoons unsalted butter
½ teaspoon kosher salt
⅛ teaspoon freshly ground black pepper

Cut the greens off the ramps. Slice the bulbs in half lengthwise, then crosswise into fine slivers. Gather the greens and cut them into very thin ribbons, about ⅛ inch wide.

    Heat the butter in a medium sauté pan over medium-high heat. When the butter is melted and bubbling, add the ramp bulbs and stir to coat evenly. Turn down the heat to low and cook the ramps until tender, about 5 minutes. Add the ramp greens and continue cooking until they are wilted and tender, 3 to 4 more minutes. Season with the salt and pepper and set aside to cool.

for the soufflés

4 tablespoons (½ stick) unsalted butter,
    plus more to butter the ramekins
¼ cup unbleached all-purpose flour
2 cups milk
3 ounces soft goat cheese
2 tablespoons plus ¼ cup grated Parmesan
3 large egg yolks
2 teaspoons kosher salt
¼ teaspoon freshly ground black pepper
4 large egg whites
1½ cups heavy cream
2 tablespoons finely minced fresh chives

Position a rack in the center of the oven. Preheat the oven to 350°F.

    Butter the bottom and sides of eight 4-ounce ramekins. (Or spray evenly with cooking spray.) Place the ramekins inside a large roasting pan. Bring a large pot of water to a simmer as you make the soufflés.

    Place the butter in a medium saucepan over medium heat. When the butter has melted, whisk in the flour until smooth. Continue whisking until the mixture turns light golden brown, 5 to 6 minutes. Add the milk in a slow, steady stream, whisking continuously to eliminate lumps. Turn up the heat and bring the mixture to a boil, whisking continuously. Turn down the heat to low and cook until the mixture is thickened and smooth, about 4 minutes. Whisk in the goat cheese and 2 tablespoons of the Parmesan. Transfer the mixture to a large bowl and let cool for 10 minutes. Whisk in the egg yolks, salt, and pepper. Stir in the cooled ramps.

Place the egg whites in the bowl of a standing mixer fitted with the whip attachment. Beat the egg whites until they hold a soft peak, 5 to 6 minutes. Using a large rubber spatula, fold one-third of the beaten egg whites into the goat cheese mixture. Add the remaining egg whites and fold them in quickly and evenly.

Divide the mixture among the prepared ramekins. Pour simmering water inside the roasting pan until it comes halfway up the sides of the ramekins. Carefully place the pan in the oven and bake for 30 to 35 minutes, or until the tops of the soufflés are puffed and golden brown.

Remove the soufflés from the roasting pan to a wire rack and cool for 20 minutes. If they are still too hot to handle, let them cool a little bit longer. Run a thin knife around the inside of each ramekin to loosen the soufflés. One at a time, turn over each ramekin and gently shake it until the soufflé releases into the palm of your hand. Quickly turn over the soufflé and place it on a baking sheet. Use a light touch. Cool the soufflés to room temperature. (At this point, the soufflés can be covered with plastic wrap and refrigerated for up to 2 days.)

to serve

Turn the oven up to 425°F.

Place the soufflés, with at least 1 inch of space between them, in a large baking dish. Drizzle the cream over the tops of the soufflés, covering them generously. Top with the remaining ¼ cup Parmesan.

Bake for 8 to 10 minutes, or until the soufflés are puffed and deep golden brown. Using a spatula, carefully transfer the soufflés to serving plates. Spoon some of the cream around the soufflés or over the top. Garnish with the chives.

TIPS AND TECHNIQUES

If serving the soufflés a day or two later, remove them from the refrigerator an hour ahead of time to come to room temperature.

Removing the soufflés from the ramekins while they are still a little warm makes it easier to release them.

SUBSTITUTIONS AND VARIATIONS

Scallions or green garlic can be substituted for the ramps. Use one bunch, or about 6 green onions or bulbs of green garlic. Adding 1 finely minced garlic clove during cooking will re-create the complex flavor of the ramps.

The same amount of blue cheese or Gorgonzola can be substituted for the goat cheese.

Ramp-Up Sunday Brunch Scrambled Eggs

There's a good reason why ramps and eggs are served at all the ramp festivals. The hillbilly breakfast trinity of ramps, eggs, and bacon is a boisterous way to begin a weekend spring day. While the other two ramp recipes here show the gentler side of ramps, these slowly scrambled eggs proclaim their oniony glory. Munching on the ramp swizzle stick in your bloody Mary is the crowning touch to complete the traditional breath treatment for your own home-based ramp festival.

[SERVES 4 TO 6]

12 large eggs
¾ teaspoon kosher salt, or more to taste
¼ teaspoon freshly ground black pepper,
    or more to taste
6 ounces cleaned ramps with greens
3 tablespoons bacon fat or unsalted butter
Bloody Marys garnished with fresh ramps
    (optional)

Whisk together the eggs, salt, and pepper in a medium bowl. Set aside while cooking the ramps.

Cut the greens off the ramps and slice them into ¼-inch strips. Cut the bulbs into ¼-inch dice.

Heat the bacon fat in a large sauté pan over medium heat until hot. Add the ramp bulbs and sauté until tender and translucent, 3 to 4 minutes. Add the greens and cook until wilted and tender, 2 to 3 more minutes.

Pour the eggs into the sauté pan with the ramps and turn down the heat to medium low. Cook, stirring constantly with a wooden spatula or spoon, gathering the cooked portion as it forms curds and stirring the curds back into the liquid to form a creamy, moist scramble. Depending on the heat, this will take from 5 to 7 minutes. For moist eggs, remove them from the pan just before they are fully cooked and still look wet. They will continue to cook a little bit more off the heat. Taste for seasoning and add more salt and pepper as needed.

TIPS AND TECHNIQUES

The slow stirring method for scrambling the eggs produces a creamy texture. For larger curds, turn up the heat slightly and stir less often.

The bacon fat gives this a southern taste and is a nice flavor complement to the ramps.

SUBSTITUTIONS AND VARIATIONS

You can add grated cheese—Monterey Jack or Gruyère, for example—to the eggs halfway through cooking. A milder, nuttier cheese will complement the flavor of the ramps.

Scallions can be substituted for the ramps. There is no need to separate the greens from the white parts of the onions when cooking.

The sautéed ramps can also be used as a filling for an omelet or in a frittata.

Fiddleheads
[Ostrich and Lady]

MATTEUCCIA STRUTHIOPTERIS; ATHYRIUM FILIX-FEMINA

Certainly a fiddlehead fern is one of the most beautiful forms on our planet. If nature makes a more graceful form, I just can't think of what it might be. How much more beautiful are they after months of bitter cold and walls of snow? How much more lovely did they seem when, in years past, they appeared as April cellars were reduced to the last grim pickled cabbages or beets? The hunger for something of vibrant green that goes crunch between your teeth must have been fierce.

The great ostrich fiddleheads of the Northeast and the lesser-known lady fern fiddleheads of the Pacific Northwest curl from the cold spring ground as tight green coils resembling the scrolled neck of a violin. These charming green spit curls emerge from the heart of the dormant winter fern. A circle of dead brown fronds lies as a shadow of last year's verdant resident fern.

The ostrich fern is what most folks think of as the true edible fiddlehead fern. Although still somewhat obscure in the rest of the country, the ostrich fern is an emblem of spring in New England and Canada. They begin to peek out in May in the southern areas of their range. As spring moves north, they often continue until mid-June in Canada and chilly parts of Maine. They're a rich emerald green color and have a distinct groove running up the stem on the inside of the curl. Bits of peanut skin–like husks are attached here and there, but you can remove these bitter scales with a little water soak and light rubbing. Because most people cook fiddleheads like asparagus, many think they taste like it too. They remind me, however, of lovely green beans.

The ostrich fern is superior in flavor to the lady fern, but it comes late to the party. The lady fern of the Pacific Northwest begins in early April, weeks before the ostrich fern. Both ferns are found in the shady, moist habitats that most ferns favor. The lady fern fiddlehead is chartreuse and, after cleaning, is quite naked in comparison to its northern cousin, whose spiral is shrouded by the infant leaves wrapped around the stem curve in front of it. Before cleaning, the lady fiddlehead has

OPPOSITE: *Lady fern fiddleheads*

a difficult-to-remove orangutan-colored fur covering it. Considerable soaking and rubbing are required to remove it. Both the lady fern's fur and the ostrich fern's peanut skin must be thoroughly removed because they contain dreadfully bitter compounds. Failure to properly clean them is the main reason for some people's distaste for fiddleheads.

However eager hungry hands are to pick these, thoughtful harvest methods are very important. As the fern wakes from its winter dormancy, the six or seven first fiddleheads are what the plant has with which to rally back to life. You can harvest only a part of the plant's strength or it can dwindle and die. Half these fiddleheads, usually two to three curls per season, are your limit. Snap these off at the base and walk away until next year. Refer to your field guides, of course, and be sure to pick the ferns only when they are tightly curled. Unfurled fronds become somewhat toxic. The fern you've left behind will become a very large, five- to six-foot-high mass of long single fronds that resemble the ostrich plumes they're named for. The ancient fern family has survived grazing dinosaurs; make sure it survives you.

The culinary playing field for fiddleheads has lots and lots of running room. There's very little European culinary tradition for fiddleheads. The Japanese, however, have a great affection for the bracken fern fiddleheads and another fern like our ostrich. Warabi, the bracken fern, is very popular in Japanese soups. Fiddlehead tempura comes from the Japanese tradition and makes great use of the fern's crunchy qualities. Canadians and New Englanders have a very special passion for fiddleheads. It's common to see fiddleheads pickled in jars, in cans, or bagged and frozen. This is still a lightly touched playground for the adventurous cook. For example, I think a pickled fiddlehead looks great coiled in the bottom of a martini.

One freakishly early spring I had some fiddleheads the day before St. Patrick's Day. I marched up to a chef and said, "Look, they're perfect. Just like the staff of Saint Patrick." I was so excited at the prospect of little Saint Patrick crosiers on an early-spring plate. The chef looked at me like I was mad. Poor thing had no poetry in his soul.

OPPOSITE: *Ostrich fern fiddleheads*

kitchen notes

CLEANING AND PREPARATION: Time, water, and patience are required here. Put the fiddleheads in a colander and run cold water through while stirring and rubbing them against each other and the colander to remove fur and scales.

COOKING METHODS: For general use, both ferns should be blanched. The ostrich fern is nicely cooked in boiling water, or steamed, for 5 minutes. Follow with an ice water bath. The northwestern lady fern, with its bitter component, benefits from blanching two times. Boil this variety for 4 minutes, drain, and boil again for 4 minutes in a new batch of boiling water. Again, follow with an ice water bath. The still slightly firm fiddleheads are ready for sauces, salads, or any wild idea.

STORAGE: After they are washed, keep fiddleheads in a plastic bag, folded not sealed, with a little moisture. No paper towel inside is necessary. They'll keep for well over a week in your refrigerator.

IDEAL FIDDLEHEADS: They should be snapping crisp, with a very tight curl. Don't use any that are unfurled. The ostrich fiddlehead should be emerald green, while the lady fiddlehead should be bright chartreuse, with no dark patches on either. The brown color of the end cut is not very important because the cut turns brown very quickly and doesn't reflect freshness. Make *sure* that the fiddleheads are rubbed clean and are free of the bitter fur or scales.

Todd Humphries's Fiddlehead and Mussel Soup

Cooking nature's little green bedsprings didn't come naturally to the likes of a girl raised in the semitropics. Mercifully, my clues came from Todd Humphries, the chef/owner of St. Helena's Martini House. Fresh from New York's revered Lespinasse, this lovely and urbane chef taking charge at San Francisco's coveted Campton Place had a wild side that the food press didn't see. Todd is a native of Regina, Saskatchewan. He's been hunting and cooking fiddleheads since before he knew the name of a single Manhattan restaurant. Providing Todd with fiddleheads is like giving a kitten string. One year he created this elegant soup as a farewell to our last batch of fiddleheads.

[SERVES 4 TO 6]

for the mussels

4 tablespoons (½ stick) unsalted butter

¼ cup thinly sliced shallots (1 large or 2 medium)

1 tablespoon thinly sliced garlic

1 fresh thyme sprig

1 bay leaf

3 pounds mussels, washed and debearded
   (discard any mussels that are cracked
   or broken)

½ cup dry white wine

1 cup chicken broth

Place the butter in a large pot over medium-low heat. When the butter is melted and bubbling, add the shallots and garlic. Cook, stirring occasionally, for 3 to 4 minutes, or until the shallots and garlic are translucent. Add the thyme and bay leaf and cook for 1 more minute. Add the mussels, stirring to coat them evenly with the butter. Cook, uncovered, for 2 minutes. Add the white wine, turn up the heat to medium high, and bring to a boil. Cook for 2 minutes to burn off the alcohol, then add the chicken broth. Bring the mixture back to a boil,

cover the pot, and turn down the heat to low. Steam the mussels until the shells open and the flesh is plump and full, about 5 minutes. Discard any that do not open.

Drain the mussels and their cooking liquid through a colander into a large pot or bowl. You should have between 2 and 3 cups of liquid. Let the mussels cool in the colander.

When the mussels are cool, remove the meat from the shells. Discard the shells and set aside the mussels in a cool place until ready to use.

for the soup

4 tablespoons (½ stick) unsalted butter

¼ cup thinly sliced shallots (1 large or 2 medium)

1 tablespoon thinly sliced garlic

1¼ pounds ostrich fern fiddleheads, cleaned

Reserved mussels cooking liquid (above)

1½ cups heavy cream

¼ teaspoon finely chopped fresh rosemary
   or ⅓ teaspoon dried

⅛ teaspoon cayenne pepper

2 teaspoons fresh lemon juice

2 teaspoons kosher salt

4 grinds of white pepper (⅛ teaspoon)

1 tablespoon finely minced fresh chives

Heat the butter in a large pot over low heat. When the butter is melted and bubbling, add the shallots and garlic.

Cook, stirring occasionally, until the shallots and garlic are tender and translucent, about 4 minutes. Add the fiddleheads. Cook, stirring occasionally, for 2 minutes. Add the mussel cooking liquid and bring to a boil. Turn down the heat to low and simmer for 5 minutes. Stir in the cream, bring back to a boil, then turn down the heat and simmer for 5 to 6 more minutes.

Remove the pot from the stove and remove the fiddleheads with a slotted spoon or strainer. Set aside ¾ cup fiddleheads. Place the remaining fiddleheads in a blender and add half the soup. Puree until smooth, 3 to 4 minutes. Add the remaining soup and, starting on low, blend briefly to combine. Add the rosemary, cayenne pepper, lemon juice, salt, and white pepper and blend briefly to incorporate. Return the soup to a clean pot.

to serve

Heat the soup just to a boil, whisking occasionally.

Place the mussels and reserved fiddleheads in a small pot, ladle in a small amount of the soup, and place over low heat. When hot, divide the mussels and fiddleheads among 4 to 6 soup bowls and ladle in the soup. Garnish with the chives.

TIPS AND TECHNIQUES

Be careful blending the hot soup: It can explode out of the blender easily if the lid is too tight. To prevent this, remove the small glass or plastic insert in the blender lid and cover the opening loosely with a kitchen towel while you have the blender running.

After blending it, the soup can be strained through a fine-mesh strainer for a smoother consistency, if desired.

For a thicker soup, peel 3 small Yukon Gold potatoes, dice them into ¼-inch cubes, and add them to the pot with the fiddleheads. Continue with the recipe as directed.

If using canned chicken broth, use half as much salt as the recipe calls for, then taste and adjust at the end.

SUBSTITUTIONS AND VARIATIONS

If ostrich fern fiddleheads are not available, lady fern fiddleheads can be substituted. The fiddleheads need to be blanched ahead of time to remove bitterness (see page 32). After blanching, proceed as for the ostrich fern fiddleheads in the recipe.

In some parts of the country, frozen fiddleheads are available. Use as directed for the ostrich fern fiddleheads in the recipe.

Fresh asparagus can be substituted for the fiddleheads. Use the same amount in weight. Remove and discard the woody part of the stems, then dice the asparagus into ¼-inch pieces. Blanch just until tender, 2 to 3 minutes, then place into an ice water bath. Proceed as for the fiddleheads in the recipe.

Spring Fry: Fritto Misto of Fiddleheads, Ramps, and Asparagus with Meyer Lemon Aioli

OK, maybe not for breakfast . . . It's embarrassing to say that I could eat this each and every spring day. Who loves pretty, crunchy, crispy fried things? Everybody! People just don't fry at home enough, considering the deliciousness it brings. The secret frying weapon is having a pan dedicated solely to having oil ready to put on a burner for frying. You'll be ready to go for at least one more fry if, after frying, you cool, strain the oil to get out the brown bits, put a tight-fitting lid and/or plastic wrap on top, place the container with oil in a cool location, and you're ready to go for at least one more fry. You'll be ready for ramp hush puppies or this great spring fry. Lemon slices, dipped and fried with the spring treats, are a sparky addition.

[SERVES 4 TO 6]

for the fritto misto

4 quarts peanut or vegetable oil

3 cups unbleached all-purpose flour

1 cup cake flour

1 large egg

2 cups buttermilk

½ teaspoon kosher salt, plus more to taste

¼ teaspoon freshly ground black pepper

1½ to 2 pounds mixed fiddleheads, ramps, and asparagus, cleaned and patted dry

Place the oil in a 6- to 8-quart pot and heat it to 375°F.

Sift together the all-purpose and cake flours and place them in a wide bowl or on a platter. Whisk together the egg, buttermilk, salt, and pepper in a large shallow bowl.

While the oil is heating, prepare the vegetables, making sure that they are dry before coating. To avoid gluey fingers, use one hand for wet dipping and the other for dry. Working with a few pieces of the vegetables at a time, dip them into the buttermilk mixture, coating them well. Lift them out, letting the excess buttermilk drip off, then drop them into the flour mixture, working quickly to coat them evenly with the flour. Shake off any excess flour and lay the vegetables in a single layer on a large parchment paper–lined baking sheet. Continue until all the vegetables are coated.

When the oil is hot, carefully add the vegetables to the pot but do not overcrowd. Fry until golden brown, 2 to 3 minutes. Give the vegetables a stir as they fry, turning any that are browning unevenly. Using a slotted spoon or flat strainer, remove the vegetables and place on a paper towel–lined baking sheet. Sprinkle with salt. Hold in a warm place while frying the rest of the vegetables. Be sure to bring the oil back up to temperature before adding the next batch.

Serve warm with the Meyer Lemon Aioli.

for the Meyer lemon aioli

½ cup extra virgin olive oil
½ cup pure olive oil
1 large or 2 small garlic cloves
1 teaspoon kosher salt
1 large egg
1 large egg yolk
Finely grated zest of 1 Meyer lemon
2 tablespoons fresh Meyer lemon juice

Combine the extra virgin olive oil and the pure olive oil in a measuring cup with a spout.

Place the garlic and salt in the bowl of a food processor. Process until the garlic is finely minced and beginning to liquefy. Add the whole egg and egg yolk. Process for 30 seconds. With the machine running, slowly begin to drizzle in the oil. As the mixture thickens, the oil can be added a little more quickly. Add the lemon zest and lemon juice and process briefly to mix in. Taste for seasoning and adjust as needed. If the aioli is too stiff, add water in ½-teaspoon increments to thin.

TIPS AND TECHNIQUES

Coating the vegetables ahead of time makes the coating adhere better when frying. This can be done up to 20 to 25 minutes ahead.

Thinner or medium-size asparagus will cook more evenly for this recipe.

SUBSTITUTIONS AND VARIATIONS

Almost any vegetable can be substituted in this recipe. Cut the vegetables into sizes that will allow them to fry quickly and evenly.

Regular lemons can be substituted for the Meyer lemons.

Fresh chopped herbs, such as chives, chervil, tarragon, basil, or flat-leaf parsley, can be added to the aioli just before serving.

Spruce and Douglas Fir Tips

PICEA, VARIOUS SPECIES; PSEUDOTSUGA MENZIESII

It's right about here that I can feel someone thinking "Just how far is too far into the wild?" You might even remember the old Euell Gibbons cereal commercial and the line "Did you ever eat a tree?" But steel-jawed gnawing on brittle-barked branches isn't our culinary quest. It's quite the opposite, actually. The tender spring tips of these trees provide a secret delight, with flavors ranging from mandarin orange peel to what I think of as "Nordic rosemary."

In spring the almost monotonous green wall of a conifer forest erupts with the beautiful bright chartreuse swelling of new growth at the end of nearly every branch. For each Douglas fir branch, the end is like a little neon green paintbrush. Spruce and true fir tips are rounder and sturdier, with a touch of blue to the baby green needles.

While picking morels, I've always enjoyed idly plucking and nibbling on this fetching greenery, as well as putting the odd few into a fresh salad. Tasting spruce tips and Douglas fir tips, in particular, has provided me with a remarkable opportunity to experience the genetic variety of wild flavors. For years I've pinched and chewed the orange peel–flavored tips of one special Douglas fir tree at the beginning of a trail leading from my house. Through time, endless trails, and the peculiar tip nibbling of many trees, I've found that each tree has a unique flavor. Some taste of lemons, grapefruit, bitter orange, or peach skin. Many are simply one-dimensionally tart or resinous. It's fascinating. This is the taste kaleidoscope of a wild forest. Tree plantations just can't offer this. I like to use grapefruit-flavored tips in salads. The orange peel–like tips are my favorites for infusing in vodka for a nice martini, a tip or two saved to float around the frozen lake of celadon-colored vodka, like a perfect toy Christmas tree (see page 324).

You can find conifers—be they spruce, Douglas Fir, other firs, balsam, or even pines—to harvest in parks and public lands almost everywhere but in the deepest South. Growers

OPPOSITE: *Spruce tips*

of (chemical-free) Christmas trees will find that your free tip pruning makes their trees bushier. There are no native spruce trees where I live, yet by watching campuses, hospitals, and even homes, I've gained access to landscaping spruce and their tips every spring.

Harvesting is easy. After finding a tree with a pleasing flavor, slide your hand along the stem toward the tips, gathering the little branches into a big clump. Pull the tips, and they pop off. Don't take more than a quarter to a third of the tips from any branch, and *never* take the tips at the top of the tree.

This tree munching takes you into largely un-explored culinary territory. Daniel Patterson, chef/owner of Coi, in San Francisco, became a fir fan after I sent him a little bag of fir tips. While I amused myself with infusing the tips and even mature needles into syrup and vodka (see pages 321 and 324), Daniel infused them into oil. This aromatic, citrusy green oil is stunning dotted on or in a sauce for fish and other wild food. Exploring the sweet path can take you to a sorbet, shortbread, and syrup drizzled on treats from waffles to wild berries. On the savory path, think of Nordic rosemary perfuming lamb, chicken, fish, and even bread. Next I'm going to try the needles for smoking meat. Explore!

ABOVE LEFT: *Douglas fir tips*

kitchen notes

CLEANING AND PREPARATION: All you need to do is remove any papery sheath remaining around the tip and trim off any excess stem.

COOKING METHODS: Our syrup recipe is superb (see page 321). A rejected experiment, however, yielded one interesting result. The ratio of 1:1:1 tips to sugar to water made a thin syrup. When this mixture was boiled until acceptably thick, the result was a delicious and utterly convincing faux golden honey.

The mature needles stripped from the stem of a favorite tree can make excellent infused vodka (see page 324).

STORAGE: Keep the tips in an unsealed bag or open container. They'll keep nicely for a week in your refrigerator. Dried tips and needles are suitable for tea.

IDEAL TIPS: Harvest only those tips with the flavor that you yourself enjoy. The tips must be fresh, young, and tender for use in a salad, a syrup, or as a savory spice.

Buckwheat Waffles with Spruce Tip Syrup

Good lord, this is half citrus and half Christmas tree! That's what I thought on the first morning in Gustavus, Alaska, when the pancakes dripping with spruce tip syrup hit my taste buds. Like any syrup, spruce tip is plenty sweet, but the orangey, piney flavors make you feel as though you're licking up the fresh green landscape.

These brown-flecked buckwheat waffles have a light, airy texture that soaks up just the right amount of this haunting syrup. This is a perfect Christmas breakfast—if you still have any syrup in December.

The first trick to remember is to watch for the spruce tips to emerge and get the syrup made in the spring. The second trick is hiding it for the next seven months until Christmas breakfast. Make extra. People are tickled pink when you give them a little bottle for Christmas. This works just as well with Douglas fir tips.

[MAKES 6 TO 8 WAFFLES]

1¼ cups sifted cake flour

¾ cup sifted buckwheat flour

¼ teaspoon baking soda

1½ teaspoons baking powder

½ teaspoon kosher salt

1 tablespoon sugar

3 large eggs, separated

10 tablespoons unsalted butter, melted
    and cooled slightly

1½ cups buttermilk

1 recipe Spruce or Douglas Fir Tip Syrup
    (page 321)

Sift the cake flour, buckwheat flour, baking soda, baking powder, salt, and sugar into a large bowl.

Whisk the egg yolks in a medium bowl until light colored and slightly thickened. Whisk the butter and buttermilk into the egg yolks.

Place the egg whites in the bowl of a standing mixer fitted with the whip attachment. Whip the egg whites until they hold a firm, creamy peak.

Make a well in the center of the flour mixture and pour in the egg yolk mixture. Using a large rubber spatula, quickly fold the ingredients together, being careful not to overmix. Quickly fold in the egg whites just until incorporated. The batter will appear slightly lumpy, with some streaks of beaten egg whites. Heat a waffle iron according to the manufacturer's directions.

Use ½ to ¾ cup of batter per waffle. Pour into the center of the waffle iron. Cook until puffed and golden. Hold in a warm oven while making the remainder of the waffles.

Serve the waffles with butter and the warm spruce tip syrup.

TIPS AND TECHNIQUES
Sifting the flours twice gives these waffles a light, tender texture.

SUBSTITUTIONS AND VARIATIONS
You can substitute whole wheat flour for the buckwheat flour.

Make pancakes using ¼ to ⅓ cup batter per pancake for small to medium-size pancakes.

Douglas fir boughs

Stinging Nettles

URTICA DIOICA; URTICA SP.

Pain and pleasure, pleasure and pain. Why do so many things that are good for us come with these two aspects of life entwined? Our beastly clever and probably desperately hungry ancestors found a sneaky way past stinging nettles' ample defenses. They unlocked the terrific flavor and the nutritional treasure chest hiding behind the burning needles covering this fine plant.

As if the superior flavor that has seduced chefs everywhere weren't enough, the dazzling nutritional content of nettles includes large amounts of protein, iron, vitamin C, and vitamin A. Nettles make vegetarian rennet, as well as fat chickens and glossy livestock after drying as hay. This tasty and troublesome weed has been with humans for so long that it's hard to tell just where it originated. Its usefulness (it even makes a beautiful linenlike fabric) has made its very presence an occasional clue to possible historical human settlements. While other sensible animals have left fresh nettles alone, humans have used nettles for food, fodder, fibers, medicine, and even strange combinations of scourges and therapy.

The delicious European species *Urtica dioica* hitched a ride to the New World and quickly colonized the rich soil beside creeks. Watch for them in late summer in moist areas, where they will stand in large groups of single-stemmed stalks from four to six feet tall. In the spring the new growth appears with pert heart-shaped leaves with plain flowers dangling beneath. Most native stinging nettles species have longer leaves but the same pointed tips, saw-toothed edges, and bountiful needles covering the tops, stems, and veins under the leaves. Nettles have a slightly "minty" look, with their square stems and opposite leaves that all but one nettle bears.

Harvesting is a delicate spring dance requiring long gloves and, ideally, your thickest pants. At the base of the angled needles is a sac of formic acid, which is quickly injected into the clumsy harvester. The burning from the acid can last from the usual thirty minutes to a more dastardly twelve hours in one nettle patch in Oregon. Armed with gloves and scissors, you harvest short stems with the top four leaves of the plant intact. It's a good thing that the patches are usually large because during the spring, you can harvest these tops just once, when the plants are usually no more than a foot tall. Although the plants will send up more stems from the lateral root system, ignore this growth; it will never taste as good as the spring tips. The plant easily sustains this harvest and returns next year looking for trouble.

Cooking disarms the needles, as does drying. *Eating these raw would be dumb,* as would be forgetting your gloves when you take the nettles into the kitchen to cook. Tongs will be your best friend when your nettles are headed for the pot.

kitchen notes

CLEANING AND PREPARATION: *Wear gloves at all times when handling stinging nettles.* Rinse the nettles, although tidy harvesting into a clean container can make washing a nonissue. The tiny flowers likely to be on the plant belong there and are excellent cooked with the leaves.

COOKING METHODS: *Never eat nettles raw.* Cook them very quickly with just the water clinging to the rinsed leaves—as you would spinach or chard—to hold their color, flavor, and nutritional content. You can mix nettles and sorrel, spinach, chard, and others to excellent effect. Use nettles in any recipe in which you would use those greens. Nettle soup is the classic European preparation. Nettles are lovely stuffed in various pastas and even on pizza. Creamed nettles beats the socks off creamed spinach. Dried nettles make a nice, healthy tea.

STORAGE: After they are harvested, they will stay perky in a plastic bag refrigerated for a good four to five days.

IDEAL STINGING NETTLES: Each should have a short, tender stem, look bright green, and have four tender leaves.

ALERT: *Wear gloves during all stages of handling: harvesting, washing, and preparation until disarmed after cooking.*

Nettle Malfatti with Brown Butter, Lemon, and Parmesan

Those of us lucky enough to have lived in Napa/Sonoma wine country for decades before glamorous food reigned and the *Michelin* stars were handed out remember when Italian American food was king. In those days, two entrées were on every menu: cannelloni and malfatti. To this day, this region is the only place I've ever found malfatti. The word means "badly made," and though malfatti are used for an odd dish or two in Italy, our wine country malfatti are unique. Local legend says that the dish was invented during the Depression by an elderly local Italian American woman faced with feeding a football team and having no pasta on hand.

This traditional and economical mixture is composed of old bread, eggs, cheese, and Swiss chard or spinach. Our use of wild nettles would probably have made this frugal woman happy. The blue-green color and richer flavor of the nettles really enhances these malfatti. A few cooks add ricotta, but we're sticking with the old way. This wonderful dish survives in just a couple of little delis in Napa. This pleasure deserves preservation.

Make the malfatti a day or two ahead for the best well-married texture, then roll the malfatti mixture into the traditional tiny breakfast sausage shapes. Vegetarians must cook this.

[MAKES 5 DOZEN]

for the malfatti

½ pound nettle leaves, cleaned (wear gloves
    at all times during handling, until cooked)
3 tablespoons extra virgin olive oil
1 medium onion, finely diced (1 to 1¼ cups)
3 garlic cloves, finely minced
½ cup flat-leaf parsley
2 teaspoons kosher salt
¼ teaspoon freshly ground black pepper
4 large eggs, well beaten
¾ cup grated Parmesan, plus ¾ cup
    for topping malfatti
1¼ cups panko bread crumbs
½ pound (2 sticks) unsalted butter,
    cut into 16 pieces
2 tablespoons fresh lemon juice
Finely grated zest of 1 lemon

Bring a large pot of salted water to a boil. Wearing gloves or using tongs, plunge the nettles into the water and cook for 3 minutes, pushing the nettles down as needed. Drain the nettles through a colander, then spread them out on a rack placed inside a baking sheet to cool to room temperature. Squeeze out any excess moisture, then chop them coarsely.

Heat the oil in a large sauté pan over medium heat. When the oil is hot, add the onion and garlic, stirring to coat with the oil. Cook, stirring occasionally, until tender, 6 to 7 minutes. Add the nettles, parsley, 1 teaspoon of the salt, and ⅛ teaspoon of the pepper and stir together. Cook for 3 to 4 minutes, then cover the pan and turn off the heat. Let sit for 5 minutes. Uncover and cool to room temperature.

Place the nettle mixture in the bowl of a food processor. Add another ½ teaspoon of the salt and the remaining ⅛ teaspoon pepper. Process until the mixture is very finely chopped. Place in a large mixing bowl.

Whisk the eggs into the nettle mixture to loosen it. Add the Parmesan and bread crumbs and work them in evenly, using a wooden spoon or your hands. Cover and refrigerate overnight, or up to 2 days.

Lightly flour a cutting board and have a bowl of flour nearby to use for shaping the malfatti. With floured hands, pinch off a rounded teaspoon (¼ ounce) of the malfatti mixture. Gently roll it between the palms of your hands to form a small torpedo shape, about 1½ inches long, with slightly tapered ends. The mixture will be moist, so keep your hands lightly floured to prevent sticking. Line up the malfatti on a floured baking sheet, close to but not touching one another. Cover and refrigerate until ready to use. (At this point, the malfatti can be frozen on a tray, then put into resealable plastic freezer bags for up to 1 month. Thaw in the refrigerator on a baking sheet before cooking.)

Place the butter in a large sauté pan over medium heat. Cook until foaming and starting to turn golden brown, 5 to 6 minutes. You will see little bits of golden brown milk solids in the bottom of the pan, and the foam will begin to turn golden brown. Remove from the heat before the color gets too dark, because the butter continues to cook for a few minutes off the heat. Hold in a warm place while the malfatti cook.

Bring a large pot of salted water to a boil over high heat. Drop in enough malfatti to fit comfortably in the pot without touching. When the water comes back to a boil, turn down the heat slightly, cook the malfatti until they bob to the surface, then cook for 3 to 4 more minutes. Lift the malfatti out of the water with a flat strainer, give them a gentle shake, then place them on a baking sheet and hold them in a warm place while you cook the rest. Bring the water back to a boil before adding the next batch.

to serve

Reheat the butter over low heat. Stir in the lemon juice and the remaining ½ teaspoon salt. Add the warm malfatti to the pan in a single layer and roll them around to coat with the butter. Sprinkle with the lemon zest and the remaining Parmesan. Serve immediately.

TIPS AND TECHNIQUES

The nettles lose their sting after cooking, so handle them with gloves before they are blanched. After that, they can be touched safely.

If you don't have a large enough sauté pan to hold all the malfatti in a single layer, divide the butter between two pans to heat them all at the same time.

If you are serving the malfatti with roast chicken or other poultry, save the pan juices and add them to the brown butter along with the lemon juice and salt.

SUBSTITUTIONS AND VARIATIONS

Swiss chard or spinach leaves or a combination can be substituted for the nettles.

Wild Spring Salad Greens

Delicious spring greens not only thrive in the wild, they are also found growing with excess gusto as weeds in our yards, fields, and vacant lots. As culinary respect for greens like purslane and chickweed grows, they are finding their way back to a place of honor in some of the gardens from which they were exiled years ago as delicious plants of untamed and unmanageable vigor.

Purslane

PORTULACA OLERACEA

Purslane begins its seasonal attempt to take over the world in late spring. Like a strange rubbery wig, purslane spreads spiderlike over the ground. Pretty it's not; tasty it is. Its fat, fleshy tongue-shaped leaves are succulent, as are its reddish stems. The crispness and tartness of its young leaves add real character to a salad. Larger leaves and the stems make a fine pickle. This crisp crunch is a treat in any sandwich. A gooey quality when cooked makes purslane a wonderful thickener for soups and an excellent pot green. A traditional vegetable in Mexico, purslane is often used there in a delicious pork stew.

You can harvest the entire plant for months, from late spring through summer, if it is wildly abundant, or just snip off some branchy arms' tips. Wash this ground hugger well. You'll find purslane thriving in full sun where no one wants it to grow—everywhere in the United States. Because of its delicious flavor and extraordinary omega-3 content, purslane is welcome again in many gardens, as it was for vast stretches of human history in Asia, Mesoamerica (it was native here too), and Europe.

Chickweed

STELLARIA MEDIA

Chickweed is a fluffy tangled bouffant of a salad green. It grows in tumbled mats of floppy weak stems with dainty opposite-positioned spade-shaped leaves. Chickweed is often impressively abundant in areas with enough moisture in sun and shade alike. It's easiest to harvest it with scissors: Just snip off the upper part of the greenery. It's wise to do this first, even if you plan to pull up the entire plant as a weed. There's also not much washing needed this way. Watch for the odd single line of little white hairs growing along the stem. This unusual trait distinguishes chickweed from similar plants, like scarlet pimpernel.

Chickweed's flavor is mild and lettucelike. It adds "loft" and an interesting texture to a salad. Many people cook chickweed, but mountains of it shrink to very little. It grows through the winter and spring in much of the country. By summer, its tender salad days are truly over.

OVERLEAF, CLOCKWISE FROM FAR LEFT: *Wood sorrel, common "garden" sorrel, dandelion, mustard and flowers, chickweed*

The Sorrels: Wood Sorrel, Sheep Sorrel, and "Garden" Sorrel

OXALIS MONTANA; OXALIS SPECIES; RUMEX ACETOSELLA; RUMEX ACETOSA

It's remarkable that three such different plants have all been lumped together under the common names *sorrel* and *sour grass*. The mean-sounding word *sour* is thrown at all of these nice plants. However, the word *sorrel* itself came from an antique French derivation of the word for "sour." I prefer to think of bright lemony tartness as the common flavor of each of these distinct plants. They are just delicious.

WOOD SORREL: Whether the *Oxalis* species called wood sorrel has violet, white, or yellow flowers, the flowers all look like shamrocks. And the various wood sorrels have their distinctive heart-shaped three leaves in common. Each little heart folds in half like butterfly wings. The yellow-flowered oxalis has small, pure green leaves and is readily found throughout the country as a common weed growing from cracks in sidewalks and in fields. The beautiful violet-flowered wood sorrel has purple undersides to its large leaves and is found on the dark forest floor. It's best to pick the youngest and smallest of all these leaves. Mature ones can be a bit chewy. Wood sorrels are gorgeous in a salad.

SHEEP SORREL: The dainty leaves of sheep sorrel are no more than two inches long and are a strange arrow shape. The lower lobes seem like floppy ears. In the spring they are usually found growing in a rosette form, though they can spread out via rhizomes. These are little leaves to pinch for harvest, but it doesn't take many to add all the lemony zest you'd want for a salad. Three of these little leaves float on the soup on the jacket of this book.

"GARDEN" SORREL: This is the feral version of the French sorrel many of us have planted in our gardens. The leaves are also arrow shaped, though the points by the stem are small. This variety is more common in the East. Like other sorrels, it adds spark to warm wilted salads.

kitchen notes

ALERT: With purslane and chickweed in particular, remember that lots of people just hate these plants. Our tasty greens are someone else's target for extermination via modern chemistry. Gather them in safe places and also watch for patchy browning as a sign of possible herbicide use.

Some people are also concerned about the presence of calcium-depleting oxalic acid in these plants. This is what gives them their lemony tang. Don't worry. Only the most deadened palates could harm themselves by eating excessive amounts of these plants.

Miner's Lettuce

CLAYTONIA PERFOLIATA

This plant is so pretty and strange looking that you might be prone to spin silly fairy stories about it. It does look like a cone collar for a fairy dog fresh from the fairy vet. (OK, I'll stop.) The beauty of this green bouquet of a plant and its unique round cone-shaped leaves makes it one of the easiest wild plants to identify. In the West blackberries and miner's lettuce are possibly the best-known wild foods. Miner's lettuce is found from Canada into Central America, but it also grows in odd spots as far east as Georgia and Vermont. In some places, names like winter purslane or Indian lettuce are used to describe it. The vitamin C in this tasty plant fended off scurvy in California gold miners, for whom it was named.

You can harvest individual stems by cutting them with scissors, or you can pull up the whole rosette-shaped plant. New plants will come next year as long as you leave most of the plants alone to set seed. Traditionally, you harvest miner's lettuce before the flower spray growing from the center of the cup-shaped leaf gets very large. Miner's lettuce is unusual, however, in that its mild, juicy flavor remains even after the plant is in full flower. This charming plant has also found fans in Europe, where it is now cultivated.

Wild Spring Greens Salad with Creamy Chive Dressing

The choices of wild greens for this salad are wide open to what's beautiful and growing nicely in your world. There's no law against adding a fine cultivated green or two. As you compose the mixture of your salad, think of a crazy quilt or musical composition where energetic variation is balanced by the harmony of its parts. Although there are no rules here, you might use more of the friendly crunch of chickweed, miner's lettuce, even purslane, while saving any or all of the sorrels for a lighter flourish of tartness.

[SERVES 4 TO 6]

for the creamy chive dressing
⅓ cup crème fraîche
⅓ cup heavy cream
1 tablespoon unseasoned rice vinegar
1 tablespoon fresh lemon juice
½ teaspoon kosher salt
⅛ teaspoon freshly ground black pepper
⅓ cup extra virgin olive oil
1½ tablespoons finely minced fresh chives

Gently whisk together the crème fraîche, cream, rice vinegar, lemon juice, salt, and pepper in a medium bowl. Drizzle in the oil, whisking constantly, until smooth and fully incorporated. Stir in the chives. Be careful not to overwhisk, or the dressing will become too thick after it sets up. It will keep 2 to 3 days, covered in the refrigerator.

Makes 1 cup.

for the salad
½ pound mixed wild spring greens, cleaned
Kosher salt and freshly ground pepper

Place the greens in a large bowl. Sprinkle with salt and pepper to taste. Drizzle with enough of the dressing to lightly coat the greens. Taste for seasoning and adjust with more dressing or salt and pepper as needed. Serve immediately.

SUBSTITUTIONS AND VARIATIONS
A sprinkling of finely grated lemon zest can be added to the dressing.

Different fresh herbs, such as chervil, flat-leaf parsley, basil, dill, or a combination, may be substituted for the chives.

Purslane Salad with Hot Bacon Vinaigrette and Garlic Croutons

This salad has absolutely everything going for it: flavor, price, omega-3, weeding. With smoky bacon, garlic, and the crunch of the purslane, it's simply scrumptious. With the deliciousness comes the bonus of frugality. In late spring you'll begin to see wild and free purslane in vacant lots, gardens, and farmland. The rampant beast that purslane can become still has small tender clusters of leaves at the tips in late May. Harvest some of this succulent green and head right back for more tender tips as they grow back with weedy relentlessness.

[SERVES 4 TO 6]

5 strips applewood smoked bacon

3 tablespoons extra virgin olive oil

¾ cup cubed ciabatta-style bread (½-inch cubes)

⅜ teaspoon kosher salt

¼ teaspoon plus a pinch freshly ground
    black pepper

2 medium shallots, finely minced

1 garlic clove, finely minced

1½ tablespoons sherry vinegar

1 teaspoon Dijon mustard

½ teaspoon sugar

1 pound purslane, tips and larger leaves only
    (5 to 6 cups loosely packed), cleaned

Position a rack in the center of the oven. Preheat the oven to 350°F.

Place the bacon in a cold sauté pan over medium heat. Slowly cook the bacon until golden brown, 6 to 8 minutes, turning once. Remove the bacon with tongs or a slotted spoon to a paper towel–lined baking sheet. Take 1 teaspoon of the bacon fat and put it in a small bowl. Leave the remaining bacon fat in the pan to finish the salad.

(There should be about 2 tablespoons.) Slice the bacon strips into ¼-inch pieces. Set aside.

Whisk 1 tablespoon of the oil into the bacon fat in the bowl. Add the bread cubes, tossing to coat evenly with the oil and bacon fat. Season with ⅛ teaspoon of the salt and the pinch of pepper. Spread the bread in a single layer on another baking sheet and bake until crisp and golden brown, 10 to 12 minutes. Set aside to cool.

Add the remaining 2 tablespoons oil to the bacon fat in the sauté pan and place over medium heat. When the fat mixture is hot but not smoking, add the shallots and garlic and cook until tender and softened, 3 to 4 minutes. Whisk in the vinegar, mustard, sugar, the remaining ¼ teaspoon salt, and the remaining ¼ teaspoon pepper. When the mixture is hot and bubbling, add the purslane. Stir quickly to coat the greens evenly with the dressing and just warm them. This should take no more than 30 seconds, or the purslane will start to lose its fresh, tender crunch. Remove from the heat. Sprinkle with some of the bacon and croutons. Serve immediately.

TIPS AND TECHNIQUES

You don't have to use all the bacon and croutons called for in the recipe. They can easily be saved for another salad or dish. Store the croutons in an airtight container at room temperature for up to 4 days. Store the bacon in a closed container in the refrigerator for up to 5 days.

SUBSTITUTIONS AND VARIATIONS

Use regular bacon if you can't find applewood smoked bacon.

This dressing can be used for tender dandelion greens or baby spinach. Again, don't heat them too long in the dressing.

A vegetarian version can be made using additional olive oil in place of the bacon fat in the dressing and croutons.

Elderflowers
[Elder Blossoms, Elder Blow]

SAMBUCUS CANADENSIS; S. CAERULEA; S. MEXICANA

Follow their perfume. Although these creamy white flowers are as big as a butter dish, their sweet citrusy aroma may strike you even before your eyes alight on the spectacle of this small tree covered with its huge, flat-faced, lacy flowers.

The magnificent elderberry tree, or elder, makes two appearances in this book. During the course of the year this most generous tree will begin spring bursting with the fragrant confection called elder blow, or elderflowers. The tender new growth of this many-stemmed tree is tipped with flowers resembling starbursts of ivory fireworks. Just a few months later, in autumn, this same tree ends the year looking gnarled and bent over like an old man under the weight of masses of ripe, blue black berries. The flavor change is every bit as extreme. The honeyed lemon flavor of the flowers gives way to the intense cassislike richness of the berries.

I've found elderberry trees everywhere from Canada to Guatemala and in all parts between the Atlantic and the Pacific oceans. The best time to begin your search for elderberry trees is in spring, when the big, distinctive flowers blare out their location in the moist places they love best: on roadsides and along creeks, ravines, and even ditches. It's not unusual to find them hunkered down in suburban settings too. However, check your field guides carefully to confirm that you're not foolishly mistaking poison hemlock's faintly similar flowers for elderflowers. Once you've located these very common trees, your "wild orchard" can provide many years of enjoyment of these spring flowers and the rich berries of autumn.

You can harvest the elderflowers for weeks because the trees tend to continue to send out their blooms even into the summer. If you want to make traditional elderflower fritters, you'll need to harvest the entire flower. Be gentle with the branches, which are quite brittle and will snap when bent too far. Snip off the bloom at the base, along with just an inch or two of the stem. Use as little stem as possible. It tastes bad and contains some toxic compounds. For most other purposes

you need to gather only the flower petals themselves. Just bend the large flower over your bag or bucket and shake or tickle the flower face gently. If the flower pollinated, most of the five petals on each of the little flowers making up the big flower head will fall. This is the best way, because after you've gathered the petals, the pollinated calyxes remain and grow into the blue black berries. While you're engaged in this romantic flower-petal-gathering foray, don't forget that the future berries will feed many beasties besides us. Be gentle and conservative; these petals provide plenty of flavor. Most people harvest more than they'll really use.

To some, elderflowers appear just a two-trick culinary pony and are fit for only elder fritters and elderflower champagne. How wrong they are. Elderflower sabayon, granita, pots de crème, milk shakes, a bouncy gelée, or a transparent jelly with whole elderflowers floating inside are just a handful of their possible delights. From cocktails (see page 324) to cosmetics elderberry blossoms can provide you with so many treasures. You may wish to do as I have and transplant one of the wild young shoots often found at the base of a mature elderberry tree to a moist piece of earth near your home.

kitchen notes

CLEANING AND PREPARATION: Don't wash these delicate blossoms. Just give them a good once-over for any unexpected little critters. Any unripe berries will fall through a colander. Discard these because they are mildly toxic.

COOKING METHODS: Rather than cooking, infusion or fermentation is the traditional path for these flowers. Put the flowers directly into cream and place in the refrigerator to infuse for three to four days, or add to a simmering liquid, then remove the pan from the heat to steep. The flowers can also be infused directly into vodka or other high-proof alcohol (see page 322). Wander the Internet for many good elderflower champagne recipes.

STORAGE: Use within three days. Store the free petals in a bowl or whole blooms on paper towel–lined sheet pans in your refrigerator.

IDEAL ELDERFLOWERS: What constitutes an ideal depends on your purpose. For fritters, newly opened flowers with well-attached little flower petals are best. For virtually all other purposes, use full-blown elder blow. These fully open and fertilized blossoms allow you to shake and harvest the tasty petals only.

OVERLEAF: *Elderflowers in liquid*

Elderflower Panna Cotta with Elderflower Syrup

Ethereal is just the right word for this dessert. While you can imagine angels spooning this creamy wonder, it is the work of an earthling to harvest the elderflowers four days before you plan to serve this. The cold steeping of the flowers in cream retains their floral essence. At the same time, any extra petals steeped in extra cream can be used for an ice cream or a milk shake. With extra petals yet, you can proceed to the more devilish work of infusing the elderflowers in high-proof alcohol for the elderflower liqueur recipe on page 325.

[MAKES 6]

for the panna cotta
2 cups elderflowers
3½ cups heavy cream
½ cup milk
2 teaspoons powdered gelatin
⅓ cup sugar
Pinch of kosher salt

Stir together the elderflowers and cream in a glass bowl or large measuring cup. Cover and refrigerate for at least 3 days or up to 4. Strain through a fine-mesh strainer, pressing to extract all the liquid. Discard the flowers. You should have 3 cups of cream. Set aside ½ cup.

Pour the milk into a medium bowl and sprinkle with the gelatin.

Place 2½ cups infused cream, the sugar, and the salt in a medium saucepan over medium-high heat. Whisk together to dissolve the sugar and salt. Heat just until the cream comes to a boil and remove from the heat. While whisking, ladle 1 cup hot cream into the gelatin mixture. Add the remaining cream, whisking until the gelatin is dissolved. Strain through a fine-mesh strainer into a medium bowl, pressing to extract all the liquid. Whisk in the reserved ½ cup cream.

Divide the mixture among six 4-ounce ramekins or dessert glasses. Cover with plastic wrap and chill for at least 6 hours or overnight. Serve with a drizzle of elderflower syrup.

for the elderflower syrup
1 cup elderflowers
3 cups sugar

Stir together the elderflowers and 2 cups water in a glass measuring cup or bowl. Cover and refrigerate for at least 3 days or up to 4.

Strain the infused water through a fine-mesh strainer into a 2-cup measuring cup, pressing to extract all the liquid. Discard the flowers. You should have 1½ to 1¾ cups liquid.

Place the infused water and sugar in a medium saucepan over medium-high heat. Whisk together to dissolve the sugar. Bring to a boil over medium-high heat, then turn down the heat and simmer for 8 to 10 minutes, or until slightly thickened. Cool before serving. The syrup will keep covered with plastic wrap or in a sealed container in the refrigerator for 2 to 3 weeks.

TIPS AND TECHNIQUES

If you make the panna cotta in ramekins, they can be turned out onto plates once they are set. Run a knife around the inside of the ramekin to loosen the panna cotta, then carefully invert the panna cotta onto a plate. Drizzle the top with the syrup just before serving.

The extra syrup can be used in several ways: to sweeten berries or sliced fruit, to sweeten iced tea or lemonade, or to drizzle over ice cream.

Fresh strawberries or apricots would be a nice complement to the delicate flavor of the elderflowers.

SUBSTITUTIONS AND VARIATIONS

Honeysuckle blossoms, citrus flower blossoms, or fragrant rose petals can be substituted for the elder-flowers. Use half the amount called for in the recipe.

summer

Lobster Mushrooms

HYPOMYCES LACTIFLUORUM

This "thar she blows," flamboyantly colored mushroom is often visible from afar. With its screaming red-orange gown, this drag queen of mushrooms is not quite what she seems. The character disguised beneath the wild color is one of the most tasteless of mushrooms, *Russula brevipes*. Its sole redeeming quality is its nice meaty texture. Mercifully, in midsummer to early fall the shellfish-flavored parasitic fungus called *Hypomyces lactifluorum* attacks the *Russula* and transforms it into the lobster mushroom that we know. This makeover takes place when lobster-colored fungus spreads over the outside of the base mushroom, eating and melting the original features of its host. Looking down on the mushroom, you'll see rather pretty orange rippling ridges where the brittle-bladed gills of the host mushroom once were. Slicing the mushroom in half, you'll notice the reddish parasitic layer all around the outside, with the white meat of the original mushroom inside. Simply, the lobster mushroom is actually two different mushrooms sharing the same mushroom body.

The common name lobster mushroom fits not just the red outside–white inside color scheme of the mushroom, but the aroma as well. The strong crustacean smell is seductive to most, yet repugnant to others who don't find this seafood quality in line with their fungal expectations. The name, color, and aroma lead inevitably to odd concoctions like lobster mushroom Newburg. But a better use for lobster mushrooms is as an excellent sidekick for halibut and most whitefish. It's a tasty and dramatic red addition to greens too.

The habitat for lobster mushrooms spreads from Nova Scotia to Oregon and from Alaska to the mountains of Mexico. In the Pacific Northwest firs are a common host. Pine is usually the host in New Mexico and Nova Scotia. Lobster mushrooms prefer oak trees in the East.

I take some comfort in knowing that even as we aging mushroom hunters totter around with bad knees and failing eyesight, we'll still be able to see these blazing orange floozies of the mushroom world scattered across the forest floor.

kitchen notes

CLEANING AND PREPARATION: Because of their broad, bowl-shaped tops, lobster mushrooms are generally very dirty on top, while the undersides will be nice and clean. Using a brush, wash them after harvest, making sure to clean out any rumpled pits in the cap. Cut the stem and look for worm holes. Cut away any blood-colored discoloration (usually soft) or just discard the whole mushroom.

A dusting of white powder is commonly seen on lobster mushrooms exposed to heat or sun. This is merely white spore matter being ejected. You can make a lobster mushroom eject its white spores by placing it upside down in the sun. A light misting with a water bottle will dissolve the spores easily.

COOKING METHODS: Sautéing, roasting, and grilling are always appropriate for lobster mushrooms. The meaty texture and great color are this mushroom's virtues.

STORAGE: These have a comparatively epic shelf life and will stay vibrant in a paper bag in the refrigerator for two to three weeks. Worms, if present, can be merrily munching during this time, however. Lobster mushrooms are of average quality dried.

IDEAL LOBSTER MUSHROOMS: The mushrooms should be firm with freshly cut stem ends, making it easy to spot any of the worm holes that can be a problem for this species. Some lobsters are not completely red orange. This pale pastel orange form is still acceptable. What is not acceptable is the softening wine red flesh, which indicates the final breakdown of the mushroom.

"Breakfast of Champignons"

LOBSTER MUSHROOM AND ROCK SHRIMP EGGS BENEDICT WITH DAZZLING HOLLANDAISE

The screamingly flashy lobster mushroom calls for some flamboyant treatment. Combining radiant red shellfish with the mushrooms seems like the ideal excess for this extravagant brunch dish. Butter poaching the mushroom not only colors the butter but also tenderizes this often tough mushroom. Because lobster mushrooms have a long shelf life, you can store these mushrooms for days after hunting until the luxury of a pampered weekend arrives.

[SERVES 6]

for the poached eggs

2 teaspoons white or cider vinegar

1½ teasoons salt

12 large eggs, at room temperature

Bring 2 inches of water to a simmer in a large sauté pan or wide saucepan. Add the vinegar and salt. One at a time, crack each egg into a small mug or ramekin, then ease the egg into the barely simmering water. Keep track of the order of the eggs as they are added to the water. Repeat with the remaining eggs, being careful not to crowd them. You may have to do this in batches. Poach the eggs for 2 to 3 minutes, or until the whites are set and the yolks are still runny. Using a slotted spoon, transfer the eggs in the order in which you put them into the water to a bowl of ice water. When the eggs are cool, transfer to a paper towel–lined baking sheet until ready to use. To reheat, return the eggs to barely simmering water for 20 to 30 seconds, or until warmed through.

for the mushrooms

½ pound cleaned lobster mushrooms,
    cut into ¼-inch slices

2 medium shallots, finely minced

2 tablespoons tomato paste

¼ teaspoon kosher salt

⅛ teaspoon freshly ground black pepper

½ pound plus 4 tablespoons
    (2½ sticks) unsalted butter

Place the mushrooms, shallots, tomato paste, salt, pepper, and butter in a medium saucepan over medium heat. Stir as the butter melts and coats the mushrooms. When the butter has completely melted, bring the mixture just to a boil, then turn down the heat and simmer for 5 minutes. Place a fine-mesh strainer over a bowl and pour the mixture through, pressing down on the mushrooms to extract all the butter. Set aside 3 tablespoons butter for sautéing the rock shrimp. Reserve the rest of the butter for making the hollandaise. Reserve the mushrooms separately.

for the hollandaise sauce
3 large egg yolks
2 tablespoons fresh lemon juice
½ teaspoon kosher salt, or more to taste
Butter reserved for the hollandaise sauce,
**   warmed**

Fill a medium saucepan with water one-quarter of the way up the sides of the pan and bring to a simmer. In a metal bowl large enough to fit inside the saucepan without touching the water, whisk together the egg yolks, 3 tablespoons water (or 2 tablespoons water and 1 tablespoon white wine), lemon juice, and salt. Place the bowl over the simmering water. Continue whisking vigorously until the mixture is thickened and light in color, 2 to 3 minutes. Remove from the heat and place the bowl on a coiled kitchen towel on the counter to hold it steady.

Slowly whisk in the warmed lobster mushroom butter, along with any sediments that have collected in the bottom of the butter. The sediments are full of mushroom flavor. Taste for seasoning, adjusting as needed. Cover with plastic wrap and hold in a warm place next to the stove until ready to serve.

for the eggs benedict

Reserved 3 tablespoons of butter
1 pound rock shrimp, cleaned
1 teaspoon finely minced garlic
Reserved lobster mushrooms
1 tablespoon finely minced fresh tarragon
6 English muffins, split
Paprika for garnish

Place the butter in a large sauté pan over medium-high heat. When the butter is hot, add the rock shrimp and garlic. Cook until the rock shrimp are just done, 2 to 3 minutes, then remove with a slotted spoon to a bowl. Place the lobster mushroom slices in the pan, stirring to coat with the liquids in the pan. Cook until the liquids have reduced to a glaze, 2 to 3 more minutes. Stir the rock shrimp back into the pan, mixing them with the mushrooms. Stir in the tarragon. Turn the heat off and cover for up to 8 minutes as you toast the English muffins.

Toast the English muffins in a toaster or under the broiler.

Rewarm the poached eggs in barely simmering water.

to serve

Place both halves of an English muffin on each of 6 plates. Divide the rock shrimp and lobster mushroom mixture among the muffins. Top each muffin with a poached egg and nap with the warm hollandaise sauce. Sprinkle the tops with paprika. Serve immediately.

TIPS AND TECHNIQUES

The lobster mushrooms and butter can be made up to 2 days ahead and refrigerated until ready to use.

Before reheating, the whites of the poached eggs can be trimmed with scissors to make them neater looking.

You can preheat a thermos or thermal beverage server with hot water, empty it, and pour in the hollandaise to keep it warm for a longer period of time.

SUBSTITUTIONS AND VARIATIONS

You can substitute butter-poached or steamed lobster for the rock shrimp. Heat the mushrooms in the reserved lobster mushroom butter, then add slices or diced pieces of lobster to the pan just to warm.

Fresh basil can be substituted for the tarragon.

Meadow Mushrooms and Fairy Rings

The description "mushroomy" gets tossed about willy-nilly without much thought. For mushroom fanatics like me, each mushroom has a distinct flavor. Chanterelles have that apricot-peel fruitiness, king boletes (porcini) are butter and cashews, black trumpets have a touch of Stilton, and so on. Here we have both the first and second mushrooms that embody the essence of "mushroomy" for me. Meadow mushrooms and their more dilute cousins, the cremini/portobello/button mushroom cultivars, are the very heart of what people commonly describe as "mushroomy." Fairy rings' intense flavor is close, but with a hazelnut earthiness.

Meadow Mushrooms, "Pinkies"

AGARICUS CAMPESTRIS

Meadow mushrooms with their bright pink petticoatlike gills are old pals to many of us plunderers of mushrooms in green fields all over the world. The original *champignon*, meadow mushrooms have always been adored by the French, who finally made the breakthrough two-plus centuries ago to the cultivation of its kissing cousin *Agaricus bisporus*—the ubiquitous grocery store button mushroom. The maligned button mushroom, which performs yeoman's duty in recipes everywhere, really is tastier than wild gourmands give it credit for.

The *Agaricus* clan of *A. campestris*, *A. bisporus*, *A. arvensis*, and a few others have pretty pink gills covered with a fragile white veil. As brown spores form in the maturing mushroom, the gills turn the color of bittersweet chocolate. The texture gets soft then, but the flavor is at its very peak. Chef François La Varenne's invention of duxelles in the 1600s certainly used the meadow mushroom for this classic cooked paste of minced mushrooms. Identification of meadow mushrooms varies in difficulty depending on where you live. A good field guide and a knowledgeable local are mandatory. The "mushroomy" smell of the meadow mushroom is utterly different from the almond extract perfume of *A. arvensis*, the horse mushroom, and others. In many regions there are unfortunate impostors that smell like a creosote-sweating telephone pole.

These white poofy mushrooms with the silky cap used to polka-dot fields, lawns, and pathways more often than they do now. The best guess is that fertilizers and seeding may have altered the ecology of old pastures. Watch for lovely old "neglected" meadows with peace-loving livestock.

Fairy Rings, Mousseron

MARASMIUS OREADES

Looking like little fairy parasols strewn in a ring on the grass, these fawn-colored mushrooms have long been associated with magical events. At the center of the ring they form is often a patch of dead grass, which was seen as sure evidence of fairies dancing in circles, dragons' scorching breath, or the devil up to the usual mischief. Old science was so much more fun. The real explanation for this delicious plague on pastures and manicured lawns is that the mushrooms' main body, the underground mycelium, digests the lawn thatch outward from a center point. Fairy rings, like tree rings, grow larger each year. Some are more than a century old. Through the years I've watched one grow five feet wider and break into an arc.

These sweet little beige bonnet-shaped mushrooms are deceptively rugged and pack huge flavor. Though the cap is only one to two inches wide, the stem buried in the grass is tall and tough. Its fibrous, rubbery stem is a great identification feature, but grab your field guide because many other mushrooms grow in rings. If you find them growing in a lawn, be mindful of pesticides.

Picking these is so comfortable that you'll find yourself scooting on grass-stained knees with a pair of scissors, snip, snipping around the ring. I cut the caps away from the skinny tough stems at this point. If the caps look dried out, pick them anyway. Fairy rings are one of the very best of dried mushrooms. In fact, rain often brings them right back to life. They often grow in sandy soil and can require serious washing: Swish them vigorously in water, letting the sand settle to the bottom of a bowl, then lift them out.

Fairy rings, or *mousseron* as they're called in Europe, have a big, robust flavor. One chef told me that he thought they tasted like what he'd always thought porcini should taste like. Beyond being extra cute, they are an extremely versatile mushroom in cooking.

Classic Meadow Mushroom Soup with Wild Mushroom and Herbed Ricotta Tartines

For a mushroom lover, the cornerstone of all recipes is a luscious mushroom soup. We regard this combo as the ultimate soup and sandwich for all the seasons of the year. Just change the type of mushroom used with the season. A bowl of this soup with a mushroom-laden tartine tucked alongside is a meal to cure all that's amiss. Our recipe has double layers of mushroom flavor. Its foundation is a rich mushroom stock. Yes, it's easier to use chicken stock and yes, the soup will be mighty tasty. It just won't be the ultimate, rich mushroom soup if you don't make the mushroom stock.

The second tier of flavor comes from the mushrooms themselves, whether they be wild meadow mushrooms, their cultivated cousins—cremini, portobellos, button mushrooms—or other wild fungi. After a jackpot of a hunt in any season, this recipe can become luxurious chanterelle soup, porcini soup, or even the wildly extravagant morel soup.

Though not intentionally so, this recipe is vegetarian and can be vegan if you omit the touch of cream and butter.

[SERVES 6]

---

for the soup

1 ounce dried porcini mushrooms, rinsed

4 cups Traditional Mushroom Stock (page 315),
    plus up to 1 more cup to thin soup, if needed

8 tablespoons (1 stick) unsalted butter

1 large yellow onion, thinly sliced

1 large garlic clove, finely minced

2 teaspoons kosher salt, or more to taste

⅛ teaspoon freshly ground black pepper,
    or more to taste

1½ pounds meadow mushrooms,
    cleaned and cut into ⅛-inch slices

2 tablespoons Madeira

1 teaspoon fresh thyme leaves

½ cup heavy cream

½ teaspoon fresh lemon juice

Place the porcini mushrooms in a medium saucepan with 2 cups of the mushroom stock. Bring to a boil, then turn off the heat and let sit for 30 minutes.

Place a large stockpot over medium heat. Add 6 tablespoons of the butter. When the butter is melted and bubbling, add the onion, garlic, ½ teaspoon of the salt, and the pepper, stirring to coat evenly with the butter. Cook until softened and starting to turn transluscent, 4 to 5 minutes. Add the meadow mushrooms and cook for 2 to 3 minutes until softened. Stir in the Madeira. Cook for 3 more minutes, then stir in the porcini mushrooms and their soaking liquid. Add the remaining 2 cups mushroom stock and the thyme. Bring to a boil, then turn down the heat and simmer for 30 minutes.

Turn off the heat. Add the remaining 1½ teaspoons salt and let sit for 5 to 10 minutes. Carefully transfer the soup to a blender and, starting on a low speed and increasing in increments, puree until very smooth. Place the soup in a saucepan and return to the stove over medium heat. Add the cream. Whisk in the remaining 2 tablespoons butter and the lemon juice. Taste for seasoning and adjust with salt and pepper as needed. Stir in additional stock if the soup needs thinning.

Divide the soup among 6 bowls and serve with the tartines.

for the tartines

1 cup ricotta

2 tablespoons finely minced garlic,
    plus 1 whole garlic clove, peeled

1 teaspoon finely chopped fresh thyme

2 teaspoons finely chopped fresh chives

2 teaspoons finely chopped flat-leaf parsley,
    plus 2 tablespoons for garnish

½ teaspoon finely chopped fresh tarragon

½ teaspoon finely grated lemon zest

¾ teaspoon kosher salt

⅛ teaspoon plus a pinch freshly ground
    black pepper

1 teaspoon fresh lemon juice

4 tablespoons (½ stick) unsalted butter

½ pound wild mushrooms, cleaned and cut into
    ⅛-inch slices

6 thick slices country bread or ciabatta (¾ inch)

Extra virgin olive oil

Fleur de sel

Place the ricotta in a small bowl. Add 1 tablespoon of the garlic, the thyme, the chives, 2 teaspoons of the parsley, the tarragon, the lemon zest, ½ teaspoon of the salt, ⅛ teaspoon of the pepper, and the lemon juice. Mix well. Set aside until ready to use.

Heat the butter in a large sauté pan over medium-high heat. When the butter is melted and bubbling, add the mushrooms, tossing to coat evenly with the butter. Add the remaining ¼ teaspoon salt and the pinch of pepper. Cook until the mushrooms have released their liquid. Continue cooking until the liquid has evaporated and the mushrooms are starting to caramelize. Add the remaining 1 tablespoon garlic during the last few minutes of cooking. Remove from the heat and hold in a warm place.

Toast the bread under a broiler or in a toaster. While the slices are still warm, rub the toasted surface with the whole garlic clove.

Spread the toasts with about 2 tablespoonfuls of the ricotta mixture. Divide the warm mushrooms among the toasts. Drizzle with the oil, then finish with a sprinkling of fleur de sel and the remaining 2 tablespoons parsley.

TIPS AND TECHNIQUES

The ricotta mixture can be made up to a day ahead and refrigerated. Remove from the refrigerator 1 hour before serving.

Have the soup warm and the ricotta mixture ready before toasting the bread slices. They are best just out of the oven or toaster.

SUBSTITUTIONS AND VARIATIONS

For the soup, you can substitute the "tamed" button, cremini, or portobello mushrooms for the wild meadow mushrooms. Almost any wild mushroom can be substituted in this recipe. Use all of one kind, or mix them half wild and half cultivated.

You can use chicken broth, beef broth, or canned mushroom broth for the homemade broth in the recipe.

For the tartines, any wild mushrooms will work beautifully.

ABOVE: *Fairy Ring (Mousseron) Mushrooms* [PAGE 81]

OPPOSITE: *Classic Meadow Mushroom Soup with Wild Mushroom and Herbed Ricotta Tartines* [PAGE 82]

Gray Morels

"Morels in the summer?" you ask. Indeed. In fact, in the grand finale of a great morel season, the still obscure yet most remarkable gray morel arrives just as the season appears to have ended. As summer heats up, the mightiest morel in both size and flavor begins to emerge from the burned, needle-covered forest floor that less than a year before had been ablaze. Morel fever strikes all morel fanatics in the spring, but it's we lucky ones in the western states whose blood comes to a full rolling boil when the first rumors of "grays" begin in the warmth of June.

More than twenty years ago just a handful of European Americans knew that gray morels even existed. I saw my very first one in 1992. It was the biggest and prettiest morel I'd ever seen. In spring mushroom pickers have always flocked to the sites of forest fires to pick morels. After the traditional "burn" conica morels had been picked, folks called it quits and headed home. Gray morels remained a secret. Nearly everyone was unaware that when the summer fired up and the rain came too, the magnificent gray morel would appear, often in huge numbers. The morel-loving Northern Cheyenne knew, however. They called them "sons of thunder," because these morels arrive with the rain and thunderstorms of summer.

Gray morels pass through stages of color that always remind me of Lipizzaner horses. The mushroom, like the horse, is born a dark charcoal gray but as it matures turns fair in color. The young mushroom, particularly the stem, is covered in short black velvety fur. This is bizarre for a morel, and absolutely fetching. As the mushroom grows, the black "hairs" stretch farther and farther apart and/or fall off, leaving the morel's creamy flesh showing through. A basket of grays ranges from soft black to nearly blond in color. A few telltale black "hairs" always remain on the stem. These are often mistaken for dirt and ash splashed from the burned landscape they grow in. The cut stem of a gray morel shows off its double and even triple walls. These thick walls not only give good support to a mushroom that can be as tall as nine inches, but it also makes them the supreme morel for stuffing.

Sadly, this regal morel does not grace the world with its presence every year. But where forest fires were and summer rains persist, it can be thrillingly abundant. I set a record years ago by making the last gray morel delivery of an unbelievable season to Mark Franz at Farallon restaurant in San Francisco on November first. After many months, grays' intense beefy richness made other morels seem a tad bland.

I'm often asked, "What's your favorite mushroom?" It's a terrible question, but if I've had a cocktail and am pushed hard into a corner, it's this great gray morel that always burns brightest in my heart.

kitchen notes

CLEANING & PREPARATION: See page 6.

COOKING METHODS: This hollow mushroom's thick walls make it the ultimate stuffing morel. It can also be cut vertically to look like an open boat and then stuffed. As with all morels, cook gray morels thoroughly.

STORAGE: Heat-loving grays are very durable. They will keep for 6 to 7 days, covered with a damp cloth, in your refrigerator. They are spectacularly good when dried in a food dehydrator.

IDEAL GRAY MORELS: Pick, or if you must, buy them while they are still gray in color with tight "pleats." For stuffing purposes, the color phase is unimportant. They become brittle when they become five-plus-inch giants. Another unusual morel, the green morel, or "pickle," fruits late also but is not as good for stuffing.

ALERT: Like all morels, gray morels must be completely cooked. *NEVER EAT RAW MORELS!*

Sean O'Toole's Braised Short Rib–Stuffed Morels

It's so hard to choose a favorite stuffing from all the years of great ones. At past years' morel parties (see page 96), Staffan Terje's (Perbacco) lardo-wrapped veal stuffing followed Tom Worthington's (Monterey Fish Market) blood pudding stuffing, which followed Toni Moore's Greek lamb stuffing, and on and on. Even in this cavalcade of morel wonders, Sean O'Toole's (Bardessono) short rib stuffing just thrilled me. My coauthor, Sarah, has simplified Sean's ambitious recipe a bit for us earthling nonchefs. The unexpected Asian flavors in the short ribs, combined with the gray morels' own beefy flavor, make my mouth water even now. Other big morels from Iowa or anywhere can work for this too.

[SERVES 4 TO 6; MAKES ABOUT 2 CUPS STUFFING]

for the short ribs

3 pounds beef short ribs,
    cut to 2- to 3-inch pieces
Kosher salt and freshly ground black pepper
2 tablespoons pure olive oil
1 large fennel bulb, cut into ½-inch dice
¾ pound shallots, thinly sliced
1 garlic head, cut in half crosswise
¼ cup coriander seeds
2 tablespoons black peppercorns
3 lemongrass stalks, cut into 1-inch pieces
½ bunch fresh cilantro
1 cup unseasoned rice vinegar
1 cup dry white wine
½ cup soy sauce
1 quart beef broth

Position a rack in the center of the oven. Preheat the oven to 425°F.

Season the short ribs all over with salt and pepper. Place them on a rack set inside a baking sheet and roast for 25 minutes.

While the short ribs are roasting, heat the oil in a large braising pan over medium-high heat. When the oil is hot, add the fennel and shallots. Place the garlic halves in the pan, cut side down. Cook, stirring occasionally, until the vegetables are tender and starting to caramelize, 5 to 6 minutes. Remove from the heat and set aside until the short ribs finish roasting.

Place the coriander seeds and black peppercorns in a mortar and crush them slightly with a pestle. (Or place them in a resealable plastic bag, open, and crush with the bottom of a small saucepan, being careful to contain the coriander seeds and peppercorns.) Place the lemongrass, cilantro, and crushed coriander and peppercorns on a 10-inch square piece of cheesecloth. Roll up and secure tightly with string. Place the bundle in the pan with the vegetables.

When the short ribs are roasted, place them in the braising pan. In a large bowl, combine the rice vinegar, white wine, soy sauce, and beef broth. Add to the braising pan and return the pan to the

heat. Bring to a boil. Fit a piece of parchment paper on top of the short ribs and liquid to cover. Place a large piece of aluminum foil on top of the parchment, gently pushing the foil down until it is directly on top of the parchment paper and tucked up against the sides of the braising pan. Seal the edges securely by crimping the foil around the edges of the pan. Place in the oven. Turn down the heat to 375°F and cook for 2½ hours.

Remove the short ribs from the braising liquid. Strain the liquid through a fine-mesh strainer into a container with a lid. When the meat is cool enough to handle, remove it from the bones and clean off any tough connective tissue or excess fat. You should have about 2 cups. Refrigerate the broth and meat, covered, until ready to use.

to finish

Reserved short rib meat

½ cup reserved braising liquid, fat removed

¼ cup finely minced scallions

2 tablespoons finely minced fresh ginger

2 Thai or small serrano chiles, seeded (optional) and finely minced

¼ cup finely chopped fresh cilantro

1½ teaspoons unseasoned rice vinegar, or more to taste

¼ teaspoon kosher salt, or more to taste

20 to 24 large gray morels, cleaned

Pure olive oil

Prepare a grill to medium heat.

Finely dice the short rib meat. Place the braising liquid in a large saucepan and bring just to a boil. Add the meat, stirring to moisten it completely. Stir in the scallions, ginger, chiles, cilantro, rice vinegar, and salt. Taste for seasoning, adding more vinegar and/or salt as needed. If the mixture is too dry, add a little more braising liquid. Cool slightly before proceeding.

Place the stuffing mixture in a piping bag with a tip small enough to fit inside the mushrooms.

Place the tip inside the mushroom and gently squeeze the piping bag, being careful not to overstuff it to bursting.

Lightly brush the morels with oil.

Place the morels on the grill and cook, turning them as they brown, for 2 to 3 minutes per side, or until the morels are cooked and the stuffing is heated throughout, 8 to 12 minutes.

Serve immediately.

TIPS AND TECHNIQUES

Season the short ribs with salt and pepper a day ahead to give them even more flavor.

You can sauté the mushrooms in a pan instead of grilling.

Creating a tight seal with no airspace between the braising liquid and the parchment and aluminum foil makes for a more concentrated, flavorful braise.

Chilling the braising liquid overnight allows the fat to rise and solidify, making it easy to remove it the next day.

Bacon-Wrapped Duck–Stuffed Morels

Ground duck with its bits of juicy fat is perfect for basting morels from the inside out. Strangely enough, with all the exquisite stuffings made and gobbled at my parties here, no one has ever used duck. This mighty duck stuffing slid inside a morel and belted around by smoky bacon is not for fat-fearing sissies.

Any leftover ground duck mixture makes an extremely good burger.

[SERVES 4 TO 6; MAKES ABOUT 2½ CUPS STUFFING]

for the stuffing
2 large boneless duck breasts, skin on
    (1¼ pounds)
4 slices smoked bacon, cut into ¼-inch pieces
¾ teaspoon kosher salt
¼ teaspoon freshly ground black pepper
2 teaspoons finely chopped fresh thyme
1 tablespoon finely minced garlic
2 tablespoons dry white wine

Trim the skin and fat off the duck breasts. Weigh out 3 ounces of skin and fat and place on a dish in the freezer. Use whatever remains in another recipe.

Cut the duck meat into 1-inch cubes and place it in a medium bowl. Add the bacon, salt, pepper, thyme, and garlic. Stir everything together well to coat with the seasonings. Cover with plastic wrap and refrigerate for at least 1 hour or up to overnight.

Just before grinding the duck meat, remove the duck fat from the freezer (freezing the duck fat enables it to grind more easily and evenly in the meat). Working quickly, cut it into ¼-inch cubes. If it gets too soft, return it to the freezer to firm up again. Mix the cubes of duck fat into the duck meat.

Place the meat in a meat grinder fitted with the coarse die and grind through. Alternatively, pulse/ chop the meat in the bowl of a food processor. The texture will not be as even in a food processor.

Put the mixture through the grinder once more, then place it in the bowl of a standing mixer fitted with the paddle attachment. Add the white wine and beat on medium-high speed for 1 minute.

Use immediately or refrigerate in an airtight container. The stuffing will keep in the refrigerator for up to 3 days. Remove from the refrigerator 1 hour before using.

for the morels
2½ cups duck stuffing (above)
20 to 24 large gray morels, cleaned
10 to 12 slices smoked bacon,
    cut in half crosswise
2 tablespoons pure olive oil
Fleur de sel

Place the stuffing mixture in a piping bag fitted with a tip small enough to fit inside the mushrooms. Place the tip inside the mushroom and gently squeeze the piping bag, being careful not to overstuff it to bursting.

Wrap each mushroom with a slice of the bacon, pressing the overlapping ends of the bacon to seal.

Heat the oil in a large sauté pan over medium heat. When the oil is hot, add the mushrooms, the overlapping ends of the bacon facedown.

Cook for 2 to 3 minutes per side, making sure that the bacon is cooked and golden brown before turning and that the sausage is fully cooked by the time the bacon is done, about 10 to 12 minutes. Hold the cooked mushrooms in a warm place until all of them are done. Sprinkle the warm mushrooms with fleur de sel before serving.

TIPS AND TECHNIQUES

The stuffing freezes very well and will keep for 1 month.

SUBSTITUTIONS AND VARIATIONS

Pancetta can be substituted for the bacon, both in the stuffing and for wrapping around the morels.

You can add a tablespoon of chopped fresh basil to the seasoning mixture when marinating the duck meat.

Ground turkey can be used as a substitute for the duck. Mince the bacon finely and stir it into the ground turkey, along with the thyme, garlic, salt, and pepper. Stuff as directed above.

Morel-Stuffing Party

In our splendid spoiled-rotten tribe of chefs and mushroom-hunting fools, the annual gray morel–stuffing party held in June here on the mountains above Napa Valley outranks the Super Bowl. Our routine is simple: Bring a great bottle of wine and a pastry bag loaded with a morel stuffing. Gooey gobs of ingenuity and delicious cunning show up inside those pastry bags. Hours and many wine bottles later, we've gobbled stuffings of wild boar, andouille sausage, veal mousse, sweet corn with cheese, fava beans stuffed and wrapped in squash blossoms, and even a memorable crawfish sausage–stuffed morel dipped in corn-dog batter on a stick. My morel-stuffed morels (think Russian dolls here) debut next year. Come morning, there's a significant herd of hungover chefs here, but the morels are always gone.

Wild Fennel

FOENICULUM VULGARE

Aromatic wild fennel has been in the "kitchen" and "medicine chest" for thousands of years. Fennel has hitched rides with immigrants across the Mediterranean, India, and China and is now found nearly everywhere. Although domesticated as Florence fennel to produce fat white bulbs, common bulbless wild fennel remains far and away the most widely used, growing as it does just out the door and down the road.

At the zenith of its life, fennel's stately silhouette is a dreamy blue-green cloud of feathery foliage crowned with umbels of yellow flowers up to six inches across. Every bit of this elegant perennial is edible and all parts, from seed to root, are laden with fennel's signature aniselike perfume and flavor.

Fennel does indeed belong here in the heart of this summer chapter, yet its usefulness for foragers spans three seasons and includes every part of its fragrant plant body. Through its life cycle the fronds, flowers, flower pollen, seeds, and old bony stalks provide a sequence of culinary treasures.

YOUNG FRONDS: In late winter or spring, at the base of the large skeleton of last year's fennel plant, new fronds with bushy hairlike "leaves" emerge. Harvest only a third of these pretty stalks, no thicker than a ballpoint pen, per plant. A few leaves and stems are lovely fresh in salads, or they can be cooked for three or four minutes. Cooking gentles the intense Pernod-like power of raw fennel. Sicilians like my friend and fellow forager Angelo Garro cook delicious traditional fennel cakes of eggs, bread, and cheese. The greens also add great flavor when tucked inside the cavity of whole fish before cooking.

FLOWERS AND POLLEN: The starburst-shaped yellow flowers are the next tasty stage of fennel's useful life. Bright as a canary, the flowers are a joy sprinkled in greens or turned into various desserts, particularly a refreshing sorbet. Crowning the flowers with gold dust is that special prize, fennel pollen. Sarah is convinced that fennel pollen is a culinary umami-loaded pixie powder that makes more than just fish extra delicious. Dusting food like lamb, chicken, or fish requires a light hand or the flavor can become medicinal. Gathering pollen is as simple as putting a bag over the flower head and shaking. Put your collected pollen on cookie sheets to thoroughly dry before running it through a sieve and putting it in a tin or colored glass bottle. Although fennel is a perennial, don't cut all the flower heads off to get the pollen—as the flowers die, they create seed. And you'll want some seeds.

SEEDS, BOTH GREEN AND RIPE: As the flowers fade, the pale green lumps on the stalk ends are the soft embryonic seeds. These are fantastic little bombs of flavor when scattered in many things, like salad, sausages, or pizza. A few weeks later, as the fennel plant matures with the end of summer, its seeds will be the dry, grooved gray seeds you know from spice bottles. From pastry to meat, you can use them all year.

STALKS: Even as fennel's life ebbs, its tall skeletal stalks, retaining a touch of green, can be broken into lengths and placed directly on coals over which to grill fish. Later yet, as they get quite dry, they become hollow. I cut them and use them as short soda straws. A sturdy fennel stalk feels good on your lips and makes even ice water delicious and elegant.

Fennel's New World habitat spreads from Canada to Patagonia. Like so many invading species, fennel thrives along and in disturbed ground like roadsides or graded soils. Fennel grows with a special intensity near the ocean, as if it's creeping toward the fish it tastes so very good with. I even found some growing out of the sidewalk in Cordova, Alaska.

kitchen notes

ALERT: Fennel thrives along roadsides, but don't pick it on the flat or downhill side. Who wants fennel nourished by road effluents? Make sure of your ID. You'd have to have bad eyes and no sense of smell, but deadly water hemlock could be mistaken for fennel.

Fennel-Dusted Halibut with Wild Fennel Broth

The marriage of wild fennel and fish is an ancient one. Wild fennel thrives along the Mediterranean shore and has been picked by fishermen and taken home with the fish. Whether stuffed into the cavity, chopped into fish stews, or burned for its flavored smoke for cooking, fennel belongs with fish. Sarah's fish-friendly mushroom stock, combined with the fennel pollen, gives a double-barreled umami blast here. This is an elegant aromatic dish from this venerable fennel-and-fish tradition.

[SERVES 6]

Six 6-ounce halibut fillets
¾ teaspoon kosher salt, plus more to taste
⅛ teaspoon freshly ground black pepper, plus
    more to taste
1½ teaspoons fennel pollen
4 tablespoons pure olive oil
2 leeks, white part only, cleaned and cut into
    ¼-inch slices
2 cups coarsely chopped fennel stalks and heads
¼ cup dry white wine
4 cups Fish-Friendly Mushroom Stock (page 315)
3 tablespoons unsalted butter
½ teaspoon fresh lemon juice
½ tablespoon finely minced fennel fronds, plus
    extra fronds for garnish
Fleur de sel

Season the halibut fillets with salt and pepper. Sprinkle ¼ teaspoon of the fennel pollen evenly on top of each fillet. Set aside in the refrigerator. Remove the fillets from the refrigerator 20 minutes before cooking and allow to come to room temperature, so the fillets cook more evenly.

Heat 2 tablespoons of the oil in a large saucepan over medium-high heat. When the oil is hot, add the leeks and chopped fennel, stirring to coat with the oil. Add ¼ teaspoon salt and the ⅛ teaspoon pepper. Cook, stirring occasionally, until the vegetables are softened and starting to caramelize, 5 to 6 minutes. Add the white wine. Stir and cook until it has reduced to a glaze, 1 to 2 minutes. Add the mushroom stock. Bring to a boil, then turn down the heat to a simmer and cook for 40 to 45 minutes, or until the liquid has reduced to about 1½ cups. Strain the broth through a fine-mesh strainer into a smaller saucepan, pressing on the vegetables to extract all the juices. Discard the vegetables.

Bring the broth to a boil over medium-high heat, then whisk in the butter, ½ teaspoon salt, and lemon juice. Cook over high heat until the broth is slightly thickened and reduced to about 1 cup, 2 to 3 minutes. It should be a rich brown color. Remove from the heat and stir in the minced fennel fronds. Hold in a warm place while cooking the fish.

Heat the remaining 2 tablespoons oil in a large sauté pan over medium-high heat. When the oil is hot, place the fillets in the pan, pollen side down. Cook for 2 minutes, or until you can see the fillets beginning to change color on the bottom and sides as they cook. Cover, turn down the heat to low, and cook for 5 to 6 more minutes, or until the fillets are cooked through. Do not turn over the fillets during the cooking process or lift the lid, allowing steam to escape.

Reheat the sauce and divide it among 6 deep plates or pasta bowls. Place a fillet in each bowl, crusted side up, and sprinkle with a few grains of fleur de sel and wisps of fennel fronds.

TIPS AND TECHNIQUES

The sauce can be made 2 to 3 days ahead just to the point of adding the butter, salt, and lemon juice. To finish, bring to a boil and proceed according to the directions.

SUBSTITUTIONS AND VARIATIONS

This dish can be made with salmon or any other firm-fleshed fish.

If you don't have fennel pollen, substitute freshly ground fennel seeds.

You can substitute store-bought fennel bulbs for the wild fennel stalks in the sauce. To get more flavor, add ½ teaspoon crushed fennel seeds when you sauté the leeks and fennel.

For a more concentrated sauce, continue reducing it to ¾ cup after you've added the butter.

You can substitute clam juice, chicken broth, or regular mushroom broth for the Fish-Friendly Mushroom Stock in the recipe. Add less salt to the recipe in this case, tasting and adjusting at the end.

Nopales
[Prickly Pear Cactus Pads]

OPUNTIA SPECIES

Their spikes are pointed right at you, but you've got a knife and you're smarter than this heavily armed vegetable. Those Aztecs were tough, but their hungry ancestors may have been tougher yet to have learned to wrestle deliciousness from the nopal cactus. During summer, this useful cactus grows the tasty thorn-studded new pads called nopales. A beloved Mexican vegetable, nopales are found not only in the Mexican section of grocers' produce shelves but also in the wilds and tucked into the landscaping of nearly every state.

Thorny and beaver tail–shaped, nopales seem to always be described as tasting like green beans, bell peppers, or asparagus. In addition to these flavors are a citrusy tartness and the slipperiness of okra. Cooking nopales makes them less *baboso*, which means "slobbery" (cuter sounding than "slimy"). Some plants are less baboso than others. In fact, in Mexico, certain nopal cacti varieties are best known for their nopales, while others are known for their sweet fruit, called tunas or prickly pear fruit (see page 297).

Look for hand-size young paddles, and grab them with tongs, thick gloves, or a big barbecue fork. The paddles will have a green sheen and curved, single-thorned "eyes" like animal claws. With a large sharp knife, slice the nopales off above the joint with the main plant, leaving a stub from which another bud can grow. Many people feel that harvesting should be done early in the morning for the best flavor and lower acidity. To clean the nopales, ignore the common suggestions of burning off the spines or cooking the pads first and removing the spines afterward. Very young nopales can be easily cleaned of thorns by wiping a dish scrub sponge sideways across the pads under running water. Or, with gloves on, it's really quite easy to just hold the base of the paddle and, with short, flat strokes of your knife, slice off the thorns with the bumps, or eyes. Then, after you've cleaned both sides, run the knife around the paddle, slicing off the entire edge. Finally, cut an inch off the tough flesh you were holding at the base of the paddle, then rinse all the spines safely away.

Now you can slice the gentled paddle into string bean–shaped strips or make one more cut for squares. These smaller pieces are called *nopalitos*.

Except in a delicious traditional juice made of nopales and pineapple, nopalitos are rarely eaten raw. There are two ways to cook them: Either grill or boil them, then add them to a cooked dish. Grilled nopales are particularly excellent for those put off by slippery textures. Steve Sando's cheese-stuffed nopales recipe that follows is a great version of a classic Mexican recipe. Cut two to four slits into the paddle toward its base until it resembles an ugly glove, coat it with oil, and grill it. After boiling nopalitos for 10 to 15 minutes with a little onion or garlic, you can add them to colorful salads, traditional Lenten scrambled eggs, or tacos. To reduce the tartness and viscousness, and even to hold color, some people add a little baking soda, tomatillo husks, or an alkaline pre-Hispanic ingredient, a mineral called *tesquisquite*, to the water (see Guidebooks and Sources, page 336).

It's easy to become fond of nopales. As one friend said, "They taste like what most green beans should taste like." Later in the year, you'll fall in love with the nopal cactus's sweet fruit called the tuna (see page 297). These two great foods make the thorny nopal cactus as inviting as a rose.

kitchen notes

PREPARATION AND COOKING: See previous page.

STORAGE: They will keep for a week refrigerated in a plastic bag.

IDEAL NOPALES: The nopales should be a maximum ½ to ¾ inch thick, be the size of a hand, and have just a single thorn per eye. If you purchase nopales, make sure that they are unwrinkled, not floppy; bright green; and the base looks freshly cut.

Steve Sando's Nopales and Heirloom Tomato Salad with Epazote

This riotously colored salad reminds me of the Mexican flag. The flavors of the world would be so flat without New World foods. Discovery of a Native American food is still possible for the many who are strangers to nopales. Steve Sando, of Rancho Gordo, shares not only a crazy passion for Mexico, but here he shares this fine version of a classic Mexican salad. For the best color and texture, harvest just the tender shiny paddles to make the nopales strips, or nopalitos. The fresher the paddles, the better the flavor. Once-unusual ingredients like epazote, tomatillos, and Cotija cheese are now widely available in Mexican and even mainstream grocery stores.

[SERVES 4 TO 6]

2 garlic cloves

2½ teaspoons kosher salt, or more to taste

1 pound nopales paddles
    (3 medium or 4 to 5 small), cleaned

3 large tomatillos with husks

1 small white onion, sliced into ⅛-inch rings
    (save the root end for cooking the nopales)

1 pound multicolored heirloom tomatoes,
    cored and cut into ½-inch cubes

3 tablespoons extra virgin olive oil

3 tablespoons apple cider vinegar,
    or more to taste

¼ teaspoon freshly ground black pepper,
    or more to taste

3 ounces Cotija cheese, crumbled

6 to 8 epazote leaves, cut into fine slivers

Finely mince the garlic with ½ teaspoon of the salt. This will break down the garlic to almost a paste.

Cut the nopales paddles in half lengthwise, then crosswise into ¾-inch strips. (If the paddles are large, cut them into thirds lengthwise.) Place the strips in a large saucepan and cover with cold water. Peel or pull off the tomatillo husks, then add them to the saucepan. Use the tomatillos for another recipe. Rinse the root end of the onion and add it and 1 teaspoon of the salt to the pot. Bring the mixture to a boil, then turn down the heat and simmer until the strips are tender and mild tasting, 8 to 16 minutes, depending on the age of the paddles. Begin tasting after 8 minutes. If the nopales taste predominantly tart, continue cooking until the flavor has mellowed. Drain and set aside to cool to room temperature. Remove the onion and tomatillo husks and discard.

Place the minced garlic, onion slices, tomatoes, oil, and vinegar in a large salad bowl. Add the remaining 1 teaspoon salt and the pepper. Stir gently to combine, then let sit for at least 20 minutes at room temperature.

When the nopales have cooled, add them to the bowl with the tomato mixture and stir gently to combine. Mix in the Cotija and epazote. Taste for seasoning, adding more salt, pepper, or vinegar as needed.

SUBSTITUTIONS AND VARIATIONS

Instead of using the tomatillo husks, add a pinch of baking soda or tesquisquite during the last 10 minutes of cooking the nopalitos.

Nopales "Grilled Cheese" Paddles with Salsa Fresca

This may appear to be a grilled cheese sandwich from outer space, but it's actually a tradition on my pal Steve Sando's (Rancho Gordo) backyard grill and on patios all over Mexico. Steve is fortunate to be able to forage for nopales next to his bean field. There may be no simpler or more delicious nopales recipe. The cuts into the paddles make them look like strange green baseball gloves, but the cuts actually keep the nopales from curling on the grill as they cook. Small paddles, freshly harvested, are the ideal for this recipe. Older paddles take longer to cook and aren't as flavorful.

[SERVES 4]

for the nopales
8 small nopales paddles, cleaned
3 to 4 tablespoons pure olive oil
Kosher salt and freshly ground black pepper
6 ounces Oaxacan string cheese,
    pulled into 2-inch strands, or
    Monterey Jack, cut into thin slices

Prepare a grill to medium heat.

Starting at the top of each paddle, cut two 3-inch slits just to the right and left of center, creating what look like three fat "fingers" in the paddle. (Larger paddles may need 3 slits.) Brush both sides of the paddles with oil and season with salt and pepper.

Place the paddles on the grill and cook for 3 to 5 minutes per side, or until tender and slightly charred. Remove the paddles to a baking sheet beside the grill. Divide the cheese among 4 of the paddles, spreading it evenly over the surface. Cover with the remaining 4 paddles and press together gently. Return the paddles to the grill and cook for 1 to 2 minutes per side, or until the cheese is melted.

Spoon the salsa fresca over and serve warm.

for the salsa fresca
1 large garlic clove
½ teaspoon kosher salt, or more to taste
2 large tomatoes or 3 roma tomatoes,
    cored and cut into ¼-inch dice
½ cup finely diced red onion
1 serrano chile, seeded (optional) and finely diced
¼ cup fresh cilantro leaves, finely chopped
2 to 3 tablespoons fresh lime juice, or more
    to taste

Chop the garlic with the salt. This will break down the garlic to almost a paste.

Combine the tomatoes, red onion, garlic, serrano chile, cilantro, and lime juice in a bowl and let sit for at least 20 minutes at room temperature. Just before serving, taste for seasoning, adding more salt and/or lime juice as needed.

TIPS AND TECHNIQUES

Make the salsa before starting the paddles so it has time to sit while the paddles grill. Removing the seeds will remove some of the heat of the chile. Keep the seeds if you like the heat.

If the paddles are really small, you may not need as much cheese as is called for. Use your judgment when assembling the sandwiches, as too much cheese will ooze out onto the grill.

Make sure the paddles are thoroughly cooked before sandwiching them with the cheese, or they will be tough and unpleasant tasting.

SUBSTITUTIONS AND VARIATIONS

You can substitute mozzarella or any other good melting cheese you prefer for the Oaxacan string cheese.

You can substitute a small can of diced tomatoes (14.5 ounces), drained, for the fresh tomatoes in the salsa recipe.

You can substitute cider vinegar for the lime juice in the salsa recipe.

Sea Beans
[Glasswort, Samphire, Pickleweed]

This peculiar succulent plant grows like an odd survivor of some long-lost world. Ancient and leafless, this plant looks like it has held forth on its salty marsh perch ever since the dinosaurs and other strange species grazed and lumbered by with mud-sucking footfalls into extinction. In the last few centuries the animals plucking its tasty green corallike branches have usually been French, English, or Mediterranean foragers. In the last decade American foodies have slogged in too.

An assortment of *Salicornia* species are liberally painted along both North American coastlines and around the rim of Europe as well. These species have mastered a challenging habitat niche that few plants can endure. Sea beans are the amphibians of the plant world, locked as they are in a limbo zone between freshwater and salt water, and between land and sea. Sea beans commonly grow in large colonies in estuaries where freshwater flows past their muddy growing beds and into salt water. They like to have their feet touched by high tide but not the buffeting surf. In another strange niche, a couple of species grow around Utah's salt lakes, the saline lakes in California, and even a brine spring in New York State.

Sea beans grow in places strewn across the globe from Greece to Alaska and from Baja California to Dover, England. In English alone, people call them by a parade of names that includes glasswort, samphire, pickleweed, sea asparagus, and even chicken claws. The more appetizing name "sea beans" has won out in restaurants. It comes from the fact that the jade green branches snap like string beans. The plant is made up of linked, juicy, capsulelike cylinders that separate like old-fashioned pop beads. They taste like the two worlds they're a part of. Sea beans are juicy and crisply green like celery, yet the juicy interior is as salty as the sea. Like oysters that can share this type of habitat, their clean, briny flavor is most refreshing.

The drab mudflats start budding green with new sea bean plants in spring. By late May their growth can be near their full ten- to twelve-inch mature height. Wait for low tide, put on your rubber boots, grab a bucket, and head into the marsh. Cut the upper four to six inches of tender tops and put them in your bucket. Harvest from the edges of the sea bean beds. It's best to avoid walking into the sea bean colonies because the plants are very brittle, and your steps butcher the plants. By August a tough fiberglasslike thread begins to form in the center of the stalks. This marks the end of the season. Soon after, the plants will turn pale and then eventually a luminous russet red as autumn spreads throughout the marsh.

kitchen notes

CLEANING AND PREPARATION: Cleaning is a simple business: Just swish briskly in freshwater. If sea beans are too salty for your taste, soak them in fresh cold water for thirty minutes, then drain them.

COOKING METHODS: Sea beans delight most of us best in their crunchy raw state, either nibbled on or added to salads. Europeans have a longer history of using sea beans (which they call samphire), and they blanch, steam, stir-fry, and sauté them. Sea beans blanched for three minutes are a perfect throne for a fish fillet. Quick cooking intensifies the green color and still keeps much of sea beans' crisp quality. As you might guess, pickling (see page 311) is a favorite cooking method worldwide. Either use a light hand or use no salt at all for dishes that include sea beans.

STORAGE: When kept moist in a closed plastic bag, sea beans will last for a surprising three weeks in your refrigerator.

IDEAL SEA BEANS: The bright four- to six-inch-long green tender tips are what you want. Avoid them when the hard, stringy core has formed inside the stem, as it does later in the summer.

ALERT: Avoid harvesting in polluted areas. Sea beans have a nasty habit of accumulating heavy metals.

Sarah's Seaside Sea Bean and Seared Tuna Salad

This is an exceptionally delicious and lovely looking variation on a salade Niçoise. Sea beans are so perfect here that it makes you wonder why they weren't always a part of this seaside salad. And be forewarned: The sea bean tartar sauce is an addictive substance. Make a double batch of the sauce and then plan to make a nice batch of batter-fried fish to dip into it a day or two later.

[SERVES 6]

for the tuna and salad
Six 4-ounce ahi tuna fillets
Kosher salt and freshly ground black pepper
6 ounces cleaned sea beans
¾ pound new or fingerling potatoes
1 cup cherry tomatoes, stemmed and halved
    (multicolored, if you can find them)
¼ cup pitted kalamata olives, cut into quarters
2 tablespoons pure olive oil
2 tablespoons finely chopped flat-leaf parsley

Season the tuna fillets with salt and pepper. Refrigerate until 1 hour before cooking.

Bring a medium saucepan of unsalted water to a boil (remember, sea beans are very salty). Cook the sea beans for 3 minutes, then drain and plunge them into ice water. Set aside ⅓ cup for the sea bean tartar sauce. Refrigerate the rest until ready to serve.

Steam or gently boil the potatoes in lightly salted water until tender, 20 to 25 minutes. Cool and cut into ¼-inch slices. Refrigerate until ready to serve.

Combine the cherry tomatoes and olives in a small bowl. Refrigerate until ready to serve.

for the sea bean tartar sauce
¾ cup mayonnaise
1 clove garlic, finely minced
½ teaspoon finely grated lemon zest
1 teaspoon fresh lemon juice
1 tablespoon capers, drained, rinsed,
    and finely minced
½ teaspoon Thai fish sauce (nam pla) or
    ¼ teaspoon anchovy paste
¼ teaspoon freshly ground black pepper
Reserved ⅓ cup sea beans, finely chopped

Combine the mayonnaise, garlic, lemon zest, lemon juice, capers, fish sauce, pepper, and sea beans in a small bowl and mix well. Refrigerate, covered, until ready to finish the salad.

for the vinaigrette
2 tablespoons finely minced shallots
2 tablespoons red wine vinegar
2 teaspoons fresh lemon juice
¼ teaspoon kosher salt
⅛ teaspoon freshly ground black pepper
½ teaspoon Dijon mustard
¼ cup extra virgin olive oil
¼ cup pure olive oil

Place the shallots, vinegar, lemon juice, and salt in a medium bowl. Stir to combine, then let sit for 15 minutes. Whisk in the pepper and mustard. Combine the two olive oils. While whisking, drizzle the oil mixture slowly into the vinegar mixture until emulsified and thickened. Set aside.

to finish
Heat a large sauté pan with the 2 tablespoons pure olive oil over medium-high heat. Alternatively, heat a grill to medium-high heat. Sear or grill the tuna to medium rare, 3 to 5 minutes per side. Hold in a warm place while assembling the salad.

to serve
Toss the sea beans with 2 tablespoons of the vinaigrette. Divide the sea beans among 6 plates, making a bed for the rest of the salad. Top with the sliced potatoes, drizzling with some of the vinaigrette. Add 1 to 2 tablespoons of the vinaigrette to the tomato mixture and spoon the mixture onto the potatoes. Sprinkle with salt and pepper. Drizzle any remaining vinaigrette over the vegetables, then top with a tuna fillet. Place a generous dollop of sea bean tartar sauce on top of each piece of tuna and sprinkle with the parsley. Serve immediately.

TIPS AND TECHNIQUES
The sea bean tartar sauce can be made up to 3 days ahead and will keep, covered, for up to 1 week in the refrigerator. It just gets better and better.

SUBSTITUTIONS AND VARIATIONS
Haricots verts or green beans can be substituted for the sea beans. Blanch them in lightly salted water.

Salmon, halibut, or any firm-fleshed fish can be substituted for the tuna.

Auntie Nemo's Sea Bean and Potato Salad

Messing about with a beloved tradition like potato salad is dangerous. If you've tasted sea beans, you'll have an "Aha, why didn't I think of that?" reaction. If you haven't tasted them, you're probably horrified at the notion of adding greenery that appears to come from another solar system to Mom's potato salad. Have faith; take the leap. The salty crunch of sea beans is brilliant and will make the typical celery seem drab ever after.

[SERVES 4 TO 6]

1 pound small Yukon Gold, new,
    or fingerling potatoes
2 tablespoons finely minced shallots
1 teaspoon red wine vinegar
1 teaspoon fresh lemon juice
½ cup plus 2 tablespoons crème fraîche
2 tablespoons mayonnaise
1 teaspoon Thai fish sauce (nam pla)
¼ teaspoon kosher salt
¼ teaspoon freshly ground black pepper
1½ ounces (½ cup) sea beans, cleaned
    and cut into ¼-inch pieces
2 teaspoons finely minced fresh chives

Steam or gently boil the potatoes in lightly salted water until tender, 20 to 25 minutes. Cool to room temperature. Cut the potatoes in half, then into ¼-inch slices. Place in a large bowl and set aside.

Combine the shallots, vinegar, and lemon juice in a small bowl and stir to moisten. Let sit for 15 minutes.

Whisk together the crème fraîche, mayonnaise, fish sauce, salt, and pepper in another small bowl. Set aside.

Add the sea beans to the potatoes and mix together gently. Stir in the shallot mixture, then the crème fraîche mixture. Taste for seasoning and adjust as needed. Stir in the chives.

TIPS AND TECHNIQUES

The salad can be made a day ahead and will keep for up to 1 week in the refrigerator. The flavors continue to develop over time.

SUBSTITUTIONS AND VARIATIONS

If you can't find Thai fish sauce, substitute ¼ teaspoon anchovy paste.

Scallions can be substituted for the shallots. There is no need to let them sit in the vinegar and lemon juice ahead of time.

Sour cream can be substituted for the crème fraîche.

Wild Summer Berries

Certainly the blackberries and raspberries in your grocery store are much more convenient. Your only yelp comes from opening your wallet rather than from thorns. The intense flavor of wild summer berries isn't found on any store shelf, however. The smaller wild berries make their domesticated brethren seem watery by comparison.

Blackberries and Raspberries

RUBUS SPECIES

I write this with purple paws. While contemplating the summer's brambly tangled richness of dewberries, thimbleberries, salmonberries, cloudberries, blackcaps, wineberries, raspberries, and so on, I can just imagine my mother's voice: "Here's the pail. Just go pick some blackberries." I always did. My mother had heard that same thing from her mother, and so on back through generations. As the most commonly gathered wild food, these ripe berries are a lifeline right back to our foraging ancestors. When sweet, ripe summer berries beckon, even my eighty-five-year-old mother hears Grandma Liller's voice and finds herself with purple lips and fingers.

Wild raspberries and blackberries are so common that I'd surely win a bet that you are within ten miles of a berry patch right now, no matter where you are. Even the few people in the whole country who've never picked them quickly recognize blackberries and raspberries as old friends. Wild raspberries, both red and blackcaps (black raspberries), are smaller and more flavorful than their domesticated kin in the grocery store. Unlike that of the blackberry clan, the core of a raspberry, the receptacle, remains on the stem and leaves the ripe berry hollow when picked. Raspberries ripen earlier, are more delicate, and have a shorter shelf life than blackberries. Blackberries are an entwined labyrinth of varieties found, thanks to birds, all over the world. Late-ripening blackberries are the most thorn endowed of all the brambles. Blackberries and raspberries are found near creeks, on disturbed ground, at the edges of woods, and very often on roadsides.

A few harvesting tips are in order for these delicate yet well-armed berries. Ripe berries need almost no pulling. They'll nearly fall into your hands. No matter how hot it is, while you pick, wear jeans, closed-toe shoes, and a jacket to cover your arms. A pair of leather gloves with the fingertips cut off is a great idea. Move slowly, because the thorns are angled to grab you as your hand moves out of the thicket. I never pick without a long stick with a nail driven into the end at a right angle. With it I can grab and pull the out-of-reach berry-loaded canes toward me. Forget picking into bags and choose a small bucket instead to help keep the berries whole and protect them from crushing. I like to put the little plastic strawberry baskets that you get in the grocery store in the bucket to keep the ripe berries intact. Relax about all those fat berries that are just out of reach. Other critters need them more than you do. If you're in bear country, do announce yourself with some bad singing. The bears will most likely flee.

Mulberries

MORUS RUBRA; M. ALBA

In Chicago, during a two-year flirtation with city life, I began to spot the first purple fruit hanging from small trees lining the sidewalks on my way to work. For several wonderful weeks both the sidewalks and I were polka-dotted purple. My boss was madly in favor of my coloration once I gave him a bowl of mulberries. This exquisitely flavored fruit seems all but invisible to people. Now it's common to see the tragic "fruitless" mulberry trees, bred to eliminate all the messy fruit.

Our native "red" mulberry, with its luscious, juicy, and screamingly purple ripe fruit, grows wild from North Dakota to Manhattan island. The white mulberry tree, introduced a couple of centuries ago, failed to launch an American silk industry but did manage to spread throughout the country. Its white fruit is abundant, but the cloying low-acid sweetness can't compare to the complex flavor of the red mulberry. Both berries are very delicate and must be used within a day or two.

Whether you forage mulberries from forests or city sidewalks, you'll find it delightful picking. With just a step stool, you can pluck away in the cool shade of these small thornless trees. More fun yet is the "purple rain" option of spreading a tarp under the tree and shaking the branches. Expect rich purple stains on everything.

kitchen notes

Wash berries, if necessary, just before using. Store the unwashed berries in layers no more than four deep in your refrigerator. Use within forty-eight hours. They can be frozen as individual berries on a cookie sheet, then put in a plastic bag for future use.

ABOVE: *Mulberries*

OPPOSITE: *Fresh Mulberry Ice Cream* [PAGE 128]

Fresh Mulberry Ice Cream

What a color! The flavor is just as dazzling. Sarah's recipe is deceptively simple. This noncustard ice cream is extremely creamy and, unlike many homemade ice creams, it keeps beautifully in the freezer for many days. Mulberries are the best berry for this vivid-colored ice cream, with wild huckleberries a close second. The *Rubra* gang—blackberries, blackcaps, and raspberries—are fantastic here as well, but be sure to strain out the seeds.

[MAKES 1 QUART]

3 cups mulberries
¾ cup sugar
¼ teaspoon kosher salt
2 cups half-and-half
1 tablespoon fresh lemon juice

Place the mulberries, sugar, and salt in a medium saucepan over medium heat. Press on the berries with a potato masher or wooden spoon to extract the juices as they heat up. Stir to dissolve the sugar and salt. Cook until the mixture just comes to a boil. Remove from the heat and pour through a fine-mesh strainer set over a bowl. Press to extract all the juices from the fruit, then discard the solids. There should be 1¼ to 1½ cups of juice. Cool to room temperature.

Whisk in the half-and-half and lemon juice. Refrigerate for at least 30 minutes or overnight.

Freeze in an ice cream machine, according to the manufacturer's instructions.

TIPS AND TECHNIQUES

The longer the mixture has to sit before being frozen, the thicker its texture. Overnight is best.

A compote made of fresh mulberries, stirred together with a little sugar and lemon juice, is a nice flourish. Let the compote sit a little bit before serving to allow the juices to dissolve the sugar and the flavors to come together.

SUBSTITUTIONS AND VARIATIONS

Many berries can be substituted for the mulberries: huckleberries, blackberries, and raspberries, among others. Taste as you go, adding more sugar or lemon juice as needed to balance the varying berry flavors.

Stephen Durfee's Blackberry "Caviar" Blinis and Crème Fraîche

You can do it the hard way or the easy way; either way this is delicious. To get the complete caviar illusion you must, by knifepoint, flick each little black membrane-covered juicy ball off the blackberry. Hold the berry by the tip and start from where the stem was. If you *have* to buy the big cultivated blackberries, cut them in half, then begin to flick off the little black "eggs." Black raspberries are hollow and easier to pick apart.

I suggest that you cajole some friends into coming early to your dinner party. Pour them a big glass of wine and give them this task. Without doubt, bitching about this fussy job will be fodder for table talk. Our friend Stephen Durfee, of the Culinary Institute of America and winner of the James Beard Award for pastry while he was French Laundry pastry chef, would pat you on the back for achieving the visual pun of his lovely dessert.

The easy (and just as tasty) way to present this is to use whole or halved berries on the blinis.

[**SERVES 6**]

for the blackberry caviar

1 pint (6 ounces) blackberries
1 teaspoon confectioners' sugar,
    plus more for garnish

Using the tip of a small sharp knife, work the pips off the core of the berry, starting at the stem end. Let the pips fall into a bowl as you work. Ideally, you want individual pips, but small clusters may come off as well. Sift the confectioners' sugar over the berry pips and very gently stir to coat with the sugar. Cover and refrigerate until ready to serve, up to 2 hours.

for the crème fraîche

⅓ cup crème fraîche
1 tablespoon heavy cream
½ teaspoon granulated sugar

Whisk together the crème fraîche, cream, and sugar in a small bowl until thickened and the mixture holds soft but definite peaks. Cover and refrigerate until ready to use, up to 2 hours.

for the blinis

⅓ cup unbleached all-purpose flour
1 tablespoon buckwheat flour
1 tablespoon granulated sugar
⅛ teaspoon kosher salt
¾ teaspoon baking powder
1 large egg, separated
¼ cup milk
1 tablespoon unsalted butter, melted

Sift the all-purpose flour and buckwheat flour into a medium bowl. Whisk in the sugar, salt, and baking powder.

Whisk together the egg yolk and milk in a small bowl. Stir into the flour mixture, just until the ingredients are moistened. Stir in the butter. Whip the egg white with a whisk in a small bowl to a soft peak, then fold it into the flour mixture, just until incorporated. Be careful not to overmix. Let the batter sit for 5 minutes at room temperature.

Heat a crepe pan or medium nonstick sauté pan over medium-low heat. Spray with nonstick vegetable cooking spray or brush with clarified butter, if needed. Drop ½ tablespoonfuls of batter into the pan, being careful not to overcrowd the pan. The batter will spread slightly as it cooks. Cook for 20 to 30 seconds, or until the edges are dry and small bubbles start to appear in the top surface. Carefully turn over the blinis and cook for 20 to 30 more seconds. Remove to a wire rack and hold in a warm place while you finish cooking the rest. You should have 18 blinis.

to finish

The blinis should be served warm, so have all the components of the recipe ready before assembling them. Work quickly as soon as the blinis are made. Arrange 3 blinis on each plate. Top each blini with a dollop of the crème fraîche mixture. Divide the blackberry caviar among the blinis. Dust the tops with confectioners' sugar just before serving.

TIPS AND TECHNIQUES

Fresh-picked blackberries are the best. The older the berries, the softer the pips and the harder it is to pick them off whole.

SUBSTITUTIONS AND VARIATIONS

Several varieties of berries can be substituted for the blackberries: small huckleberries or blueberries, black raspberries, red or yellow raspberries, or marionberries, for example.

indian
summer

Chanterelles

CANTHARELLUS CIBARIUS; C. FORMOSUS; C. CALIFORNICUS

I fell in love with chanterelles in the mid-1970s. We became engaged a few years later after I wandered into a wood and my knees went weak at the sight of gold chanterelles spangling the ground as far as I could see. Not long after, we married, when I found that there was nothing I'd rather do than make my living bringing my chanterelles to chefs (to their great delight) and seeing these mushrooms become beautiful food. All these decades later I still feel joy with each and every one I find, no matter if it's my millionth chanterelle.

Beyond in my heart, chanterelles occupy a huge chunk of the forests all over the world. From Zimbabwe to Vancouver Island, Siberia to Costa Rica, Saskatchewan to uptown New Orleans, their graceful golden form is a familiar sight to foragers worldwide. One day while I was delivering chanterelles, a very excited man rushed up to me on the sidewalk and gushed, "We *love* these in my country." He was fresh from Nigeria. On our continent, they range from the tiny, very fragrant chanterelles from the pines of Nova Scotia to the largest chanterelles in the world—those thriving under California live oaks. The chanterelles' symbiotic relationship with trees is so wide ranging (Douglas fir, hemlock, spruce, aspen, oak, etc.) that I cannot generalize. You'll need to discover the secrets of and the host tree for chanterelles in your own world via your mycological society or kindly fellow hunters, particularly the mushroom-crazed Polish and Russian ones.

In just a few decades I've lived through French chefs not believing chanterelles grew in America to people thinking that chanterelles grew under the sea to now having nearly everyone recognize a chanterelle when they see one. Chanterelles are even sold at Costco!

In the course of merrily draining three bottles of cabernet with Michael Ruhlman as he was coauthoring the now-legendary *French Laundry Cookbook*, one of the ideas he later quoted me on during bottle number one was that the chanterelle is the "workhorse" of the mushroom world. This is still true. There is no mushroom more versatile. Its texture when cooked is as tender as a gently cooked oyster. Its flavor has a toasty, gently nutty quality that flatters nearly everything with which it's paired. The famous apricot aroma and pepper taste (it has the name *pfifferling* in German) of the raw chanterelle become a faint base note after cooking. (You can taste this essence clearly in the Chanterelle Vodka recipe on page 322.)

Chanterelles are the fungal kingdom's most generous gift to those of us who love to hunt and eat wild mushrooms. The floral beauty of each chanterelle belies its surprising sturdiness and worldwide abundance. The easily identified chanterelle is the perfect wild mushroom with which to begin a long-term relationship with the forest. My patches and I have been together for nearly thirty years. Go find yours.

kitchen notes

CLEANING AND PREPARATION: Cleaning begins with tidy picking. Brush the mushroom while harvesting and peel or cut the dirty base off before putting it in your basket. Chanterelles grow rather slowly and have been through numerous rains by the time you pick them. Don't be afraid to wash them if they're dirty. See page 326 for more details.

COOKING METHODS: Whether you sauté, roast, grill, or butter poach them, chanterelles may be the most versatile of all mushrooms. From ham and eggs to halibut, they harmonize with almost everything.

STORAGE: Yet another joy of chanterelles is their remarkable shelf life. Most species will hold beautifully in your refrigerator for two weeks after a big hunt. Dried chanterelles are like shoe leather, but they are nice for infusing vodka.

IDEAL CHANTERELLES: No matter the type of chanterelle, it should be clean and dry enough that its stem yields little or no water when pinched, but not so dry that the cap edges are browning. In most of the world chanterelles are bug free, but in the few areas where bugs have become gourmets, watch for little holes.

Luscious Chanterelle and Corn Chowder

In 1983, during a delivery of my chanterelles to Patty Unterman at Hayes Street Grill in San Francisco, I mentioned that "it's too bad that chanterelles and corn are nearly the same color, because they go so well together." Patty loved that idea, and by the following week, chanterelle-crowned polenta cakes were already a favorite on her menu. We now take this pairing of chanterelles and corn for granted; this wonderful flavor duo is a completely American contribution to world cuisine. Corn-wary Europeans never saw this coming. Chanterelles and corn having a good swim together in Sarah's great chowder is another riff on this fine duo.

Have all the ingredients ready before starting as the soup comes together quickly once you begin.

[MAKES 6 CUPS]

2 ounces smoked bacon (about 2 strips),
    cut into ¼-inch dice
3 tablespoons unsalted butter
½ cup finely diced yellow onion
1 medium celery stalk, finely diced
1 large garlic clove, finely minced
¾ pound cleaned chanterelles, cut into ½-inch dice
1 cup fresh yellow or white corn kernels
    (from 2 ears of corn)
1 large Yukon Gold potato, peeled and
    cut into ½-inch dice
3 tablespoons unbleached all-purpose flour
1 teaspoon chopped fresh thyme
1½ teaspoons kosher salt, or more to taste
¼ teaspoon freshly ground black pepper
1 small bay leaf
1 quart Traditional Mushroom Stock (page 315)
1 cup heavy cream
½ teaspoon fresh lemon juice, or more to taste

Place the bacon in a large stockpot over medium heat. Cook until just starting to brown, 3 to 4 minutes, then add the butter. When the butter has melted, stir in the onion, celery, and garlic. Cook until tender and translucent, 4 to 5 minutes. Add the chanterelles and cook for 3 to 4 more minutes, or until the mushrooms are softened and tender. Stir in the corn and potatoes and cook for 2 to 3 minutes, or until they begin to soften.

Sprinkle the flour evenly over the vegetables in the pot and stir to coat them with the flour. Add the thyme, salt, pepper, and bay leaf. Add the mushroom stock, stirring continuously to prevent lumps from forming. Bring the soup to a boil, then turn down the heat and simmer for 20 minutes, or until the potatoes are tender.

Remove the bay leaf. Stir in the cream and lemon juice. Taste for seasoning, adding more lemon juice and/or salt as needed.

SUBSTITUTIONS AND VARIATIONS
Russet or new potatoes can be substituted for the Yukon Golds.

Frozen corn can be substituted for the fresh.

Canned chicken broth can be substituted for the mushroom stock. Use less salt; taste and adjust the seasoning at the end.

Grilled Quail with Chanterelles, Pancetta, and Soft Polenta

For both Sarah and me, fall is branded with the memories of our big fathers toting home these little birds. This recipe could as easily be called our "Daddy's Bagged Georgia Quail over Grits with Bacon and Wild Mushrooms." This is just so delicious. Little game birds nested beside "Italian grits" with corn-loving chanterelles draped over the browned birdie skin is as autumn as autumn can be.

[SERVES 6]

for the quail

12 boneless quail
Kosher salt and freshly ground black pepper
12 thin slices pancetta

Cut the wings off the quail at the breast and set aside to make the sauce. Season the quail lightly with salt and pepper. (Or brine them ahead of time; see Tips and Techniques on page 141.)

    Wrap each quail with a slice of the pancetta, overlapping the slices on the back of the quail. Place on a baking sheet and refrigerate until ready to use, up to 4 hours. Remove from the refrigerator 1 hour before cooking.

for the quail jus

1 tablespoon pure olive oil
2 thin slices pancetta, cut into ¼-inch dice
Reserved quail wings (above)
⅓ cup finely diced onion
1 garlic clove, finely minced
½ teaspoon kosher salt
2 cups homemade chicken stock

Heat the oil in a medium saucepan over medium-high heat. Add the pancetta and cook until softened and just starting to brown, 2 to 3 minutes. Add the quail wings, stirring to coat with the oil. Cook for 5 to 6 minutes, stirring occasionally, then add the onion, garlic, and salt. Continue cooking until the wings are browned and the onion and garlic are tender, 4 to 5 more minutes. Add the chicken stock, scraping the bottom of the pan to incorporate all the cooked bits. Bring to a boil, then turn down the heat and simmer until reduced to about ¾ cup liquid, 12 to 14 minutes. Strain through a fine-mesh strainer, discard the solids, and set aside until ready to cook the chanterelles.

for the chanterelles

3 tablespoons unsalted butter
½ pound cleaned chanterelles, torn into
    ½-inch pieces
½ teaspoon kosher salt
⅛ teaspoon freshly ground black pepper
2 garlic cloves, finely minced
Reserved quail jus (above)
2 tablespoons finely chopped flat-leaf parsley

Heat the butter in a large sauté pan over medium-high heat. When the butter is melted and bubbling, add the chanterelles, tossing to coat evenly with the butter. Add the salt and pepper. Cook, stirring occasionally, until the mushrooms have released their liquid. Continue cooking until the liquid has evaporated and the mushrooms are starting to brown and caramelize.

Add the garlic and cook for 1 more minute. Add the quail jus and turn the heat to high. Cook for 1 to 2 minutes, or until the pan juices are slightly thickened. Turn off the heat and hold the mushrooms in a warm place until it's time to finish the dish.

for the polenta

1 teaspoon kosher salt, or more to taste
¾ cup polenta or coarse-ground cornmeal
2 tablespoons unsalted butter
2 tablespoons grated Parmesan
¼ teaspoon freshly ground black pepper,
    or more to taste

Place 4 cups water and the salt in a medium saucepan. Bring to a boil. Slowly add the polenta, whisking continuously to prevent lumping. When the mixture returns to a boil, turn down the heat to a simmer and cook, stirring frequently, for at least 35 minutes, or until the polenta is tender. You may need to whisk in additional water, ¼ cup at a time, if the polenta gets too thick while cooking.

Whisk in the butter, Parmesan, and pepper. Taste for seasoning, adding more salt and/or pepper as needed. Thin with additional water, if needed. Remove from the heat, cover, and hold in a warm place while you grill the quail.

to finish

Prepare a grill to medium-high heat.

Place the quail on the grill, back side down, and sear the ends of the pancetta slices together. Cook for 5 to 6 minutes, then carefully turn over the quail, being careful to keep the pancetta slices intact. Cook for 5 to 6 more minutes, or until just cooked through. Remove the quail from the grill and let rest for 5 minutes before serving. (You can pull them off earlier if you like your quail medium rare.)

Stir the polenta, adding water, if needed, to thin the texture. Rewarm the mushrooms.

For individual servings, divide the polenta among 6 deep bowls or dishes. Top with 2 quail per person and spoon over some chanterelles and jus. Garnish with the parsley.

For family style, spoon the polenta into the center of a large platter. Lay the quail down the middle and spoon over the chanterelles and jus. Garnish with the parsley.

TIPS AND TECHNIQUES

Brining the quail a day ahead gives them more flavor and makes them more moist and succulent when cooked. Use a proportion of 2 tablespoons kosher salt to 2 quarts water, plus 1 bay leaf, 3 fresh thyme sprigs, and 1 crushed garlic clove for the brining mixture.

The quail jus can be made a day ahead and refrigerated in an airtight container overnight or up to a week. Homemade chicken stock is best here, but you can use water instead, for a lighter flavor. If using canned chicken broth, use less salt and adjust the seasoning at the end of cooking.

The brined quail can be wrapped with the pancetta and refrigerated for up to 6 hours before cooking. It's best to do it the day it will be cooked and served, not a day ahead.

SUBSTITUTIONS AND VARIATIONS

Bone-in quail can be substituted for the boneless quail. Adjust the cooking time, using an instant-read thermometer for accuracy.

Cornish game hens can be substituted for the quail. Split them in half and proceed as for the recipe. The cooking time will be longer, so use an instant-read thermometer for accuracy.

Other fresh herbs, such as basil, thyme, or chives, can be added to the mushrooms.

Louisiana-Style Chanterelle Hash

WITH . . . ROASTED CHICKEN, EGGS, SAUSAGE, BOUDIN, PORK CHOPS, CATFISH, MUSHROOM GRAVY, RIB-EYE STEAK, SHRIMP, ROAST RABBIT, FRIED CHICKEN . . .

My pal Donald Link, chef/owner of Herbsaint and Couchon restaurants in New Orleans, is another chef I've deliberately infected with the mushroom-hunting virus. One day he called giggling like a kid to report that he'd just picked eight pounds of Louisiana chanterelles. I could hear loud thunder in the background because he was hunkered down under a porch in a thunderstorm at the time.

Donald let Sarah mess around with his great chicken/chanterelle hash recipe, turning this into a chanterelle hash side dish. When we pondered what this hash would go with, the list went on and on. I can't really think of much of anything that doesn't taste better with this fantastic hash alongside. Make plenty. While recipe testing, Sarah's ever-moderate sidekick Sam gobbled up nine patties.

[MAKES 12 CAKES]

---

2 large Yukon Gold potatoes

4 ounces smoked bacon (about 4 slices),
    cut into ¼-inch dice

¼ cup pure olive oil, plus ½ to ¾ cup more
    for cooking the cakes

1 cup finely diced yellow onion

3 large garlic cloves, finely minced

1 jalapeño chile, seeded, finely diced (optional)

1 tablespoon finely chopped fresh thyme

1 pound cleaned chanterelles,
    cut into ¼-inch dice or torn into thin shreds

2 teaspoons kosher salt

¾ teaspoon freshly ground black pepper

Pinch of cayenne pepper

2 tablespoons unbleached all-purpose flour,
    plus ½ cup for dusting cakes

½ cup Traditional Mushroom Stock (page 315)

Place the potatoes, whole and unpeeled, into a large pot of salted water. Bring to a boil over medium-high heat and cook until they are very tender, about 20 to 25 minutes. When they have cooled to room temperature, peel them and cut into ¼-inch cubes. You should have about 2 cups.

Place the bacon and the ¼ cup oil in a large sauté pan over medium heat. Cook until the bacon is just golden brown, 3 to 4 minutes. Add the onion, garlic, jalapeño, and thyme and cook until tender, 4 to 5 minutes. Add the chanterelles, turn up the heat to medium high, and cook until the mushrooms are tender and any excess liquid has cooked off, 4 to 5 minutes.

Stir in the potatoes, 1½ teaspoons of the salt, ½ teaspoon of the black pepper, and the cayenne. Mix well. Sprinkle the 2 tablespoons flour evenly over the mushroom mixture, stirring to coat with the flour. Add the mushroom stock, stirring quickly as the mixture comes together and thickens, 1 to 1½ minutes. Turn the mixture out onto a baking sheet to cool. Pressing lightly on the mixture at this point will help to form firmer cakes.

Divide the cooled mixture into 12 portions and shape them into rounded patty-shaped cakes. Place the ½ cup flour in a small bowl with the remaining ½ teaspoon salt and the remaining ¼ teaspoon pepper. Dip each cake into the flour, coating it evenly and shaking off any excess before placing it on a baking sheet. Let the cakes sit for 10 minutes before cooking.

Place enough oil in a large sauté pan to come ¼ inch up the sides, ½ to ¾ cup. Place the sauté pan over medium-high heat. When the oil is hot, place the cakes in the pan, being careful not to crowd them. You may have to cook them in batches. Cook until golden brown, 4 to 5 minutes, then carefully turn them over and cook for 4 to 5 more minutes. Remove them to a wire rack placed over a baking sheet and hold them in a warm place while you cook the remaining cakes.

Serve alone or as a side dish.

TIPS AND TECHNIQUES

You can refrigerate the mixture overnight. It will help set it and make shaping the cakes easier.

The cakes can be cooked in a mixture of olive oil and bacon fat, if desired, for a richer flavor. Vegetable or canola oil can also be used.

SUBSTITUTIONS AND VARIATIONS

Canned chicken broth can be substituted for the mushroom stock. Use less salt, adjusting the seasoning at the end of cooking the hash mixture.

Russet or new potatoes can be substituted for the Yukon Golds.

Puffballs

CALVATIA GIGANTEA; C. BOONIANA;
C. CYANTHIFORMIS/LYCOPERDON PERLATUM; L. PYRIFORME

Puffballs are probably the biggest reason that foragers like me become menaces behind the wheel during mushroom season. A glimpse of a round white anything on a grassy background can cause swerving and speeds dropping from sixty miles per hour to five. It might be a dozing lamb, a lost soccer ball, one of those awful white pumpkins, or please, please, please, a giant puffball. There's not a soul who hasn't seen and kicked a leathery puffball just to see its poof of brown spore dust erupt, but what you really want is to find that fat puffball earlier, when it's fresh and white and thumps like a ripe melon.

There are many varieties of tasty puffballs, and they fall into two general shapes. Puffballs of the genus *Calvatia* are roundish and range from the size of a quail egg to that of a small propane tank. Those of *Lycoperdon* are the size and shape of regular and small lightbulbs. The lives of all puffballs are similar. They grow rapidly into their given shapes and both have a globe-shaped chamber the color and consistency of a marshmallow or a nice, chalky goat cheese. This is the delicious stage of interior whiteness that we want to harvest them in. Exterior size, particularly with the giant puffball, can't tell you whether the puffball is a creamy, edible white throughout. The only way is to slice the puffball from top to bottom and look inside. Watch for a stain in the middle that may be yellow to green to brownish. These colors are the spores forming as the puffball begins the process of turning into the kickable sack of smoky spores that is its final destiny. If you see a color forming in the white center or the faint outline of an embryonic mushroom inside, give it up and toss the mushroom. The first scenario could upset your stomach. The second means that it isn't a puffball and it could be the egg stage of one of the perilous or poisonous *Amanita* mushrooms.

You can spot giant puffballs and their kin in old pastures and meadows from Indian summer through fall everywhere but the Far West, where our *C. booniana* usually appears in early summer.

It tends to reappear in the same field and some years is ludicrously abundant. For example, the same afternoon I found an eleven-pound puffball, a rancher pulled into my mushroom buyer's place with his pickup truck *filled* with giant puffballs. This remarkable sight was repeated until I had to ask him not to bring in more than eighty pounds at a time. The overflow became many messy BLTs using puffball slices as white bread. My chefs were cutting shapes out of the big puffball slices for fungal creations, and vegetarians were merrily slicing into puffball steaks all over San Francisco.

This very safe mushroom family still merits a trip to your field guide, where you'll find fanciful things like absurd meringue-peaked puffballs or that the peculiar genus name *Lycoperdon* translates from the Latin as "wolf flatulence."

kitchen notes

CLEANING AND PREPARATION: A wipe with a washcloth cleans puffballs nicely. The outer skin can be a bit leathery and may require peeling. Slice giant puffballs like bread. Peeling the lightbulb-shaped *Lycoperdon* is like skinning an Easter marshmallow bunny, but the interior is quite tasty.

COOKING METHODS: Breading and frying puffball slices like cutlets is the traditional path. A coating of some kind and/or fast cooking keep them from absorbing too much cooking fat. They make delightful French fries or chips too.

STORAGE: Use within two days, or harvest a slice at a time from the living puffball. Puffballs are not very good as dried slices, but they're excellent ground up and added to your mushroom powder.

IDEAL PUFFBALLS: When cut open, your puffballs should be homogenously white throughout, like giant marshmallows, with no little bug trails.

Chicken-Fried Puffball Steaks with Creamy Mushroom Gravy

The truck stop of my wild dreams would have this dish on the menu breakfast, lunch, and dinner. As much as I love chicken-fried steak, puffball steaks are a colossal improvement on the weird meat that's usually in this old favorite. The cultivated abalone mushroom or giant king oyster mushroom works for the "steaks" too. This classic mushroom gravy recipe will make you find and really use your grandma's gravy boat. Don't forget biscuits.

[SERVES 6 TO 8]

for the puffballs

1 large egg

¾ cup buttermilk

2 teaspoons kosher salt, plus more to taste

1⅛ teaspoons freshly ground black pepper

1¼ cups unbleached all-purpose flour

Pinch of cayenne pepper

¼ teaspoon paprika

1 pound puffball mushrooms,
    cleaned and cut into ½-inch-thick slices

Vegetable or canola oil

Whisk the egg in a medium bowl. Whisk in the buttermilk, ½ teaspoon of the salt, and ⅛ teaspoon of the pepper. Set aside.

Place the flour, the remaining 1½ teaspoons salt, the remaining 1 teaspoon black pepper, the cayenne, and the paprika in a medium bowl. Whisk until combined.

Line a large baking sheet with parchment or waxed paper.

Dip each mushroom slice into the buttermilk mixture, coating evenly. Lift out, letting the excess drip off. Drop the slice into the flour mixture and turn to coat evenly. Remove the mushroom slice, lightly shaking off any excess flour, and place on the prepared baking sheet. Repeat until all the mushroom slices are coated. Let them sit for 5 to 10 minutes at room temperature before cooking. This helps hold the mixture on the mushrooms as they fry, giving them a thick, crunchy crust.

Add enough oil, approximately ½ to ¾ cup, to come ¼ inch up the sides of a large sauté pan and place over medium-high heat. When the oil is hot, add the mushroom slices to fill the pan without crowding. Cook until golden brown, 3 to 4 minutes. Turn over the slices and cook for another 3 to 4 minutes, or until golden brown. Remove the mushrooms to a wire rack placed over a baking sheet and sprinkle lightly with salt. Hold in a warm place while you cook the rest of the mushrooms. Serve warm with the creamy mushroom gravy.

for the creamy mushroom gravy

4 tablespoons (½ stick) unsalted butter

½ pound cremini, button, or chanterelle
    mushrooms, stems removed,
    cut into thin slices

1 teaspoon finely minced garlic

1½ teaspoons kosher salt

¼ teaspoon freshly ground black pepper

3 tablespoons unbleached all-purpose flour

1½ teaspoons Porcini Powder (page 312)

2 cups Traditional Mushroom Stock (page 315)

½ teaspoon fresh lemon juice

2 tablespoons heavy cream

Place the butter in a large sauté pan over medium-high heat. When the butter is melted, add the mushrooms, tossing to coat with the butter. Cook, stirring occasionally, until the mushrooms have released their liquid, 2 to 3 minutes. Continue cooking until the liquid has evaporated and the mushrooms are beginning to brown, 2 to 3 more minutes. Add the garlic, salt, and pepper and cook for 1 minute. While stirring, sprinkle the flour and porcini powder over the mushrooms to coat evenly. Add the mushroom stock, stirring constantly to avoid lumps as the mixture thickens. Turn down the heat and simmer for 5 minutes. Add the lemon juice and cream and cook for 1 minute more. Taste for seasoning, adjusting as needed.

TIPS AND TECHNIQUES

Slice the puffballs in the manner that will yield the most surface area.

When coating the puffballs, use one hand for the wet mixture and one for the dry. This prevents both hands from getting sticky with batter.

The gravy can be made a day ahead and reheated just before cooking the puffballs.

SUBSTITUTIONS AND VARIATIONS

Many wild or cultivated mushrooms can be substituted for the mushrooms in the gravy recipe (no shiitake, maitake, or matsutake, however).

Canned chicken or mushroom broth can be substituted for the traditional mushroom stock in the recipe. Use less salt and adjust the seasoning at the end.

Fresh herbs, such as thyme, parsley, basil, rosemary, or tarragon, can be minced and added to the gravy just before serving.

Cuitlacoche
[(Huitlacoche) Corn Smut]

USTILAGO MAYDIS

We've all smacked up against that edgy place that is our first experience of things unknown to us—sex, the first raw oyster, great bourbon, a foreign land—and so the flavors of the world widen. This experience isn't always pretty, however. In Mexico, I remember spotting the hideous pile of cuitlacoche ("wheat-la-coach-eh") just as I was taking the first bite of a quesadilla with telltale blackness oozing from its edges. My *"Qué horror"* was fast followed by an American "Wow." That same great quesadilla is reborn on page 153.

Who knew that yucky corn smut had such a sublime flavor? The Aztecs, Tlaxcalans, and several other New World peoples did. Culinary thrill seekers may be disappointed to find that the taste under the nasty appearance is the comforting flavor you might expect from a nice Indian grandma's kitchen. Those to whom I've fed cuitlacoche describe it as warm, musky, earthy, base note of corn, creamy, deep, and unctuous. It has an indefinably familiar flavor. Its high protein and umami content seem to enhance all it touches. Poor cuitlacoche suffers not only from a ghastly physique but also from unrealistic and unfair expectations created by those who compare it to a truffle. Cuitlacoche is a subtle flavor experience hidden behind the face of a culinary gargoyle.

If you wonder what's wild about cuitlacoche other than its appearance, remember that it's still a wild fungus, even though the host it invades is the ever-so-tamed corn plant. The same corn smut (cuitlacoche) that is viewed as a disastrous blight in the United States is embraced in much of Mexico as a delicious blessing that dramatically increases the value of the crop. There's something powerful about a people who welcome this wild fungus predator even as it strikes the most essential, indeed sacred, of their foods—corn. Cuitlacoche's best translation from the Aztec Nahuatl is "excrement of the lords (gods)."

Foraging for cuitlacoche in our world is a strange scavenger hunt. Ask corn growers at your farmers' market if they've seen any in their fields. Some farmers may be embarrassed to admit that this "scourge" has made an appearance in their crop. Some might sell you some or possibly ask you to help "weed" it out of their fields. Drought conditions or excess moisture on corn untouched by fungicides creates the ideal conditions for cuitlacoche. Even then you must forage through the corn rows before you spot the odd ear with galls erupting from the husks. A few clever U.S. farmers are inoculating their corn with corn smut, but at this point they find that peddling the delicious smut often meets with perplexed consumers. Perhaps it's the perfect spooky Halloween ingredient. Squash-"oranged" masa tamales stuffed with black cuitlacoche, anyone?

kitchen notes

CLEANING AND PREPARATION: Peel the husks off, then untangle and remove the silk from the cuitlacoche. Slice down the cob to remove the cuitlacoche galls. It's OK if a few corn kernels end up in your pile of cuitlacoche. Washing the cob is your call, but if you choose to do it, do so before slicing the cob.

COOKING METHODS: In Mexico the usual first step is to sauté onions, then add the cuitlacoche. As it cooks, it turns a glorious black. From there, cuitlacoche can take traditional paths into tamales and gorditas, for example, or blaze inky new trails into ravioli, lasagna, or other, yet unexplored, territories.

STORAGE: Cuitlacoche left on the cob will keep in the refrigerator for one week. Once cut off, it lasts about twenty-four hours. It freezes nicely off the cob in a plastic bag. Thaw overnight in the refrigerator before using.

IDEAL CUITLACOCHE: Boy, oh boy, there's no beauty prize awarded here, but it is best kept on the cob until the day of use. The fully ripe galls should be silver gray, firm as a grape, and never dry inside. Cuitlacoche's flavor is best when the tasty blobs have matured at two to three weeks of age. Don't worry if the odd gall has split—this reflects its ripeness. Frozen cuitlacoche is very good, and canned, available in many Mexican grocery stores, is actually not bad. (See Guidebooks and Sources, page 336.)

Pesticides are not a serious issue. Cuitlacoche tends to grow in poorly kept farms; it won't grow if fungicides are used.

Cuitlacoche and Squash Blossom Quesadilla

When I go mushroom hunting with my pals in Mexico, I have to start in the great food city of Puebla. I jump into my Poblano friends Nuria and Fernando's car, and the street food tour begins. Fabulous cuitlacoche quesadillas made by a tiny Indian woman are always the goal of my pilgrimage. I can't wait to take this book to this gifted street chef to show her the picture of our version here. I hope we've made her proud.

We've used yellow corn masa, but white or blue is traditional. If you can find the little sprouted pearl-size onions with green tops, use them in place of the scallions. Daylily petals are an easily found and delicious substitute for the squash blossoms. This recipe calls for a *comal* (a round, flat Mexican griddle), a tortilla press, and Oaxacan cheese, all of which are inexpensively available at a Mexican grocery. See substitutions at the end of the recipe.

[MAKES 6]

for the filling

1 tablespoon plus ¾ cup pure olive oil
    or canola oil
¼ cup finely minced white onion
1 large garlic clove, finely minced
¾ pound cuitlacoche
1 tablespoon finely slivered epazote,
    plus 12 leaves, slivered
½ teaspoon kosher salt
2 poblano chiles, roasted, peeled, seeded,
    and cut into ¼-inch strips
6 squash blossoms, cleaned, stems and
    stamens removed, torn into ½-inch strips
4 ounces Oaxacan string cheese,
    torn into thin 2-inch strands

Heat the 1 tablespoon oil in a large sauté pan over medium heat. When the oil is hot, add the onion and garlic, stirring to coat evenly with the oil. Cook for 2 to 3 minutes, or until softened and starting to turn translucent. Stir in the cuitlacoche and any of its liquid, the slivered epazote, and the salt. Lower the heat and simmer until any liquid has evaporated and the cuitlacoche is tender, 8 to 10 minutes. Set aside.

for the tortillas

1 cup masa harina, yellow or white
½ teaspoon kosher salt

Combine the masa harina and salt in a small bowl. Add ¾ cup plus 3 tablespoons hot water, mixing it in by hand until the mixture is smooth and moist. The water will absorb into the masa as you work it. Pat the dough into a ball and return it to the bowl. Cover with plastic wrap and let sit for 30 minutes before shaping.

to finish

Place the ¾ cup oil in a small bowl. Have the filling ingredients, the oil, and a small ladle near the stove.

Heat a comal or large cast-iron skillet over medium-high heat. Keep the comal or skillet hot as you proceed with the recipe.

Prepare a tortilla press: Cut the side and bottom seams from a quart-size resealable plastic storage bag, giving you two equal-size pieces of plastic. Lay one of the pieces on the bottom of the tortilla press.

Divide the dough into 6 pieces and roll each piece into a ball. Keep the balls covered with plastic wrap or a kitchen towel as you make each tortilla to prevent the dough from drying out.

Place a ball of dough just off center, away from the handle, in the tortilla press. Cover with the second piece of plastic. Press the tortilla. Open the press and gently peel off the top layer of plastic. Turn the tortilla over into the palm of your hand and gently peel off the top layer of plastic. Place the tortilla immediately on the hot comal or skillet.

Cook the tortilla for 30 seconds. Turn it over and quickly begin to assemble the quesadilla, placing the filling ingredients just off center of the tortilla: 2 tablespoons of the cuitlacoche mixture, 1 tablespoon poblano chiles, some of the remaining epazote, and some of the squash blossoms, finishing with 1 to 2 tablespoons Oaxacan string cheese. Fold the tortilla in half over the filling and press down with a spatula.

Ladle 1 to 2 tablespoons oil onto the empty part of the comal and slide the quesadilla over into the hot oil, moving it around to coat it evenly with the oil. Cook for 45 seconds to 1 minute, or until crisped and golden brown. Turn over the quesadilla and cook for another 45 seconds to 1 minute, adding more oil, if needed, to crisp and brown the bottom. The filling should be heated through and the cheese melted.

Remove the quesadilla to a plate and repeat with the remaining tortillas. Serve the quesadillas whole or cut into quarters.

TIPS AND TECHNIQUES

The filling ingredients can all be prepared up to 2 days ahead of time.

Have everything ready and assembled to make the cooking process go quickly and smoothly. Depending on the size of your comal or skillet, you can make 2 to 3 quesadillas at a time.

The quesadillas are best eaten right out of the pan, but they can be cooked and kept in a warm oven until all of them are made.

Giving the tortilla press an extra push at the end will make the tortillas come out round and even.

The masa dough absorbs more liquid the longer it sits, which can cause the dough to dry out. You can add a little extra water if this happens and reshape the balls.

Peeling the plastic off the pressed tortilla slowly helps prevent tearing the tortilla. With practice, it will get quicker and easier.

VARIATIONS AND SUBSTITUTIONS

String cheese or Monterey Jack can be substituted for the Oaxacan string cheese.

Canned green chiles can be substituted for the poblano chiles.

Canned or frozen cuitlacoche can be substituted for fresh.

Cuitlacoche Soup with Crema Mexicana Spiral

Those of you who have never ended up cold and wet after a long day of mushroom hunting high up in the mountains of Mexico may not understand that the traditional bowl of velvety black cuitlachoche soup waiting in a warm Indian kitchen is the most comforting of soups. Yes, I'm actually calling a pre-Hispanic dish made from an almost-unpronounceable fungus "comfort food." Our mushroom stock adds a special flavor layer in this recipe.

Crema Mexicana is a particularly good version of sour cream found in the Mexican food section of your grocery.

[MAKES 6 CUPS]

4 tablespoons (½ stick) unsalted butter

1 cup finely minced white onion

3 large cloves garlic, thinly sliced

1 poblano chile, roasted, peeled, seeded, and cut into ½-inch dice

1 pound cuitlacoche, fresh or frozen

1 tablespoon finely slivered epazote

1½ teaspoons kosher salt

¼ teaspoon freshly ground black pepper

1 quart Traditional Mushroom Stock (page 315)

⅓ cup crema Mexicana

Lime wedges (optional)

Heat the butter in a large stockpot over medium-high heat. When the butter is melted, stir in the onion and garlic. Sauté until the onion and garlic are tender and starting to turn translucent, 2 to 3 minutes. Add the poblano chile and cook for 1 to 2 more minutes. Stir in the cuitlacoche, epazote, salt, and pepper and cook for 3 to 4 minutes more, stirring occasionally.

Add the mushroom stock. Bring to a boil, then turn down the heat, cover, and simmer for 20 minutes.

Puree the liquid in a blender in batches until very smooth. For safe blending of hot soup, fill the blender only halfway and start on low, increasing the speed incrementally. Return the soup to the heat before serving and bring back just to a boil.

Swirl the crema Mexicana in a spiral pattern on the top of each bowl of soup just before serving. Serve with lime wedges, if using.

TIPS AND TECHNIQUES

The soup can be made several days ahead and will keep, covered in an airtight container, for up to 1 week in the refrigerator.

The crema Mexicana can be put into a squirt bottle to make the swirl. Another method is to place the crema in a small resealable plastic bag and snip off one corner to make a kind of piping bag.

SUBSTITUTIONS AND VARIATIONS

Canned cuitlacoche can be substituted for the fresh or frozen. Use the equivalent weight for the recipe.

Canned chicken broth can be substituted for the mushroom stock. Use less salt and adjust the seasoning at the end.

Crème fraîche or traditional sour cream can be substituted for the crema Mexicana.

A canned roasted green chile can be substituted for the poblano chile.

Blewits

CLITOCYBE NUDA OR LEPISTA NUDA; L. SAEVA

Not everyone salivates while gazing happily upon a plate of savory lilac-colored food. Bluish purple food worries most people, but not we mushroom hunters proudly clutching our baskets of blewits. What's not to adore about the beautiful blewit? It is extraordinarily delicious. It grows with wild abandon and is found from remote forests right into backyards. Walt Disney couldn't have created a more adorable mushroom. Imagine Michael Caine in *Alfie* saying, "Blue hat," and you have the old-time English origin of the endearing name "blewit."

If you see one, you're certain to find several more blewits tucked into the duff. It'll be the one with the stunning violet blue color that catches your eye first. Each mushroom in the blewit "village" will be a slightly different shade, which ranges from blue violet to lavender to beige mauve, depending on dryness and fading with age. The cap can feel like the finest suede. There's frequently a hatlike dome in the middle of the two- to five-inch cap. What a pretty hat it would make. Any ripple in the cap edge forms a sweet shape like the spout of a creamer. The full beauty of a blewit is revealed after you pick it and look at its gills. The gills are even more vividly bluish than the rest of the mushroom.

I've placed blewits here in the Indian summer chapter because Indian summer is when they appear in the most northern regions. They also could be put in autumn and even early winter. I find them in temperate California in the early winter, when they add outlandish purple highlights to my gold chanterelle patches. Cold weather triggers their fruiting from the organic debris that they, as saprophytic mushrooms, depend on. Unlike host-tree–dependent mycorrhizal mushrooms, blewits can be found in leaf litter in deep forests, in compost piles, in areas where wood chippers/shredders have created debris piles, or, as last year, even surrounding a pile of alpaca droppings. Once you find blewits, go back again because more will appear.

Unique as they seem, blewits are not the only amethyst-colored mushrooms. Crack open your field guide and watch for any rust stains on the stem that indicate a harmless but similar mushroom. One terrific look-alike, a blewit cousin, is found in gourmet markets. This "field" blewit, *Lepista saeva*, is cultivated in Europe and imported to the United States. It is equally delicious and can be purchased throughout the year.

Before you start rattling pans in the kitchen, take a moment to admire the blewit's beauty and then inhale the aroma of this mushroom. To some, the blewit's heady perfume smells strongly fruity. For me, it's a rich floral scent, like that of those little square French violet candies. The intense flavor makes me head for the sour cream for the Russian treatment. Shallots and parsley are good company for blewits, but garlic doesn't seem at home. With all its many virtues, the blewit adds a final gift by holding its beautiful color even after it's cooked.

kitchen notes

CLEANING AND PREPARATION: This is a tidy mushroom from the stem up. Cut off the base of the mushroom, which is a blob of forest debris held together by the bright blue, cottony mycelium attached to it.

COOKING METHODS: Blewits make great duxelles and are particularly good in eggs. The lavender color remains after cooking. The cultivated field blewit is equally delicious.

STORAGE: Cook the mushrooms within forty-eight hours of picking. Little hopping bugs love blewits and will take them over.

IDEAL BLEWITS: The vivid purple mushrooms are usually the youngest, but the mushrooms are delicious even if their color is a faded bluish beige.

ALERT: Never eat wild mushrooms raw, but particularly not this one. It's reputed to contain dicey compounds that can cause indigestion but are neutralized by cooking.

Pappardelle with Blewits, Pearl Onions, and Celery Root

On a cold dreary day—perfect mushroom-hunting weather, of course—Sarah and I stomped around a hill in Napa Valley that was surrounded by vineyards yet was crowned with a vibrant forest island right on its top. Sheer stubborn persistence led us to a big patch of purply mushrooms at the summit. Afterward, despite exhaustion, Sarah's hunger and great culinary gifts turned our basket of blewits into this hearty, earthy pasta dish. Yum!

[SERVES 4 TO 6]

10 ounces pearl onions
4 slices smoked bacon, 4 ounces,
    cut into ¼-inch slices
2 garlic cloves, finely minced
1 medium shallot, finely minced
1 medium celery root head, peeled and
    cut into ¼-inch cubes
1 teaspoon kosher salt, or more to taste
¼ teaspoon freshly ground black pepper,
    or more to taste
¼ cup dry white wine
1 cup chicken broth
1 tablespoon finely minced fresh thyme
2 tablespoons extra virgin olive oil
½ pound blewits, cleaned and sliced
    into ¼-inch slices
8 ounces dried pappardelle
2 tablespoons unsalted butter,
    at room temperature, cut into 4 pieces
½ teaspoon fresh lemon juice, or more to taste
4 tablespoons grated Parmesan
1 tablespoon finely minced flat-leaf parsley

Bring a large pot of water to a boil. Cook the pearl onions for 3 minutes. Drain. When cool enough to handle, peel and set aside.

Place the bacon in a large sauté pan. Place the pan over medium heat and cook until the bacon is golden brown and crisped, almost 6 to 7 minutes. Remove the bacon from the pan using a slotted spoon and set aside on a paper towel to drain.

Add the garlic and shallot to the drippings in the pan and cook, stirring occasionally, until tender and translucent, 3 to 4 minutes. Add the celery root, ½ teaspoon of the salt, and ⅛ teaspoon of the pepper to the pan and cook until tender and starting to caramelize, 5 to 6 minutes. Add the pearl onions and white wine. Cook until the wine is almost evaporated, then add the chicken broth and thyme. Bring to a boil, cover, then turn down the heat and simmer for 10 minutes, or until the celery root is tender. Set aside in a warm place.

Heat the oil in another large sauté pan over medium-high heat. When the oil is hot, add the blewits, tossing to coat evenly with the oil. Add the remaining ½ teaspoon salt and ⅛ teaspoon pepper. Cook, stirring occasionally, until the mushrooms are tender and starting to turn brown and caramelize.

Set aside in a warm place while you cook the pappardelle.

Bring a large pot of salted water to a boil. Cook the pappardelle according to the instructions on the package.

While the pasta is cooking, reheat the celery root mixture in the large sauté pan. Add the mushrooms to the mixture. Drain the pasta, saving some of the cooking water. Add the pasta to the mushroom mixture. Add the butter, lemon juice, and 2 tablespoons of the Parmesan. Mix together, using tongs or 2 large spoons, adding a splash of the pasta cooking water, if needed, for more moisture. Taste for seasoning, adding salt, pepper, and lemon juice as needed. Top with the remaining 2 tablespoons Parmesan and the parsley. Serve immediately.

TIPS AND TECHNIQUES

If you like a "wetter" pasta, add more butter and pasta cooking water as you mix together the pasta with the other ingredients. You could also use extra virgin olive oil instead of butter for this purpose.

SUBSTITUTIONS AND VARIATIONS

You can substitute ¾ pound fresh pappardelle for the dried in the recipe. Cook until just tender and proceed as for dried pasta in the recipe.

Other mushrooms can be substituted for the blewits: hen of the woods, chanterelles, or porcini, for example.

Frozen pearl onions can be substituted for fresh. Thaw and add to the celery root as directed in the recipe.

Rose Hips

ROSA RUGOSA; R. CAROLINA; R. EGLANTERIA; OTHERS

To a romantic, the rose provides a long list of glorious things: beauty, ethereal symbolism, love tokens, perfume. But after all the lovely rose petals have fallen, we earthbound foragers are called by its radiant but peculiar seedpod, the rose hip. This cherrylike fruit ornaments the fading rosebush. Yet some of us gatherers of wild things know the more tawdry side of the rose. To get through the flame-colored rose hips to the lemony rose flavor and treasure trove of vitamin C locked inside, you have to detour around many seeds and their needlelike fibers. These tiny, innocuous seeds are the devilish source of itching powder. Dastardly precomputer little children have dropped these itchy seeds down the backs of too many shirts. When these same seeds drop down your gullet, they do not always go gently through the good night of your digestive tract. The French gave these seeds the not-so-poetic name *gratte-cul*, which means "itchy butt." Most, but not all, indigenous peoples deprived of modern fine-mesh strainers also looked upon them as a pain in the derriere.

You can easily navigate and strain your way around this prickly problem to turn wild rose hips into exquisite jellies, jams, purees, teas, and my favorite, syrups like the recipe included here (see page 321). The extracted then sweetened rose hip juice works well as a granita or even for Popsicles. Less known is the traditional rose hip soup that Nordic children like my late husband lapped up, unaware of the vitamin C hidden in its deliciousness. Another hip surprise was chef Todd Humphries's exquisite rose hip and crab apple jelly placed like a gemstone beside fois gras.

Wild roses run riot all over the countryside. The sturdy wrinkled rose *Rosa rugosa*, with the biggest and most delicious of hips, thrives near the sea in the East and even in Alaska. Elsewhere, mixtures of the dog, Carolina, sweetbriar, and California roses grow in banks along roads and at the edges of pastures in all parts of the country except southern Florida. The rose variety is of less importance than the size of its rose hips and the individual bush's flavor. Harvest the plump *R. rugosa* hips as the weather chills. Other varieties are traditionally harvested after a frost. This makes

snapping the hips off the stems easy. Though rose hips can still be found as red as rubies hanging on bare branches in the snow, it's best to pick them while they are still fresh and plump. Bite and taste the flesh covering the rose hip's seeds before picking because there's surprising variation in flavor among bushes that look the same. A tumbled mix of varieties adds a fine complexity to every rosy concoction.

kitchen notes

CLEANING AND PREPARATION: Before rinsing, snap off any extra stem and dangling "tails." Cut large hips in half and scoop out the seeds, or boil them for 5 to 10 minutes and pass them through a food mill. Though tedious, removing the seeds is necessary if you're going to make a jam, puree, or soup. If you're making a jelly or syrup, it isn't necessary. It's a rare case where making jelly is easier than making jam because the seeds remain in the jelly bag (see illustration page 304). Pectin or some apples are required for jelling.

COOKING METHODS: Because of rose hips' high ascorbic acid content, use enamel or stainless steel cookware. Chopping the rose hips before boiling or using a juice/steamer device is a good way to extract the juice.

STORAGE: When I don't have time to process the hips, I bag, seal, and freeze them until I have time. Drying rose hips in a dehydrator for your winter tea is always a good idea.

IDEAL ROSE HIPS: Big plump rose hips are what you'll want. Gather them before they begin to shrivel. Mixed varieties that pass your taste test will add complexity to food you create from them.

ALERT: Wild roses are rarely sprayed, but garden roses often are. Be mindful of sprays and the use of systemic insecticides.

Rose Hip and Pistachio Baklava

Saturated with beautiful rose hip syrup, this baklava has a haunting floral-citrus complexity that people just cannot leave alone once they've tasted it. It's shocking how quickly it vanishes. This rosy syrup is also wonderful atop yogurt, panna cotta, pancakes, biscuits, ham, fresh berries or ice cream, or to saturate a sponge cake. Tea or lemonade sweetened with the syrup is a fine luxury for the self-pampering forager.

[MAKES 36 PIECES]

for the syrup

1½ cups Rose Hip Syrup (page 321)
½ cup honey
2 tablespoons rose water
1 tablespoon fresh lemon juice

Combine the syrup and honey in a small saucepan and bring to a boil. Turn down the heat and simmer for 20 minutes. Remove from the heat and whisk in the rose water and lemon juice. Set aside.

for the baklava

½ pound (2 sticks) unsalted butter, melted
    and kept warm
8 ounces shelled pistachios (1¾ cups),
    finely chopped
3 tablespoons sugar
½ teaspoon ground cardamom
Pinch of kosher salt
1 pound phyllo dough, thawed

Position a rack in the center of the oven. Preheat the oven to 325°F.

Brush the bottom and sides of a 9 x 13-inch baking pan with 4 tablespoons of the melted butter. Set aside.

Combine the pistachios, sugar, cardamom, and salt in a small bowl and mix well. Set aside 2 tablespoons of the mixture to sprinkle on top of the baklava.

Lay the phyllo sheets out on a clean work surface. If necessary, cut the sheets ahead of time to the size of the pan. Use any leftover dough for another recipe. Cover with plastic wrap, then with a damp kitchen towel, as you work to keep the dough from drying out.

Place 1 sheet of phyllo dough in the bottom of the pan. Brush lightly with some of the remaining melted butter. Work quickly, but gently, with the phyllo dough. A light touch with the brush while buttering will keep the dough from tearing. Lay another sheet down, repeating the process until you have placed 4 sheets of dough in the pan. Scatter one-third of the pistachio mixture evenly over the dough. Layer 4 more sheets of phyllo in the pan, buttering between each sheet. Scatter another one-third of the pistachio mixture. Layer on another 4 sheets as directed, and scatter with the remaining one-third of the pistachio mixture. Finish by layering on 8 sheets of phyllo dough, spreading each with the remaining butter.

Starting from one corner and using a sharp knife, make 7 evenly spaced diagonal cuts across the top layers of the phyllo dough. Turn the pan and make 7 more cuts, creating diamond-shaped pieces. Cut through only the top layers of the phyllo, not to the base of the pan. Using your fingertips or a spray bottle, lightly sprinkle the top of the dough with cold water.

Bake for 50 to 55 minutes, or until golden brown. Remove to a wire rack and cool completely before finishing.

to finish

Reheat the syrup just until it comes to a boil. Remove from the heat.

Using a sharp knife, cut through the scored lines in the baklava all the way down to the bottom of the pan.

Using a small ladle, drizzle the syrup evenly over the top of the baklava, allowing it to soak in as you go. The contrast between the cooled baklava and the warm syrup allows for better absorption of the syrup into the pastry. Make sure to cover the top surface evenly and use all the syrup. Sprinkle with the reserved pistachio mixture. Let sit for at least 1 hour before serving.

To keep, wrap tightly and store at room temperature for up to 7 days.

TIPS AND TECHNIQUES
If you have broken or torn sheets of phyllo, use them in the middle and save the whole sheets for the top.

SUBSTITUTIONS AND VARIATIONS
Blanched almonds, walnuts, or pine nuts can be substituted for the pistachios.

Huckleberries

VACCINIUM MEMBRANACEUM/GLOBARE (COMPLEX);
V. OVATUM; GAYLUSSACIA SPECIES

I know I should approach each of the wild berries with equanimity of spirit, reflecting their diverse qualities, but good lord, I just can't help it—huckleberries are my darlings. When they're ripe, a basket always rides shotgun up front with me. The powerful perfume saturates the cab of my truck and makes me wish for bath salts smelling that luscious.

The quaint word *huckleberry* is a big purple umbrella of a word with a confusing gang of some of the world's most delicious berries huddled underneath. Befuddling even taxonomists, the *Vaccinium* clan genealogy includes huckleberries, blueberries, and even cranberries woven closely together. Huckleberries are, as a general rule, those varieties with blacker berries, no frosty "bloom" coating, a stronger acidity/sugar balance, extra "juiciness," and intense flavor. The birthmark of the huckleberry and blueberry tribe is the distinct crown-shaped feature at the bottom of the berry. This is the same feature that you see on every cultivated blueberry in the grocery store. This familiar crown is a very safe identification marker for the whole family.

Huckleberries can be sorted roughly into three groups. In the high country of the western states, the "mountain" huckleberry of the Rockies and Cascades is a pea-size, red-violet berry. This huckleberry, beloved by cowboy, grizzly, and children alike, is North America's most popular huckleberry and the most widely gathered. In the East, the *Gaylussacia* species so loved by Henry David Thoreau and Mark Twain is another fine berry. It often intermingles ecumenically with low-bush blueberries. The Pacific coastal evergreen huckleberry has a dainty blue-violet berry with thicker skin and an excellent sugar/acid balance. Both pretty and tough, these two- to ten-foot-tall shrubs should be used for training NFL linemen. Many are the times that I've had to plow through thick walls of these to pick the many varieties of mushrooms that grow under them.

These three tribes, strewn across this big continent, have surprisingly similar habitats. They all thrive in acid soils and clearings with abundant sunlight and have a special zeal for areas where fires have been. Watch for them on the edges of clearings or along the sides of roads. Their lust for light is the major connection between huckleberries and the fires that open the canopy.

The harvesting of huckleberries between July and October boils down to three main methods:

1. Handpicking each berry is tedious, but the cleanliness of this method virtually eliminates the grooming routine described below in the Kitchen Notes.

2. "Raking" bushes with a berry rake imitates a bear's claw attached to a scoop or can. As you comb through a berry-covered branch, berries, accompanied by some leaves, fall into the scoop. Some tribal peoples used salmon backbones as berry rakes.

3. "Beating the bushes" involves spreading a tarp under a berry-covered bush and patting the branches with whisk brooms or paddles, then collecting the berries on the tarp.

The exceptionally intensely flavored huckleberry shares with its blueberry cousin a famously rich antioxidant and B vitamin content. Though these two berries share many things, the fork in the road is their route to domestication. Though blueberries were tamed decades ago, huckleberries continue to defy any realistic form of cultivation. You can taste the wildness.

kitchen notes

CLEANING AND PREPARATION: Cleaning huckleberries is a journey with many possible routes. If you handpick the berries, they should be very clean and the following project unnecessary. Comb picking or bush beating results in bountiful debris along with the berries. Creating a ramp to roll the berries down is the best way to winnow the berries from the debris and stems. The ramp can be as simple as a wide board wrapped in a rough old blanket or a long strip of screen/hardware cloth curved into a gutterlike trough. The holes in the screen should be smaller than the berries. The berries roll on while the leaves, little unripe green berries, and stems are caught by the screen or rough blanket. Little baffles added to your ramp make a nice cleansing bounce into the bucket at the end. The larger mountain huckleberries drop their stems easily this way, but the coastal evergreens are less cooperative. For them, I often freeze the berries on cookie sheets. As I roll the berries firmly like little ball bearings, the stems fall off easily.

COOKING METHODS: If you're baking the berries, you need not go crazy destemming every berry. The few stems will get tender in the baking. Huckleberries freeze spectacularly.

STORAGE: The fresh berries have a surprisingly long shelf life. You can keep them for about ten days in an airtight plastic bag in your refrigerator. Beyond this, however, freezing is ideal. Probably no fruit freezes better. Drying makes huckleberry "raisins."

Huckleberry Lemon Pudding Cake

This dead-easy old-fashioned cake pulls a great magic act in the oven. At the end of baking, as you turn over the ramekin, the berry-topped batter has separated into a sponge cake crowned with a gloriously gooey pudding and berry top layer. Huckleberries and lemon are a dynamic flavor pairing that gives great vigor to this sentimental favorite recipe. Other little berries, like wild blueberries, high-bush cranberries, or wild currants, are nice here as well.

[MAKES 8]

for the cakes

4 tablespoons (½ stick) unsalted butter, at room
    temperature, plus extra for buttering ramekins
⅔ cup plus 2 teaspoons sugar,
    plus extra for coating ramekins
1 cup huckleberries, cleaned and stemmed
⅛ teaspoon kosher salt
2 tablespoons finely grated lemon zest
4 large eggs, at room temperature, separated
5 tablespoons unbleached all-purpose flour
¾ cup milk
½ cup fresh lemon juice
1 cup heavy cream

Position a rack in the center of the oven. Preheat the oven to 325°F.

Butter eight 4-ounce ramekins. Sprinkle the insides of the buttered ramekins with sugar to coat, gently shaking out the excess sugar. Divide the huckleberries among the prepared ramekins, covering the bottoms evenly. Place the ramekins in a roasting pan with deep sides. Bring a large pot of water to a simmer while you make the cakes.

Place the butter, the ⅔ cup sugar, the salt, and the lemon zest in the bowl of a standing mixer fitted with the paddle attachment. Mix at medium speed until smooth and creamy. Add the egg yolks, one at a time, beating well after each addition. Stop the mixer and scrape down the sides of the bowl. With the mixer on low, add the flour and mix until well combined. Slowly add the milk to make a smooth batter. Add the lemon juice and mix well. Pour the batter into a large bowl.

Thoroughly wash and dry the mixer bowl. Remove the paddle attachment and insert the whip attachment. Place the egg whites in the clean mixer bowl and whip until they hold firm, creamy peaks.

Fold one-third of the egg whites into the lemon mixture. Quickly but thoroughly, fold in the remaining two-thirds. Divide the batter among the prepared ramekins. Pour the simmering water into the baking dish until it comes halfway up the sides of the ramekins.

Carefully place in the oven and bake for 45 minutes, or until the cakes are puffed and golden. Remove the ramekins to a wire rack and let sit until warm or at room temperature.

Clean and dry the mixer bowl and whip attachment. Add the cream and the remaining 2 teaspoons sugar and whip until the cream holds a medium-soft peak. Refrigerate until ready to use.

for the compote

½ cup sugar

1½ cups huckleberries, cleaned and stemmed

Grated zest of ½ lemon

1 teaspoon fresh lemon juice

Pinch of kosher salt

Combine the sugar, ¼ cup water, the huckleberries, the lemon zest, the lemon juice, and the salt in a small saucepan over medium-high heat. Bring to a boil, stirring gently to dissolve the sugar and being careful not to break up the huckleberries. Boil for 1 minute, then remove from heat and cool to room temperature before serving.

to serve

Remove the cakes from the ramekins while they are still slightly warm and before chilling.

Run a thin knife around the inside edges of the ramekins to loosen the cakes, being careful not to cut into them. Turn each ramekin upside down into the palm of your hand and gently shake to release the cake. Immediately turn the cake right side up and place it on a serving plate. Top each cake with a generous spoonful of compote and a dollop of whipped cream. The cakes can be served warm, at room temperature, or chilled.

TIPS AND TECHNIQUES

If there are a few stems left on the huckleberries, they will soften in the cooking process and not be noticeable.

The cakes are best made the day of serving, but they can be made a day ahead and refrigerated, covered.

The compote can be made several days ahead and stored in an airtight container in the refrigerator.

SUBSTITUTIONS AND VARIATIONS

Frozen huckleberries work well.

Nicole Plue's Huckleberry and White Chocolate Blondies

Pastry chef Nicole Plue and her chef, Richard Reddington, of Redd in Yountville, California, are beyond fond of huckleberries. Knowing of Nicole's affection for them, I asked her for a recipe. Instead of one of the gloriously sophisticated desserts she's known for, she gave us these homey, scrumptious, very American blondies. You won't find a better blondie recipe, let alone one from a James Beard pastry chef of the year. It also works very well with wild blueberries, lingonberries, wild currants, and other small berries.

[MAKES 32]

8 ounces white chocolate,
     chopped into ½-inch pieces
5 tablespoons unsalted butter,
     cut into ½-inch pieces
2 large eggs
½ cup sugar
1 teaspoon pure vanilla extract
1¼ cups cake flour, sifted
Pinch of kosher salt
1½ cups fresh huckleberries,
     cleaned and stemmed

Position a rack in the center of the oven. Preheat the oven to 325°F.

Spray a 9 x 13-inch baking pan with nonstick vegetable cooking spray.

Add water to a medium saucepan to come 2 inches up the sides of the pan. Place over medium heat and bring to a simmer.

Place the white chocolate and butter in a medium bowl and place the bowl over the simmering water. Make sure the bottom of the bowl does not touch the simmering water; otherwise the bowl will be too hot. Stir together the mixture until melted and smooth. Hold off the heat in a warm place.

Place the eggs, sugar, and vanilla in the bowl of a standing mixer fitted with the whisk attachment. Beat on high for 3 to 4 minutes, or until the mixture is thick and pale colored.

Fold the egg mixture into the white chocolate, just until combined. Fold in the flour and salt, working quickly so as not to lose the volume of the batter, just until combined. The batter should be thick and satiny. Spread it evenly into the prepared pan, using an offset spatula. Scatter the huckleberries evenly over the surface of the batter.

Bake for 35 to 40 minutes, or until the top is puffed and golden brown. Remove to a wire rack and cool to room temperature before cutting into 1½ x 2-inch blondies.

TIPS AND TECHNIQUES

Store in an airtight container. The blondies will keep for up to 1 week at room temperature.

autumn

Porcini
[King Bolete, Cèpe]

BOLETUS EDULIS

This sumptuous mushroom is an international culinary superstar. Its many common names reflect the heritage and languages of its passionate fans. Although the French name *cèpe* was once the most common name, it is now best known in the world by the Italian name *porcini*. This magnificently handsome mushroom is justly called "the king" in this country. Adored and sought after far and wide in the western world, the king bolete is, without doubt, the Elvis of the mushroom world. There is a point when rain, temperature, and season all align in a magical way, which sets the stage for the king bolete season to begin. Every region has its special scripted sequence, often even beginning in late summer. In the coastal West, the kings appear two weeks after the first big rains, just as the long dry season ends. The waiting reminds me of some love affair; you anticipate the arrival with a quaking fervor, experience the harvest with the intensity of a wanton porcini-besotted creature, and then watch the mushroom slowly vanish as the porciniless world returns. It's a glorious few weeks, yet the king's appearance is never long enough.

This mushroom has dozens of pet names and a variety of looks. The English name "penny bun" describes perfectly my favorite and the most common *B. edulis* type. The mushroom is rotund and fantastically bulbous stemmed and sports a cap as golden brown as toasty bread. In places like the Oregon coast, *B. edulis*'s small, pale cocoa brown cap is carried on a very long straight stem. The cap may be rusty colored, blondish, or even cream white when pulled from under the soil, yet local fans recognize and love all these regional variations. This sounds more confusing than it is. However varied, all in the *Boletus* genus have a spongy pored layer of vertically arranged tubes where a standard-issue mushroom would have gills. The fat stem is spread with a reticulated pattern that looks like a netting of fine beige blood vessels. The king bolete, or porcini, has numerous close and delectable cousins, like the queen bolete, *B. regineus (B. aereus)*; the white bolete, *B. barrowsii*; and the bay bolete, *B. badius*. All these are worthy finds or substitutes for the beloved king bolete.

Just as the king bolete's complexion and figure vary regionally, so does its preferred tree partner. It's a mycorrhizal mushroom with a taste for pine trees, but it is also found among other conifers, oaks, and birch trees. The best place to begin looking is near the edge of a grassy clearing, alongside the proper tree for your region. Once you've found a patch, you'll likely have about five weeks to haunt it. These massive meaty mushrooms grow shockingly fast. You can return to pick every three or four days. As the season ends, consider letting the mushrooms just grow out. The spores will fly afield, and you can get a good look at how hulky they can get, unless Bambi chomps them down to a nub first.

There may be no mushroom more fun to hunt. You can walk into a patch and find a porcini with a cap the size of a steering wheel and a stem as wide as a cantaloupe, while next to it under a hump of pine needles will be a perfect porcini button the size of a key lime. It behooves a good porcini hunter to watch for every hump, then to fall to your knees and pat-pat your hands over the ground, feeling for the little buttons under the leaf litter.

Just as king boletes or porcini in different locales have a variable look, they also vary in intensity of flavor. The essence of that flavor is a fleshy, buttery, toasted hazelnut one. Although I've relished king boletes from atop mesas in New Mexico, in central Michigan, and in many other places, the archetype of porcini flavor is still found in Italy. Italian porcini vary in flavor and usage as well, as the mushroom changes from a white-pored button to a yellow-pored teenager to an aging olive- then brown-pored older mushroom. It's the olive brown spores' development that makes this color change. The young buttons are ideal as perfect slices cooked or shaved raw into a salad (raw mushrooms are indigestible and should be forbidden except in small amounts like this one exception). The larger yellow-pored porcini are superb grilled. The older ripe and olive-pored porcini may be soft, but they have great flavor. Use them for fillings or dry them.

From Alaska to South Africa, there is no mushroom more widely loved than the king bolete, the porcini, the cèpe, the *steinpilz*, and on and on. Each name is cried with joy in woods worldwide.

kitchen notes

CLEANING AND PREPARATION: For cleaning, see page 326. The photos there are far better than my babbling. Good preparation does begin in the woods. Trimming the dirty base off not only keeps most of the dirt in the woods where it belongs, but also gives you a chance to leave the mushroom in the woods if you see too many worm holes.

COOKING METHODS: "How do I cook thee? Let me count the ways." These mushrooms are delicious cooked in nearly every way I can think of: sautéing, grilling, roasting, and so on. I think you could substitute porcini for the generic mushroom in almost any recipe and be thrilled with the results.

STORAGE: It's a race to eat them before porcini-loving critters (worms) beat you to it. Enjoy fresh porcini within forty-eight hours of picking. Store them in an open container in the refrigerator. They freeze and dry very well indeed (see Wild Pantry, page 331).

IDEAL PORCINI (KING BOLETE/CÈPE): The vast majority of chefs would say that the young, fat, very firm buttons with white spores are the ultimate. Personally, I love the larger, slightly more mature mushroom with yellowing spores. When you find these, eat them first. They're softer textured and more perishable, but they have a richer flavor.

Savory Cèpe Flans

Boletus edulis wears its French common name, *cèpe,* here for this French custard–inspired recipe. While the other cèpe (porcini or king bolete) recipes in this section use the mushroom in big fleshy slices, this recipe distills the luscious buttery flavor of the cèpe into this luxurious custard. Absolutely use the highest quality, most aromatic dried cèpes, or porcini, you have or can find. These flans can be used as a first course or as a decadent side dish, perhaps for beef or veal. The fresh cèpe slices are a perfect crown for the flans but they're perfectly glorious made without them, which allows you to make this anytime.

You may prefer to eat this in private while moaning softly.

[MAKES 4]

2 ounces dried cèpes (porcini, king bolete)
    mushrooms, rinsed
½ teaspoon Porcini Powder (page 312)
2½ cups heavy cream
2 garlic cloves, 1 clove smashed and 1 clove
    finely minced
1 fresh thyme sprig
4 large egg yolks
1 teaspoon kosher salt
¼ teaspoon freshly ground black pepper
3 tablespoons unsalted butter
¼ pound fresh cèpes (porcini, king bolete)
    mushrooms, cleaned and cut into thin slices
½ tablespoon finely chopped flat-leaf parsley

Position a rack in the center of the oven. Preheat the oven to 325°F.

Place four 4-ounce ramekins in a roasting pan with deep sides. Have a pot of simmering water ready.

Place 1 ounce of the dried cèpes in a small saucepan with 2 cups cold water. Bring to a boil, then turn off the heat and let steep for at least 30 minutes or up to 1 hour. Place a fine-mesh strainer over a medium bowl or large measuring cup. Pour the mushrooms and their liquid through the strainer, pressing on the mushrooms to extract all the liquid. Save the mushrooms for another use.

Place the liquid back in the small saucepan over medium-high heat. Reduce the liquid to ¼ cup. Turn off the heat and whisk in the porcini powder until dissolved completely. Set aside.

Place the remaining 1 ounce dried cèpes, the cream, the smashed garlic, and the thyme in a medium saucepan over medium-high heat. Bring just to a boil, then turn off the heat and let steep for 1 hour. Place a fine-mesh strainer over a large bowl. Pour the mushroom mixture through the strainer, pressing on the solids to extract all the liquid. Discard the solids. Whisk in the cèpes liquid. Measure the liquid. You should have approximately 2 cups. (If you have more, add 1 more egg yolk for up to ½ cup extra liquid.)

Whisk together the egg yolks, ½ teaspoon of the salt, and ⅛ teaspoon of the pepper in a large bowl. While whisking, slowly ladle in ½ cup of the cream mixture. When the mixture is smooth, continue adding the remaining cream until it is all incorporated. Be careful not to create too much froth while whisking. Strain the cream mixture through a fine-mesh strainer into a pitcher or large measuring cup with a spout. Divide evenly among the 4 ramekins. Pour the simmering water into the roasting pan to come halfway up the sides of the ramekins. Cover the pan with aluminum foil.

Bake for 20 to 25 minutes, or until the flans are just set. Remove from the roasting pan and set on a wire rack to cool slightly before serving.

to finish

Place the butter in a medium sauté pan over medium-high heat. When the butter is melted and bubbling, add the sliced cèpes, the remaining ½ teaspoon salt, and the remaining ⅛ teaspoon pepper. Cook until the mushrooms have released any liquid. Continue cooking until they are dry and starting to brown and caramelize, 4 to 6 minutes. Stir in the minced garlic. Divide evenly among the 4 ramekins, spooning the cooked cèpes on top of the flans. Garnish with the parsley.

Serve immediately.

TIPS AND TECHNIQUES

The flans can be made ahead and gently reheated in the oven or microwave. Be careful not to overheat; they are delicate and will become too soft.

The flans can be made in 6 smaller pots de crème vessels. They can also be made in 2-ounce ramekins and, after cooling a bit, turned out onto plates as a side dish. Run a knife around the inside of the ramekins to loosen each flan, then carefully invert them onto plates. This will make 8 servings.

SUBSTITUTIONS AND VARIATIONS

Substitute dried morels for the dried cèpes. Use the porcini powder that the recipe calls for or make a powder from the dried morels by grinding them in an electric spice grinder, then sifting them through a fine-mesh strainer.

Gerber's Porcini Panini with Teleme and Caramelized Onions

Every family has its favorite dishes, and this porcini panini is in our chefs' foray tribe's top five. Certain recipes, like some songs, resonate with the flavor of a magical time and place. During a particularly good porcini-hunting weekend, John Gerber (one of the early French Laundry alumni) made this simple sandwich. It's a rare delight for a chef to use an expensive ingredient in a very basic way. The simplicity of perfectly ripe teleme cheese oozing between slices of grilled porcini on crispy bread is perfection. It's what I want right now—if I could only eat this photograph.

[SERVES 4]

for the caramelized onions

2 tablespoons pure olive oil
1 large onion, halved and cut into ⅛-inch slices
½ teaspoon kosher salt
¼ teaspoon freshly ground black pepper

Heat the oil in a large sauté pan over medium-high heat. When the oil is hot, add the onion, salt, and pepper. Stir to coat with the oil. Cook, stirring frequently, until the onion starts to brown and soften. Turn down the heat to low and continue cooking, stirring occasionally, until the onion is very soft and tender, about 25 minutes. Cover the pan, turn off the heat, and let sit for 10 to 15 minutes. Cool to room temperature.

for the mushrooms

½ cup extra virgin olive oil
2 garlic cloves, finely minced
½ teaspoon finely chopped fresh thyme
¼ teaspoon finely chopped fresh rosemary
¾ to 1 pound porcini mushrooms
    (king boletes, cèpes), cleaned
Kosher salt and freshly ground black pepper

Prepare a grill to medium heat.

Combine the oil, garlic, thyme, and rosemary in a small bowl. Slice the porcini into ¼-inch slices and place on a baking sheet. Brush both sides of the mushroom slices with some of the oil. Season with salt and pepper.

Grill the mushrooms for 2 to 3 minutes per side, or until they are tender and golden brown. Remove from the grill and hold in a warm place.

4 ciabatta-style rolls or 1 ciabatta loaf,
     cut into 4 segments

½ cup Porcini Butter (page 319)

8 ounces teleme cheese, at room temperature,
     cut into ⅛-inch slices

Using a serrated knife, slice a thin portion of the top
crust off the rolls or bread segments to make them
flat. Slice them in half crosswise, preferably no more
than ½ inch thick. Trim off any excess bread if the
halves are too thick.

Heat a sandwich or panini press.

Spread the insides of the bread halves with
1 tablespoon of porcini butter each. Spread 1 to
2 tablespoons of caramelized onion on the bottom
half of each sandwich. Divide the porcini among
the sandwiches, placing them in a single layer on
top of the onion. Top with the teleme. Close the
sandwiches. Brush the tops and bottoms of the
bread with the remaining oil mixture, adding more
oil to the bowl, if needed. Cook in a sandwich press
until the cheese is melted and the bread is crusty
and golden brown.

Serve immediately.

TIPS AND TECHNIQUES

*The caramelized onion can be made ahead of time
and kept in the refrigerator, covered in an airtight
container, for up to 1 week.*

*The porcini slices can be pan grilled, sautéed,
or roasted in a hot (425°F) oven if a grill is not
available.*

*The panini can be made in a large sauté pan on
top of the stove, using a slightly smaller sauté pan as
a press. Heat the small sauté pan as well to crisp the
top of the sandwich. You can also press the sandwich
with a spatula while cooking, then turn it to brown the
other side.*

SUBSTITUTIONS AND VARIATIONS

*Grilled king oyster mushrooms are the ideal substitute
for the porcini, but chanterelles, portobellos, or other
meaty mushrooms will do nicely.*

*Regular butter or another compound butter—
garlic, herb, or Parmesan—can be used instead of the
porcini butter.*

*A hearty whole-grain bread can be used instead
of the ciabatta. Make sure the slices are no thicker
than ½ inch.*

Porcini³: Porcini-Dusted Rib Eye with Porcini Butter and Grilled Porcini

[OR THREE KINGS AND A RIB EYE, OR EDULIS REX³]

Porcini means "little pigs." This porcini-to-the-third-power recipe (or porcini cubed) is a veritable wallow of porcini excess. Moderation during the heat of porcini season is for tepid, lifeless fools. Make this rib eye when more and more of a fantastic thing is exactly what you want. The way I see it, the porcini season is so very brief that promiscuous indulgence is a sort of prayer of gratitude to the porcini god.

[SERVES 4]

Four 8-ounce or two 16-ounce rib-eye steaks
    (1½ to 2 inches thick)
Kosher salt and freshly ground black pepper
2 teaspoons Porcini Powder (page 312)
½ cup extra virgin olive oil
2 garlic cloves, finely minced
1 pound porcini mushrooms
    (king boletes, cèpes), cleaned
½ cup Porcini Butter, softened (page 319)
Fleur de sel
Minced fresh chives or flat-leaf parsley

Season the steaks generously all over with salt, pepper, and ½ teaspoon of the porcini powder per steak. Loosely cover with plastic wrap and refrigerate overnight. Remove the steaks from the refrigerator 1 hour before cooking.

Prepare a grill to medium heat.

Place the oil and garlic in a small bowl. Slice the porcini into ¼-inch-thick slices. Place on a baking sheet and brush with the oil mixture on both sides. Season with salt and pepper.

Grill the rib eyes for 7 to 8 minutes per side for medium rare, or until the internal temperature of the steaks is 130° to 135°F. When done, divide the porcini butter among the steaks, spooning it on top

and letting it melt into the steaks as they rest. Hold in a warm place while you grill the porcini.

Place the porcini slices on the grill and cook for 2 to 3 minutes per side, or until tender and golden brown.

Slice the steaks or serve them whole on plates or a platter, topped and surrounded by the grilled porcini. Sprinkle the fleur de sel and chives over the top.

TIPS AND TECHNIQUES

Seasoning the steaks a day ahead allows time for the flavors to penetrate beyond the surface of the meat, giving them a more delicious taste when grilled.

Allow the steaks to rest for at least 6 to 8 minutes before serving, for optimal tenderness and juiciness.

SUBSTITUTIONS AND VARIATIONS

Any cut of steak suitable for grilling can be substituted for the rib eyes. Season them in the same way, the day before, and grill according to the specific cut.

King oyster mushrooms are the best substitute for the porcini. They are particularly good if they are brushed with oil and dusted with porcini powder. Portobellos, chanterelles, or other meaty mushrooms work well too.

Porcini: Porcini-Dusted Rib Eye with Porcini Butter and Grilled Porcini [PAGE 189]

Maitake, or Hen of the Woods

GRIFOLA FRONDOSA

There are a few things I'm a bit smug about having done in the mushroom world. Up near the top of my list is having persevered in popularizing maitake or hen of the woods. Years ago chefs were very slow to accept maitake's untraditional mushroom look and texture. Yet I believed so strongly in this culinary and even medicinal powerhouse that I gave away boxes of them to chefs for a very long time. Some kitchens used these free mushrooms for staff meals. At a "family meal" at Masa's in San Francisco we discovered how remarkable they were on pizza. Very slowly (and expensively, for me) chefs fell in love with this mushroom. It's now one of the three most popular mushrooms I sell.

Maitake are one of the few mushrooms found both in the wild and also within the growing rooms of some bold mushroom growers. It's a compliment to this mushroom that I persist in my devotion, even though my half of the country has nary a wild maitake in it. We in the mushroom-rich West must look enviously eastward to the states where maitake are a common edible mushroom.

The Japanese maitake cultivation breakthrough in 1979 and finding the American grower who used the techniques to grow them here led me to this great mushroom. Unlike so many tamed-down wild things, maitake are magnificent tasting both wild and when cultivated.

This is an impressive-looking wild mushroom. The Japanese describe it as a fluttering cluster of butterflies. The less poetic European and American description is of a mouse-colored, round, fat hen with its feathers all ruffled out, hunkered down on a nest. There's no typical mushroom cap structure, but instead fan- or feather-shaped petals attached to stemlike forking branches. These are joined to a central dense mushroom core. A single maitake can be a monster. A five-pound mushroom is typical, but a hundred-pound specimen has been found that was larger than a German shepherd. Typically, the wild maitake is about one foot wide and roundish in shape.

As large as maitake are, they're very well camouflaged. They grow from the base of hardwoods, usually oaks, and often have dead leaves tucked up around them. When you walk through a forest, it's like looking at the moon—you can see only the half of the tree facing you. As you explore, try walking on curved routes through the forest to see the flip side of the tree trunks. Keep your eyes peeled for maitake (see page 193), cauliflower mushrooms (see page 209), sulfur shelves, and beefsteak mushrooms. All are easily identified fantastic edibles and all grow from the sides of living or dead trees. The search is really worth it, because when you do find maitake or any of these other three mushrooms, you can harvest that same spot for years. The mushrooms will grow back nearly every season.

To harvest a maitake, you'll need a decent-size knife. Cut the mushroom cleanly and gently from the tree. You may have to remove it in layers. Turn the edges toward the ground while tapping the mushroom. Some debris and leaf matter will likely tumble out. On the underside, you'll see tiny white pores where you'd expect gills to be. Luckily, bugs are not as fond of this mushroom as we are. An extremely large maitake can be tough and have a slightly bitter flavor component.

Maitake cultivation has made this great mushroom more widely known every year in more realms than just the kitchen. An Internet search will dazzle you with the array of teas, supplements, and other health food products featuring the maitake mushroom. This polysaccharide-rich mushroom is regarded as a T-cell stimulant by some and has been used by AIDS patients. Others hold it in high esteem as a breast tumor suppressant. While the merits of ongoing research are sorted out in Western medicine, in Chinese and Japanese medical traditions this mushroom's place has been secure for centuries.

Maitake or hen of the woods is a magnificent mushroom. Life does indeed seem fair when something can taste very good, be very big, and actually be good for you.

kitchen notes

CLEANING AND PREPARATION: This is the point when cultivated organic maitake can seem like a brilliant idea. Wild maitake can be challenging to clean: Slice the mushroom into layers, then give them a good rinse or brushing. The base can be tough, though some people like this texture.

COOKING METHODS: There is a distinct flavor difference between roasting or grilling the maitake at high heat and sautéing it. The caramelized flavor of the crispy edges of the mushroom when it has been grilled or roasted is my favorite. Some folks prefer the mushroomy and yeasty flavor that it has when it is sautéed. Millennium, a San Francisco vegan restaurant, wood smokes whole maitake heads with great success. Pickling is a wise option if you've suddenly won the twenty-plus-pound maitake lottery.

STORAGE: Maitake will hold nicely for five days in a paper bag or open plastic bag.

IDEAL MAITAKE: The flesh should be crisp and the stem zone white. Any yeasty or beerlike aroma means the mushroom is too old.

ALERT: The confusing name "chicken of the woods" belongs to a totally different mushroom, *Laetiporus sulphureus* or *L. gilbertsonii*. This mushroom is also known as the sulfur shelf. Although edible and popular, it requires different cooking methods, and many people are allergic to it.

Maitake Pizzetta

This recipe is deceptively simple. There is a single star here: Maitake gives a solo performance on a stage of perfect crust. The complexity of this mushroom shines best when it is cooked at the high caramelizing heat required by the pizzetta. Like many chefs, Sarah is not a chowhound, but she is unable to stop eating this when it comes out of the oven.

I have a sentimental attachment to this mushroom on pizza. It was a staff meal pizza and the kitchen buzz it created that began to open the kitchen doors to maitake. All these years and hundreds of recipes later, a pizza or pizzetta is still my favorite way to eat this mushroom.

[MAKES 6]

for the dough
1 package (¼ ounce) active dry yeast
1 tablespoon extra virgin olive oil,
plus more to oil the bowl
1½ teaspoons kosher salt
2 cups unbleached all-purpose flour,
plus more for shaping and rolling out dough
½ cup cake flour

Combine 1 cup warm (105° to 110°F) water and the yeast in the bowl of a standing mixer. Stir briefly to combine and let sit for 8 to 10 minutes, or until the yeast is foamy and active. Stir in the oil, salt, all-purpose flour, and cake flour and stir just until combined.

Attach the bowl to the mixer fitted with a dough hook and knead the dough on medium speed for 5 to 6 minutes, or until the dough springs back lightly when touched. The dough will be slightly sticky. Don't add any extra flour to the bowl. A moister, stickier dough makes for a tender and crispy crust.

Turn the dough out onto a lightly floured board and quickly shape it into a ball. Brush or rub the inside of a large bowl with oil. Place the dough in the bowl, giving it a few turns to lightly coat it with oil. Cover the bowl with plastic wrap and set in a warm place for 1½ hours, or until the dough has doubled in size. Punch down the dough, shape it back into a ball, then cover and let rise for 1 more hour.

Punch down the dough and place it on a lightly floured board. Divide the dough into 6 pieces, shape them into balls, and place them on an oiled baking sheet. (The balls can be refrigerated overnight at this point. Remove them from the refrigerator 1 hour before baking.) Cover the balls of dough loosely with plastic wrap and let sit for 30 minutes before rolling out.

1½ to 2 pounds maitake mushrooms,
　　cleaned and torn into petals

½ cup plus 3 tablespoons extra virgin olive oil

½ teaspoon kosher salt

¼ teaspoon freshly ground black pepper

2 tablespoons finely minced garlic (4 to 5 cloves)

¾ cup grated Parmesan

Fleur de sel

¼ cup coarsely chopped flat-leaf parsley
　　(optional)

Position a rack in the center of the oven. Place a pizza stone on the rack and preheat the oven to 550°F.

Toss the mushrooms with the 3 tablespoons oil, the salt, and the pepper in a large bowl. Place in a single layer on a baking sheet and roast in the oven for 5 to 7 minutes, or until the mushrooms are caramelized and crisped. Cool before assembling the pizzettas.

Have a lightly floured pizza peel ready.

Place the remaining ½ cup oil in a small bowl. Stir in the garlic.

On a lightly floured surface, roll a ball of dough into an 8-inch circle, about ⅛ inch thick. Place on the floured pizza peel. Spoon some of the oil mixture onto the center of the dough and spread it evenly over the surface, leaving a 1-inch margin around the edges. Scatter a single layer of mushrooms over the oil mixture, then top with 1 or 2 tablespoons of the Parmesan. Slide the pizzetta from the peel onto the stone and bake until the edges are puffed and golden brown, 8 to 10 minutes. Remove to a wire rack and sprinkle with fleur de sel and parsley, if using. Serve immediately.

TIPS AND TECHNIQUES

The dough can be kneaded by hand rather than in the mixer. After stirring the ingredients together, turn the dough out onto a lightly floured surface and knead until smooth and the dough springs back when touched, 5 to 6 minutes.

The dough can be made and placed, covered, in the refrigerator to rise slowly overnight. Remove from the refrigerator and shape the dough into balls. Let rest at room temperature, covered with plastic wrap, for 1 hour before rolling.

Roasting the mushrooms allows any moisture to cook off before adding them to the pizzettas. Wet mushrooms will make a soggy pizzetta.

SUBSTITUTIONS AND VARIATIONS

Almost any type of mushroom can be used in this recipe. Oven roast or sauté the mushrooms first to cook off any moisture.

You can substitute a number of cheeses for the Parmesan, including Asiago, fontina, Manchego, provolone, or mozzarella. You can also make a blend of several cheeses.

Maitake Bread Pudding

In the tasty maitake pizzetta, it's all about the caramelizing high-heat method of cooking this mushroom. In this recipe, sautéing the same mushroom results in a moist, deeply earthy flavor. Maitake, or hen of the woods, is unusual in that two different flavor profiles emerge depending on the cooking method.

This dense, delicious bread pudding can certainly stand alone as an entrée. We think it's at its best, however, upstaging a nice roasted chicken. As you might imagine, it's simply wonderful the next day.

[SERVES 4 TO 6]

About 6 ounces brioche, crusts trimmed,
cut into ½-inch cubes (4 cups)
2 tablespoons unsalted butter,
plus extra for the baking dish
¾ pound maitake mushrooms, cleaned and
torn into large petals
1 teaspoon kosher salt
¼ teaspoon freshly ground black pepper
1 bunch green onions, white parts and
some of the green, finely minced
2 garlic cloves, finely minced
½ cup dry white wine
2 tablespoons finely minced fresh chives
1 cup heavy cream
1 cup milk
4 large eggs, well beaten
¼ cup grated Asiago
¼ cup plus 2 tablespoons grated Parmesan

Place a rack in the center of the oven. Preheat the oven to 350°F.

Butter a 2-quart shallow baking dish. Have a larger baking dish that will hold the 2-quart baking dish nearby. Bring a large pot of water to a simmer while preparing the pudding.

Place the brioche cubes on a baking sheet and toast until just golden brown, 8 to 9 minutes. Set aside to cool.

Heat the butter in a large sauté pan over medium-high heat. When the butter is melted and bubbling, add the mushrooms, tossing to coat them evenly with the butter. Add ½ teaspoon of the salt, ⅛ teaspoon of the pepper, the green onions, and the garlic and mix well. Cook, stirring occasionally, until the mushrooms have released their liquid, then continue cooking until the pan is almost dry. Add the white wine and cook until it has evaporated. Stir in the chives and set aside to cool.

Stir together the cream and milk in a large bowl. Whisk in the eggs, the remaining ½ teaspoon salt, and the remaining ⅛ teaspoon pepper. Add the Asiago, ¼ cup of the Parmesan, and the cooled mushrooms and mix well. Add the toasted brioche cubes, gently stirring them in, then press them into the liquid to fully moisten them. Set aside for 10 to 15 minutes while the brioche absorbs some of the liquid.

Pour the brioche mixture into the prepared baking dish. Sprinkle the top evenly with the remaining 2 tablespoons Parmesan. Place this dish inside the larger baking dish. Pour in the simmering water until it comes halfway up the sides of the pudding dish.

Bake until the top of the pudding is puffed and golden brown, about 1 hour. Remove to a wire rack and let the pudding sit for at least 10 minutes before serving.

TIPS AND TECHNIQUES

The pudding can also be baked without the water bath (bain-marie), but it will cook more quickly. Begin to check for doneness after 40 minutes.

This pudding reheats very well. Cover with aluminum foil and place in a 350°F oven for 30 minutes, or until heated through.

SUBSTITUTIONS AND VARIATIONS

You can use other types of bread for the pudding, such as French bread, country bread, or ciabatta. Trim off any hard crusts before cutting the bread into cubes.

Although rarely true in other recipes, here almost any mushroom really can be substituted for the maitake. Cook as directed in the recipe.

Other cheeses can be substituted for the Asiago, including Gruyère, Comté, Jarlsberg, or Manchego.

Matsutake

Fragrance, flavor, money, power, and even phallic imagery are all at play here in this very complex mushroom. After the Italian white and Perigord truffle, matsutake is the most prized mushroom in the world. While the passion that the Italians and the French have for their truffles is intense, the most proper of Japanese tourists go slack jawed and swoon at the sight of my baskets of matsutake. This great mushroom, once the province of Japanese nobility, is revered as a supreme gift within the world of corporate royalty. The prestigious number-one and -two-grade matsutakes have closed caps with the veil over the gills completely, or nearly so, touching the stem. A large phallus-shaped number-one matsutake shadowed by a fern within a wooden box is a potent gift acquired at an often stunning price.

My commercial mushroom picker pals still fondly remember the night in the early 1990s when a single huge matsutake sold at a little buy station in Oregon for $417. Lord knows what it sold for in Japan.

There's no doubt that the lucky recipient of that glorious mushroom did exactly what all who know matsutake do: They gently raise the mushroom to their nose, close their eyes, and inhale deeply. It's all about the fragrance with matsutake. David Arora in his book *Mushrooms Demystified* describes it as a smell "between red hots and dirty socks." David's socks must smell better than mine, because to me it's a hybrid scent of cinnamon and barnyard mud. A little thumbnail scratch on the stem releases a wave of scent that words just can't articulate.

This legendary mushroom is probably the greatest barely explored ingredient in Western kitchens. Cooking matsutake is a different ball game. Preserving the fragrance is a worthy goal. Traditional dishes like *dobin mushi*, a dashi-based soup; lidded casseroles; or simply rice, all cooked with matsutake, can be served and uncovered at the table, releasing the steamy aroma. Our grilled matsutake pouch recipe holds the scent inside aluminum foil. I love playing with fibrous stems of matsutake by pulling strips from top to bottom like string cheese. Toss these in the sauce on page 205, mound them on an oyster, and stand right there as it broils. As a general rule, "matsies" are not thought to be at their best sizzling in butter in a sauté pan. Many a chef would disagree, however. The exciting future repertoire for this mushroom in European and American cooking traditions is still being born.

Matsutake is known as the pine mushroom in Japan and Canada. The disappearing red pine forests of Japan are diseased and now support few of the native brown matsutake. Japanese immigrants to the United States and Canada found western forests flush with our native white matsutake being savored only by bears, deer, and the remote Hoopa tribe. There are bittersweet stories of Japanese men in World War II internment camps being taken out as logging laborers and finding matsutake during their lunch breaks in the forest. Immigrants began the New World matsutake business.

Matsutake are found dotted across America, from Maine to California. It's in the West, however, that you hit what some of us call the "matsie line." Beginning up in northern British Columbia in August, matsutake are found in pine forests that continue south into the western states. In California the matsutake discards the pine as its mycorrhizal marriage partner and takes up with a bevy of trees, like tan oaks, manzanita, madrone, and others. Farther south yet, matsies surface in Oaxaca, Mexico, and Guatemala. Beyond this, who knows? Wherever matsies are found, it always seems that the soil is sandy or old volcanic activity is nearby.

Lazy though it may sound, a good place to begin hunting autumn matsutake is a good Japanese market. If you find matsies, ask if they're local. Pick up a mushroom and really smell it. This scent memory is a prime identifying tool in the field. Other mushrooms can look a little like matsutake, including a deadly *Amanita* or two, but no impostor wears its perfume. If you have a local mycological society, members can give you clues or the exact habitat profile for your area. When you finally see a dirty white mushroom, it's a good sign if it doesn't pull out easily. Slide your knife into the ground sideways and at a 45-degree angle toward the stem base in the ground. With a lever action, a push down on the knife handle will pop the mushroom up from the ground. Check your field guide and smell the mushroom. If the mushroom passes these tests, search carefully in that entire area. Matsies grow in arcs around the host tree and are often found in sizable patches. Though young matsie buttons hide deep in the duff, watch or feel for the bumps and never rake the surface. You can return and sustainably harvest these patches for years.

For twenty years the quest to satisfy the Japanese hunger for matsutake has resulted in major matsutake discoveries in places from Morocco to Bhutan. However, the growing wave of matsutake entering Japan now breaks upon a young Japanese generation that finds fried chicken and hamburgers sexy and matsutake to be old-fashioned. Japanese youth's sad loss is our gain. As prices drop on matsutake, American chefs are being unleashed to go wild with a culinary treasure that had for years been flown away across the Pacific, far, far from home. European chefs are almost entirely ignorant of this legendary mushroom.

kitchen notes

CLEANING AND PREPARATION: First trim off the tough tip of the stem and look for worm holes. Be careful never to touch the gills; they'll stain an ugly cinnamon brown. Hold the mushroom by the stem or by the cap edges, as if you were holding a basketball. A triangular piece of dampened hard foam or a firm sponge is an ideal tool to use to wipe off any dirt. Once it is clean, thin slices are wise with this dense-textured mushroom.

COOKING METHODS: See above.

STORAGE: Closed-veil grades one and two will keep for six days; open caps (grades three to five) keep for four or five days. Cleaned matsies will freeze well enough for soup and rice but are inferior dried.

IDEAL MATSUTAKE: Any Japanese chef would choose a large, thick, tightly closed-veiled number-one matsutake with intense fragrance. Matsutake's phallic shape and fertility connotations make some American chefs' insistence on "baby" matsutake (a low grade in Japan) somewhat amusing. The matsie should be clean but still retain the earthy base of the stem and a little touch of soil. Most of us, however, are utterly happy with a matsutake with an opened cap with margins rolling inward, so long as the gills are clean and without brown stains.

Foil-Wrapped Matsutake with White Soy and Ginger

All fired up to mushroom hunt as always, Todd Humphries of Martini House in St. Helena, California, correctly guessed that we'd nab matsutake on one particular chefs' foray. He had packed white soy sauce, a terrific ingredient many of us had never seen before. With a handful of other ingredients and a roll of aluminum foil, he made these delightful surprise packages. Like kids, we watched them puff up like Jiffy Pop. Lean forward, cut your packet open, and inhale as the perfectly preserved perfume of the matsutake curls right up to your nose.

[**SERVES 4 TO 6**]

3 tablespoons white soy sauce or 2 tablespoons
    soy sauce plus 1 tablespoon water
2 tablespoons sake
3 tablespoons mirin
¼ teaspoon freshly grated ginger
1 green onion, white and pale green parts only,
    finely minced
½ teaspoon fresh lemon juice
½ teaspoon vegetable or peanut oil,
    plus more to brush packets
1 pound matsutake mushrooms, cleaned

Whisk together the white soy sauce, sake, mirin, ginger, green onion, lemon juice, and oil in a medium bowl.

Slice the mushrooms lengthwise into ¼-inch slices. Lay out four to six 12-inch square pieces of aluminum foil on a flat surface. Brush the surface of the foil with oil. Divide the mushrooms among the foil squares, fanning the slices slightly in the center of each square. Brush the soy mixture over the mushrooms, enough to coat them generously. Fold in the sides of each packet, then fold the opposite sides together, rolling or tucking in the edges so that the mushrooms are snugly enclosed and the liquid won't leak onto the grill.

Prepare a grill to medium heat.

Place the aluminum foil packets over the heat, fold side up, and cook until they are fragrant and sizzling inside, about 8 minutes. Check inside a packet at this point to make sure the mushrooms are tender. Continue cooking for 1 to 2 more minutes, if needed.

Remove from the grill and let sit for 1 to 2 minutes before serving.

TIPS AND TECHNIQUES

Save any extra marinade to brush on after cooking or drizzle over noodles or rice.

The packets can also be cooked in the oven. Preheat the oven to 425°F. Place the foil packets on a baking sheet and cook for 8 to 10 minutes, or until fragrant and sizzling. They also cook wonderfully on top of a woodstove.

SUBSTITUTIONS AND VARIATIONS

Shiitake, king oyster, or oyster mushrooms are the best substitutes for the matsutake, but others, like cremini, will also work well. Cut off the stem and clean the gills before slicing.

Hiro Sone's Chawan Mushi with Matsutake

Many of the common partners to other mushrooms—cream, butter, and garlic—fit matsutake mushrooms as badly as clothes do a cat. It took a nanosecond to turn to my friend Hiro Sone, chef/owner of Terra in St. Helena and Ame in San Francisco, for this recipe. Hiro is not only a great chef and fine guitar player, he's also a Japanese mushroom-hunting country boy. I can still see his face when he found his first American matsutake.

Hiro's comforting, custardy *chawan mushi* is so soft and jiggly that it just dances at the edge of gravity. It is so tender that it just barely holds together. This gentle dish lets the matsies shine. When matsutake have vanished, this versatile custard works well with other mushrooms, as well as scallops, lobster, and, certainly, wild *uni* (sea urchin eggs).

Kombu is a special dried seaweed used to make the dashi broth. You'll find it in Asian markets or health food stores.

[SERVES 6]

for the dashi broth
Two 3 x 2-inch kombu pieces
2 cups loosely packed dried bonito flakes

Clean the kombu with a damp paper towel. Place it in a saucepan with 6 cups bottled or filtered water and set aside for 20 minutes.

Place the pan over low heat, taking about 30 minutes to bring to a boil. The slow heating time brings out the rich umami essence of the kombu. Just before the water comes to a boil, remove the kombu. Add the bonito flakes, bring to a boil, then turn down the heat and simmer for 6 to 7 minutes, skimming off any foam that comes to the surface. Remove from the heat and let the bonito flakes settle. Gently ladle the broth through a fine-mesh strainer lined with a double layer of cheesecloth. Let gravity do the work; don't push on the mixture. The broth will be clearer.

for the chawan mushi
12 large prawns (large shrimp),
    peeled and deveined, tails removed
12 sugar snap peas, cut in half and
    blanched until just tender
6 asparagus spears, cut into ½-inch pieces,
    blanched until just tender
3 small matsutake mushrooms,
    cleaned and cut into ⅛-inch slices
3 large eggs
2 cups dashi broth (above)
2½ tablespoons white soy sauce or
    1½ tablespoons soy sauce
    plus 1 tablespoon water
3 tablespoons mirin
½ teaspoon kosher salt

Position a rack in the center of the oven. Preheat the oven to 325°F.

Place six 6-ounce mugs or Japanese teacups in a roasting pan with deep sides. Bring a large pot of water to a simmer.

Steam or blanch the prawns until just cooked. Cool slightly, then cut into thirds. Divide the prawns, sugar snap peas, and asparagus evenly among the 6 cups.

Set aside one-quarter of the sliced matsutake. Divide the remaining slices among the cups.

Whisk the eggs in a medium bowl. Whisk in the dashi broth, white soy sauce, mirin, and salt. Strain the mixture through a fine-mesh strainer into a bowl. Divide the mixture among the cups. Carefully pour simmering water into the roasting pan to come two-thirds of the way up the sides of the cups. Cover the pan with a sheet of parchment paper, then with aluminum foil, sealing the cups in tightly.

Cook for 40 to 45 minutes, or until the chawan mushi are just set. (They are delicate custards and will have a slight wobble if jiggled gently, even when set.) Make the glaze while the custards cook.

for the glaze

1 teaspoon cornstarch
½ cup dashi broth (above)
1 teaspoon soy sauce
1 teaspoon mirin
Pinch of kosher salt
6 thin strips of lemon zest
1 tablespoon minced fresh chives

Stir together the cornstarch and 2 teaspoons cold water in a small bowl. Set aside.

Place the dashi broth, soy sauce, and mirin in a small saucepan over medium heat. Bring to a boil, then turn down the heat and simmer for 2 minutes. Stir in the salt.

Restir the cornstarch mixture and whisk it into the glaze until the glaze thickens. Stir in the reserved matsutake. Set aside until the custards are done.

to serve

Remove the chawan mushi from the water bath. Bring the glaze back to a boil. Carefully spoon it over the tops of the chawan mushi, being careful not to break the surface. Make sure to get some matsutake on each custard. Serve with a slice of lemon zest and a sprinkling of chives.

TIPS AND TECHNIQUES

The dashi broth will keep for 2 to 3 weeks in an airtight container in the refrigerator. Make it ahead of time to have on hand.

Chef Hiro Sone uses a chawan mushi cup that looks like a teacup with a lid. This is the most traditional way to serve the dish.

SUBSTITUTIONS AND VARIATIONS

Instant dashi, found at Asian markets, can be used if you don't have time to make the broth from scratch.

Lobster, scallops, or crabmeat can be substituted for the prawns. Cook the lobster or scallops briefly as indicated for the prawns in the recipe.

If you can find it, chef Hiro Sone recommends using fresh yuzu zest for the garnish instead of lemon zest. Yuzu is a Japanese citrus that is relatively difficult to find fresh in the United States.

Other vegetables, such as okra, fresh peas, or snow peas, can be used in the chawan mushi.

Cauliflower Mushrooms

SPARASSIS RADICATA; S. CRISPA; S. HERBSTII

The cauliflower mushroom is exquisite. Like a clump of lovely ivory coral, it would look at home in the pristine waters of a tropical reef. Yet for some reason most people who find this beautiful fungus can't resist the urge to pick it up and put it on their head like a ludicrous wig. I see this over and over again. When foraging, you can find great serenity in one moment and then you're channeling Harpo Marx the next. Foraging brings out the playful child in us.

Just look at this mushroom. It challenges good descriptions. It was called a bouquet of egg noodles or bouquet of ribbons by one perceptive writer. Pictured here is the ruffle-edged western cauliflower mushroom with its curly lettucelike edges. The cauliflower of the eastern states is very similar, but with straighter, more rigid and widely spaced branched edges. The scientific names are currently a mess, but they will be tidied up by future DNA work. Whatever the scientific name, the cauliflower mushroom is easy to identify. It is well known and adored in China, Japan, North America, and Europe.

Like maitake, this mushroom grows at the base of a stump or weakened tree. Barring horrid conditions, it will fruit in the same spot each year. Again, like hen of the woods, it can be spectacularly large. The easily spotted white cauliflower mushroom can range from a fungal Moby Dick–size forty-pound behemoth down to more typical three- to five-pounders. Each year I harvest one tree with a cauliflower in the ten- to fifteen-pound range. If you're lucky, you may have to face the struggle of carrying from the woods a fungus with the bulk and weight of a sleeping five-year-old kid. Aha! Maybe our ancestors started putting them on their heads just to get them back to the campfire.

Cauliflowers have a worldwide preference for pine trees, but they are also found on other conifers and some oak trees. You usually stumble upon a cauliflower while looking for other mushrooms. Moving in a zigzag fashion through the woods and eyeing all stumps and tree bases helps. Although a tree may have more than one cauliflower "head" growing on it, the fungus is usually limited to a solo bearing tree in a forested area. When you do find a cauliflower mushroom, consider whether to harvest the mushroom at that moment or wait for it to grow more. If it is small with the ridges very close together, you might wait a few days. It can more than double in size. Do harvest it while it is still creamy white. Older specimens turn yellowish and can get buggy and tough.

There are important niceties to observe during and after harvesting. Pick properly, and you can come back each year for your own sustainable and secret cauliflower tryst. Never, ever try to pull or tear the mushroom from the tree. Use a big sharp knife and cut off the mushroom without jiggling or gouging excessively close to the base of the mushroom and the tree bark. You want the body of the fungus within the tree to be undamaged and ready for next year's encore performance. After you've harvested it, cleaning the cauliflower mushroom can be a challenge. Step one begins just after you've cut it from the tree. Use the extra bag each clever hunter should always carry and put the mushroom into the bag or cover it with the bag immediately. This prevents more forest debris from entering the labyrinthine channels of this mushroom's ornate surface.

The cauliflower in your hands will be not only something of special beauty, but also one of the most extraordinarily flavored of all mushrooms. Its fragrance, my favorite of all mushrooms, is an odd combination of citrus, fungus, and freesias.

kitchen notes

CLEANING AND PREPARATION: You'll always have to wash cauliflowers. Cut them into large slices resembling the pictures of a brain scan. This way the crannies are accessible for a good wash. Slosh the slices vigorously up and down in a bowl of water. Place them on a towel or wire rack to drain and air-dry. Discard any tough cartilaginous pieces around the base.

COOKING METHODS: Most books will tell you to cook this mushroom long and slowly. This is fine, but don't be afraid of the pleasing al dente quality of this mushroom. The thinner outer portion is delicious stir-fried, for instance. A single mushroom can start the day in a quiche and end it next to a roast.

STORAGE: Mercifully, because of their large size, they'll last at least five days in the refrigerator, if covered with a damp cloth. They dry well and are popular as such in Chinese grocery stores. I like them better cooked into something like the superb oxtail soup here, then frozen.

IDEAL CAULIFLOWER MUSHROOMS: Cauliflower mushrooms should be white or creamy white and as clean as possible. The edges should be crisp with little or no browning. The bases of the mushrooms should be firm and free of the bugs that usually attack the base first. This type of mushroom is rarely sold in markets.

Cauliflower Mushrooms in Oxtail Broth

The beauty of cauliflower mushrooms is obvious. Yet cooking these mushrooms confounds even the most nimble cooks. This deceptively drab-colored oxtail soup is my favorite way to cook them. Strips of cauliflower mushrooms drift about in the rich, dark broth like delicate noodles. Noodles have never tasted this good. It's like a magic trick to those who don't know that these seemingly messy noodles are actually a mushroom, until the intense flavor hits their taste buds. Making this the day before not only makes the flavors richer but it also allows you to easily remove the layer of congealed fat for a clearer broth.

[SERVES 4 TO 6]

4 pounds oxtails

2 teaspoons kosher salt, plus more to taste

¼ teaspoon freshly ground black pepper,
 plus more to taste

2 tablespoons pure olive oil

2 yellow onions, cut into ½-inch dice

2 carrots, cut into ½-inch dice

2 celery stalks, cut into ½-inch dice

4 garlic cloves, thinly sliced

Bouquet garni: 4 fresh thyme sprigs,
 2 flat-leaf parsley sprigs, 2 bay leaves

½ pound cauliflower mushrooms,
 cleaned and torn into petal-size pieces

2 tablespoons finely minced fresh chives

Place the oxtails in a shallow baking dish and season generously with salt and pepper. Cover with plastic wrap and refrigerate overnight.

Heat the oil in a large stockpot over medium-high heat. When the oil is hot, add the oxtails in a single layer and brown them on all sides, turning and rotating them onto their sides to brown them evenly. Remove them from the pot and set aside.

Add the onions, carrots, celery, and garlic to the pot and stir. Lower the heat to medium and cook until the vegetables are softened and starting to caramelize, 5 to 6 minutes. Return the oxtails to the pot and add 3 quarts cold water and the bouquet garni. Bring to a boil, then turn down the heat to a gentle simmer and cook, covered, for 3 hours.

Strain the soup into a bowl, pressing on the solids to release all the liquid, through a fine-mesh strainer lined with cheesecloth and discard the solids. Refrigerate overnight.

to finish

Remove the layer of fat from the top of the broth.

Bring the broth to a boil in a large pot over medium-high heat. Whisk in the salt and pepper. Add the mushrooms. Turn down the heat and simmer for 8 minutes, or until the mushrooms are tender.

Divide the soup among 4 to 6 bowls and top with the chives.

TIPS AND TECHNIQUES

For a heartier version of the soup, save the cooked oxtails, remove the meat, and add it to the broth along with the mushrooms.

SUBSTITUTIONS AND VARIATIONS

For a very quick version of this soup, simply heat homemade or canned beef or chicken broth and add the mushrooms. Cook as directed in the recipe.

Maitake is the best substitute, but sliced oyster, button, or cremini mushrooms can also be substituted for the cauliflower mushrooms.

Cauliflower Mushroom and King Trumpet Spring Rolls

The most precious aspect of the cauliflower mushroom is its fragrance. Its next very special quality is the crispness of its flesh. Even after cooking, the cauliflower mushroom has the al dente texture (but not flavor) of stir-fried cabbage. More than twenty years ago very few people knew cauliflower mushrooms, yet clever Cindy Pawlcyn, chef/owner of Mustards Grill, Go Fish, and Cindy's Backstreet Kitchen, recognized its qualities immediately when I gave her a pretty specimen. With it she made wild mushroom spring rolls, using the cauliflower mushrooms as the perfumed "crunch" inside. This recipe is a memory of that dish. When you cut the wrapper open, be sure to inhale the vapors carrying the unique perfume of this mushroom.

[MAKES 12]

3 tablespoons soy sauce

3 tablespoons dry sherry

2 teaspoons sugar

2 teaspoons unseasoned rice vinegar

¼ cup plus 2 tablespoons chicken broth

1¾ teaspoons kosher salt

¼ teaspoon plus 3 pinches
    (⅛ teaspoon) freshly ground black pepper

1 tablespoon cornstarch, plus more for
    dusting the pan

4 quarts peanut or vegetable oil for frying

¼ cup vegetable oil

½ pound king trumpet mushrooms,
    cut into ⅛-inch slices

1 tablespoon finely minced garlic
    (2 to 3 small cloves)

1 pound cauliflower mushrooms, cleaned
    and broken or sliced into 1-inch pieces

4 cups thinly shredded (¼ inch) Napa cabbage

⅓ cup finely minced scallions (about 3)

1 teaspoon grated fresh ginger

12 spring roll wrappers

1 large egg, well beaten

Whisk together the soy sauce, sherry, sugar, rice vinegar, ¼ cup of the chicken broth, 1 teaspoon of the salt, and ¼ teaspoon of the pepper in a small bowl or measuring cup.

Stir together the remaining 2 tablespoons chicken broth and the cornstarch in a ramekin or small bowl. The chicken broth must be cold or at room temperature to mix smoothly with the cornstarch. Set aside.

Place the 4 quarts peanut oil in a large (6- to 8-quart) pot. Heat the oil to 350°F.

Heat 2 tablespoons of the vegetable oil in a large sauté pan or wok over high heat. When the oil is hot, add the king trumpet mushrooms, tossing quickly to coat with the oil. Add ¼ teaspoon of the salt and a pinch of the pepper. Cook, stirring and tossing, until the mushrooms are tender and starting to brown. Add 1 teaspoon of the garlic and cook for 1 more minute. Remove to a large bowl.

Wipe out the pan, place it back over high heat, and add 1 tablespoon of the vegetable oil. When the oil is hot, add the cauliflower mushrooms, tossing quickly to coat with the oil. Add ¼ teaspoon of the salt and a pinch of pepper. Cook, stirring and tossing, until the mushrooms have cooked dry and are starting to brown. Add 1 teaspoon of the garlic and cook for 1 more minute. Add the cauliflower mushrooms to the king trumpets in the bowl.

Wipe out the pan, place it back over high heat, and add the remaining 1 tablespoon vegetable oil. When the oil is hot, stir in the cabbage, tossing to coat with the oil. Add the remaining ¼ teaspoon salt and pinch of pepper. Stir in the scallions, the ginger, and the remaining 1 teaspoon garlic. Cook, stirring frequently, until the cabbage is wilted and tender, 4 to 5 minutes. Add the cabbage to the mushrooms in the bowl and stir together.

Wipe out the pan and place over medium-high heat. When the pan is hot, add the mushroom mixture, stirring to heat through. When the mushroom mixture is hot, stir in the soy sauce mixture and mix well. Restir the chicken broth mixture, then pour it over the mushrooms, stirring it in quickly. The mixture will thicken as you stir. It should be firm enough to shape, but not too gluey. Add a little water, if needed, to thin it out slightly. Cool to room temperature before rolling.

to finish

Lay out 1 spring roll wrapper on a clean surface. Place ¼ cup of the mushroom mixture in a corner, leaving a ½- to 1-inch margin at the edges. Fold the corner of the wrapper snugly over the mixture and begin to roll, pulling the wrapper tightly against the mixture. At the halfway point, brush the edges of the wrapper with beaten egg, then fold in the sides to enclose the filling. Continue rolling. Brush the tip of the wrapper with egg and press it firmly to seal the roll. Place on a cornstarch-dusted baking sheet and finish assembling the rest of the rolls.

Ease as many spring rolls into the hot peanut oil as can fit comfortably without crowding. Cook for 3 to 4 minutes, turn them, and cook for 3 to 4 more minutes, or until the spring rolls are an even golden brown. Remove and place them on a paper towel–lined baking sheet. Hold in a warm place while you cook the rest.

Serve whole or cut in half.

TIPS AND TECHNIQUES

Cooking each ingredient separately allows it to retain its individual flavor in the mixture.

Keep the spring roll wrappers covered with a kitchen towel as you work with them. They dry out and become brittle otherwise.

SUBSTITUTIONS AND VARIATIONS

Oyster mushrooms can be substituted for either or both of the mushrooms in this recipe.

Bok choy can substitute for the Napa cabbage. Place it in a colander after cooking and before adding it to the mushroom mixture, if needed, to drain off any excess liquid.

Juniper Berries

We all know the flavor of juniper berries because we all know gin, at least in my crowd. It's ironic that gin was invented by the Dutch as a juniper-infused medication, yet four hundred years later its reputation rests on the deliciously debilitating classic martini. The juniper berry's place in most homes is usually limited to that gin bottle. While gin can certainly lead to spicy wildlife, the juniper berry as a spice can lead to wild game.

The distinctive resinous tang of juniper berries has always had a special place in wild game cookery. Those of you lucky enough to have wild pig, duck, venison, or other game to cook in your kitchen are bound to have dried juniper berries in your spice rack. The strong and bright flavor of these berries stands up to and balances the bold flavor of game. It seems to be a perfect match, smelling as these berries do of some piney landscape. Germans, Alsatians, and Hungarians marry the berries with cabbage in formidable dishes. It's hard to imagine choucroute or sauerkraut without them.

Juniper is one of the few spices that grows wild in the Far North. It can be found throughout the northern hemisphere. The rugged *Juniperus* clan has found its special niche in areas with meager rocky or sandy soils. It thrives in spooky terrain landscapes like the western high plains deserts or the windblown ocean sides of the Atlantic. The common juniper, *Juniperus communis*, is the most abundant conifer in the world. Its low profile sprawls over wide expanses of the upper half of our planet. Other junipers are substantial trees, like the western juniper, *J. occidentalis*, with its dramatic gnarled limbs. Junipers are abundant in less ethereal settings as well. Every landscaped suburban insurance office seems to be literally knee deep in them. Whatever the species, and wherever the juniper is, the odd berry it bears and the aroma set it apart from other conifers.

As you begin to spy junipers, you'll notice berries only on the female plants. Pick a fresh berry and look closely. It's actually a little cone that has evolved into an enclosed berry. You'll see what was once the conifer cone edges. Inside the skin is a more or less juicy interior with one to four tiny seeds. The berries vary in size from one-quarter to one-half inch, and most take a full two years to go from a resinous green to a frosty bloom-covered purple globe. This is when they reach their peak of flavor. Junipers can have both one- and two-year-old berries hanging. Their size and flavor vary slightly among species. Western or Utah juniper berries can be juicy, sweet, and a half inch in diameter. Others, like the common landscaping junipers *J. chinensis* and *J. communis*, have dense, flavorful small berries. At a distance, the vegetation may have a frosty blue hue. Upon looking closer, that blue haze will be ripe violet juniper berries sprinkled throughout the greenery.

Picking juniper berries is easy work because you don't need many of these strong-flavored little fruits. In the autumn the ripe berries drop to the ground. If you come across ripe berries, spread a tarp and give the bush a good shake and you'll have a shower of berries. Handpicking works, but it's a bit slow because the berries are positioned in the forks of the scaly branches. A pound or three is all most people need at home.

It's puzzling as to why juniper berries are not used more. The popularity of gin is a testament to people's affection for the flavor of juniper, yet its culinary use remains within the special province of game and cabbage.

kitchen notes

CLEANING AND PREPARATION: Just rinse and shake the berries in a colander or screen to remove any pieces of vegetation.

COOKING METHODS: Juicy fresh or thawed frozen juniper berries are ideal in marinades. Wine, cider, cloves, allspice, and citrus are all common partners. Fresh or frozen berries don't have to be removed before eating because cooking makes them tender. If using dried juniper berries, either grind them or put them in cheesecloth and remove them before serving. Juniper branches added to a smoker impart great flavor.

STORAGE: If you have a juniper bush or tree nearby, just pluck the berries as you need them. The ripe berries will hang on the bush for months. If you're not that lucky, pick the ripe berries where you can. They'll keep fresh in your refrigerator for weeks in a jar or plastic bag. They're also excellent frozen. Tuck them into a handy part of your freezer for easy grabbing. Drying is the standard method of preservation.

IDEAL JUNIPER BERRIES: The berries should be fully ripe with purple skins whose color doesn't rub off. When squeezed, sweetish juice will ooze out. I prefer fresh or frozen to dried.

Juniper-and-Maple-Glazed Duck

I doubt you've ever run into a recipe that uses the essential taste of two trees to season a little duck. There's a big, dynamic flavor working here in the balance among resinous juniper, sweet maple, and bright orange peel. Sarah modestly suggests making a double batch of glaze as an option. Please, just make a double batch. A nice little puddle of this delicious glaze on the plate is heaven into which to touch each forkful of duck meat. After duck, goose is my second choice of other excellent options, like quail or pork, to serve with this glaze.

[SERVES 4]

for the brine

One 4- to 5-pound duck
1 cup kosher salt
¼ cup sugar
3 bay leaves, crushed
1 tablespoon fresh or frozen
    juniper berries, crushed
6 strips orange zest
1 teaspoon black peppercorns
3 garlic cloves, crushed
4 fresh thyme sprigs, chopped coarsely
6 quarts water

Rinse and pat dry the duck.

Place the salt, sugar, bay leaves, juniper berries, orange zest, peppercorns, garlic, and thyme in a container large enough to hold the duck and the brine. Heat 1 quart of the water to boiling. Add the water to the dry ingredients and stir until the sugar and salt are dissolved. Stir in the remaining 5 quarts of water. Let cool to room temperature. Submerge the duck in the brine and refrigerate overnight, or up to 2 days.

One hour before cooking, remove the duck from the brine and drain in a colander or on a rack placed inside a baking sheet. Pat the duck very dry before roasting.

for the glaze

1 tablespoon dried juniper berries
½ cup maple syrup
2 tablespoons soy sauce
2 teaspoons finely grated orange zest

Position a rack in the center of the oven. Preheat the oven to 450°F.

Place the juniper berries on a baking sheet and toast in the oven for 3 to 4 minutes. Be careful not to overtoast them. They will become fragrant when ready, but quickly turn acrid and bitter if burned. Remove and cool to room temperature. Grind the berries into a powder using a spice grinder or mortar and pestle.

Combine the maple syrup, soy sauce, orange zest, and powdered juniper berries in a small saucepan over medium-high heat. Bring to a boil, then turn down the heat slightly and cook at a vigorous simmer, whisking occasionally, for 1½ to 2 minutes, or until the glaze is slightly thickened. Hold in a warm place while you roast the duck. Set aside one-quarter of the glaze to use when serving the duck.

for the duck

Line a roasting pan with aluminum foil and place a wire rack inside. Truss the duck, pat very dry, and place on the rack. Cook for 30 minutes.

Remove the duck from the oven and turn down the heat to 350°F. Carefully pour off the excess fat in the pan.

Prick the skin of the duck all over with a fork. Brush with one-third of the remaining glaze and return the duck to the oven. Cook for 15 minutes. Baste with another third of the glaze. Cook for 15 more minutes and baste with the remainder of the glaze. Cook for 30 more minutes, or until the internal temperature of the duck is 175° to 180°F.

Hold in a warm place to rest for at least 10 minutes.

Serve the reserved glaze alongside the duck.

TIPS AND TECHNIQUES

You can make a double batch of the glaze to have more for serving with the duck. Cook the mixture for 2 to 3 more minutes to achieve the same thickness. Any extra will hold in an airtight container for up to 2 weeks in the refrigerator.

Lining the roasting pan with aluminum foil makes cleanup much easier.

SUBSTITUTIONS AND VARIATIONS

This brine and glaze will also work with a 3- to 4-pound boneless pork loin. Trim excess fat from the loin and brine the pork loin as for the duck. Roast at 350°F, basting with the glaze until the internal temperature reaches 145° to 150°F, about 1 to 1¼ hours.

Honey can be substituted for the maple syrup. The cooking time for the syrup will be slightly less, so watch carefully as it cooks.

The glaze can be used with goose, quail, or other game birds.

Juniper-Rubbed Pork Loin with Prunes and Savoy Cabbage

Maybe we all have an inner Alsatian peasant longing for a dish just like this. As nights get colder and colder, the fruits of autumn—newly dried prunes, cabbage, and a harvested hog—are woven together with the wild piney flavor of juniper berries. Dried berries work very well, but ripe, juicy juniper berries lend a hint of sweetness that elevates this dish. Freeze any extra-ripe berries. They freeze beautifully.

[SERVES 4 TO 6]

for the juniper rub
1½ tablespoons kosher salt
1½ tablespoons juniper berries
½ teaspoon black peppercorns
2 bay leaves
2 garlic cloves, finely minced
2½- to 3-pound boneless pork loin

Place the salt in a small bowl. Using a mortar and pestle or a mallet, crush the juniper berries and peppercorns. Add to the salt. Crumble the bay leaves and add them, along with the garlic, to the bowl. Mix everything well. Press the salt mixture evenly over the entire surface of the pork loin. Place in a shallow pan, cover lightly with parchment paper or plastic wrap, and refrigerate at least 6 hours or overnight. Remove from the refrigerator 1 hour before roasting.

for the prunes and savoy cabbage
4 slices smoked bacon (about 4 ounces), cut into ¼-inch strips
1 medium yellow onion, finely diced
1 medium head savoy cabbage, cored and cut into ¼-inch slices
1 teaspoon kosher salt
¼ teaspoon freshly ground black pepper
½ cup dry white wine
1 cup chicken broth
6 ounces pitted prunes, cut in half

Position a rack in the center of the oven. Preheat the oven to 350°F.

Place the bacon in a large braising pot or dutch oven over medium heat. Cook the bacon until golden brown, about 6 to 7 minutes. Remove the bacon from the pot using a slotted spoon and drain on a paper towel–lined baking sheet. Leave the bacon fat in the pot.

Place the pork loin in the pot and brown it on all sides, approximately 3 to 4 minutes per side, or until golden brown. Remove the pork loin from the pot and set aside.

Place the onion in the pot and cook, stirring occasionally, until it is tender and translucent, about 3 to 4 minutes. Add the cabbage to the pot, stirring to combine it with the onion. Add the salt and pepper. The cabbage will begin to wilt and shrink as it starts to cook. Stir in the wine. Turn up the heat to medium high and cook until the wine is reduced and almost gone. Add the broth, prunes, and reserved bacon to the pot and mix well. Place the pork loin on top of the cabbage mixture. When the broth is bubbling, cover the pot with a lid or aluminum foil and place it in the oven. Roast for 30 minutes covered, then remove the lid or foil and cook for another 15 to 20 minutes, or until the internal temperature of the pork loin is 140° to 145°F.

Remove from the oven. Remove the lid or foil and tent the pot loosely with foil. Let rest for 15 minutes before serving.

TIPS AND TECHNIQUES

Be sure to crush the juniper berries completely to release the flavors.

SUBSTITUTIONS AND VARIATIONS

Pancetta can be substituted for the bacon.

Regular cabbage can be substituted for the savoy cabbage. Be sure to slice it thinly, and cook it for a few more minutes before adding the wine.

Elderberries

SAMBUCUS CANADENSIS; S. CAERULEA; S. MEXICANA

Once upon a time not so long ago, elderberries were held in extremely high esteem by humans. Elderberry trees fed us. They got us drunk, provided medicine, and protected us from witches. Everybody knew elderberry trees. They offered everything from fruit to flutes and cosmetics to weapons. The elder has earned its own myth from the Bible as the tree Judas was hanged from. Legends tell of the elder as both a tree used by witches and the tree you plant outside your door to protect you from the same harpies. I'm quite sure I would have gone up in flames as a witch, since I can't leave elderberry trees alone. The elderberry has been too fine an ally for it now to be so forgotten.

In California in autumn the fragrant and frothy white elderflowers described in the spring chapter (see page 63) ripen into small purple black berries frosted with a white bloom. Big clusters of these berries hang heavily on single stems all over these shrubby trees. It's the perfect time to identify the tree because, as you'll find in your field guide, in autumn the poisonous hemlock can't be mistaken for the berry-laden elder. Don't throw caution totally out the window, though, because only the flowers and the ripe berries of the elder are safe to eat. All the other parts—leaves, green berries, twigs—*are toxic.* The berries *must be cooked* to not only be perfectly safe, but also to gain the rich black currantlike flavor they're known for. Be careful, but not alarmed. There are many foods, like rhubarb, potatoes, or tomatoes, whose poisonous leaves call for the same parameters for caution. The flavor of raw elderberries is not very sweet or impressive. Yet their mushy, seedy character is magically changed by cooking them with a touch of sugar. Their flavor becomes deeply complex and haunting.

Finding and harvesting elderberries is not much of a challenge for the foraging diehard. Elderberries are quite common. If you first spotted them flowering in the spring, you'll notice that come summer you'll often see late flowers and early berries on the same tree. Whether in the desert, lush forests, or mountains, elder trees like their feet moist in zones like creeks, ditches, and roadsides. Sometimes they're dreadfully hard to ignore. Mounds of elderberry trees with cascades of elderberries flaunt themselves along I-80, for instance, but ignore them you must if their toes sit in polluted road runoff.

Not only are elderberries rather easy to find, but they're easy to harvest. What a generous tree! It's the indulgent rich uncle of the wild-foods world. Uncle elder's fruit may be purple, but it must also be ripe enough to taste a touch of sweetness in these never-very-sweet berries. Though they must be cooked for safety, it won't hurt to taste just a little bit raw; just avoid picking any green berries. If the berries are ready for harvest, the trick is to get the small ones detached from the tiny stems. An excellent and common method is to use a big fat-toothed comb. Gently bend the berry bunch over your bucket and comb the berries off the little stems. *Gently* is the important word here because these larger brittle branches are hollow, hence their traditional usefulness as flutes, whistles, arrow shafts, and blowguns. You can also snip off the whole head of berries and groom it at home with a comb or fork. I often cut the whole clusters off and place them in the short cut-down cardboard boxes that soda pop is sold in. Fill the cardboard tray, then use another tray as a lid. This protects the berries nicely from squashing. Place your stack of these in the freezer. After the berries are frozen, smacking the boxes against a surface will break the stems from the berries. Pour the berries into a big-holed colander. They sift out very nicely, like little ball bearings, from the stemmy bits. You can also roll them over a kitchen towel–covered sheet pan. The berries roll away (careful!), leaving the broken stems behind.

Don't get carried away with the ease of harvest and take more berries than you need. Leave most of the berries behind for the birds, who also adore them. In autumn they need plenty of fuel for migration.

Beyond a splendid reputation for the elderberry's rich portlike flavor (it was actually used to fraudulently enhance port wine's flavor) is its soaring reputation as another superfood. Added to its colossal vitamin C content is massive antioxidant power. Health food stores are laden with elderberry elixirs for arthritis, viral flu cures, weight loss, and more. All this, and they're wickedly delicious too.

kitchen notes

CLEANING AND PREPARATION: See previous page.

COOKING METHODS: Elderberries must be cooked for both flavor and safety concerns. We have two stunning recipes here, but sometimes it's hard to get past making jelly, since elderberry jelly is the best on the planet (see page 320). One nice trick when you make a sauce is to reserve some whole berries while you cook and strain the rest. Return a few whole berries to your sauce to give a little caviarlike "pop" in your mouth. Elderberries contain seeds, but they are extremely tiny and add a pleasant crunch to most foods.

STORAGE: Refrigerate and cook elderberries within three days. The berries freeze well for future use. Many people dry them too. Take care with drying because the berries shrink into tiny balls and can fall through drying trays.

IDEAL ELDERBERRIES: The deep blue berries should have a hint of sweetness and be largely stem free.

ALERT: The berries and flowers are the only nontoxic parts of the elderberry tree. Always cook the berries before eating them.

Spice-Roasted Venison with Elderberry Port Sauce

This is a soulful dish, rich and deep purple. More than a hundred years ago elderberries were used to improve the flavor of some port wine. What was then a sneaky flavor enhancement makes great good sense in this excellent game sauce. The robust, almost wine-grapey taste of this sauce flatters the venison perfectly. While a fruit-tinged game sauce is a classic, this sauce has an unusual depth and the unexpected textural charm of the tiny elderberry seeds.

[SERVES 4]

for the venison

½ star anise, finely ground in spice grinder
¼ teaspoon ground allspice
¼ teaspoon ground cloves
½ teaspoon ground cinnamon
½ teaspoon kosher salt
¼ teaspoon freshly ground black pepper
One 1½-pound boneless venison short loin
2 tablespoons pure olive oil

Combine the star anise, allspice, cloves, cinnamon, salt, and pepper in a small bowl.

Trim the venison loin of any fat and silver skin. Evenly coat the loin with the spice mixture and refrigerate, loosely covered, overnight, or up to 2 days. Remove from the refrigerator 1 hour before roasting.

Position a rack in the center of the oven. Preheat the oven to 350°F.

Place the oil in a large sauté pan over medium-high heat. When the oil is hot, add the venison loin. Sear on all sides, 2 to 3 minutes per side.

Place on a rack inside a roasting pan. Roast for 20 to 25 minutes for medium rare, or until the internal temperature of the venison is 130° to 135°F. Let rest for 10 minutes before slicing. Serve with the elderberry port sauce.

for the elderberry port sauce

2 medium shallots, finely minced
1 garlic clove, finely minced
½ cup port
1 tablespoon red wine vinegar
¾ cup elderberries
¾ cup veal demi-glace
½ teaspoon kosher salt
¼ teaspoon freshly ground black pepper
2 tablespoons unsalted butter
½ teaspoon finely chopped fresh thyme

Place the shallots, garlic, port, vinegar, and ½ cup
of the elderberries in a small saucepan over
medium-high heat. Bring to a boil, then turn down
the heat and simmer, reducing the liquid to ⅓ cup,
5 to 6 minutes. Place a fine-mesh strainer over a
small bowl or measuring cup and pour the sauce
through. Press on the solids to extract all the liquid,
then return the sauce to the pot. Discard the solids.

Add the demi-glace, salt, and pepper and the
remaining ¼ cup elderberries to the saucepan.
Bring to a boil, then turn down the heat and simmer
until the sauce is reduced to about 1 cup, about
15 minutes. Just before serving, whisk in the butter
and thyme.

TIPS AND TECHNIQUES

*The flavor of star anise is best if it is ground just
before using.*

*The demi-glace, available in the freezer sections
of grocery stores, gives this sauce a richness that
balances the tart and sweet flavor of the elderberries.*

SUBSTITUTIONS AND VARIATIONS

You can substitute huckleberries for the elderberries.

*This sauce will work well with duck breasts
or pork loin or tenderloin. You can use the spice
rub as well, or omit it and simply season with salt
and pepper.*

Elderberry "Membrillo" / Elderberry Jellies

This recipe has a dual personality and purpose. Membrillo is the traditional jellylike paste made with quince. Like quince, elderberries aren't sweet by nature, yet they both have rich fruit flavor. It is a rare quality for a food to be able to swing from the savory to the sweet side of the kitchen so easily. Sarah and I very much wanted to have a wild ingredient to add its character to a cheese course. The intense currant flavor of this elderberry "membrillo" holds its position nobly on any cheese plate.

Beyond having a membrillo, the southern girl in each of us requires that a candy recipe have a place at the wild table too. This is no simple sweet, however. Foraging friend Gretchen's success with huckleberry jellies inspired us. The complex flavor of elderberries is on full display in these sophisticated, frosty purple squares.

This recipe comes together rapidly. Have all the ingredients assembled and ready for action beforehand.

[MAKES 1½ POUNDS "MEMBRILLO" OR 48 CANDIES]

---

2 pounds elderberries, stems removed
2 cups sugar, plus more for coating candies
Pinch of kosher salt
2 tablespoons fresh lemon juice
One 3-ounce package liquid pectin

Line a 7½-inch square baking pan with plastic wrap, pressing it flat onto the bottom and up the sides of the pan, with a generous margin on the edges. Set aside.

Place the elderberries in a medium saucepan over medium-high heat. Bring to a boil, then turn down the heat and simmer for 6 to 8 minutes, or until the berries have released their juices. Place a fine-mesh strainer over a large container and pour in the berries and their juices. Press firmly on the fruit to extract all the juice. Discard the berries. You should have approximately 2 cups of juice.

Place the juice in a medium saucepan over medium-high heat. Whisk in the sugar, salt, and lemon juice. Bring to a boil, whisking to dissolve the sugar. When the mixture reaches a boil, whisk in the pectin and place a candy thermometer on the side of the pan. Cook, stirring continuously with a wooden spatula or spoon, until the temperature reaches 225°F, 15 to 18 minutes. As the mixture cooks down and thickens, the surface will become very bubbly and shiny. Remove from the heat and immediately pour the liquid into the prepared pan. Place on a wire rack to set at room temperature for about 2 hours.

for the jellies

Turn the elderberry mixture out onto a sugared cutting board. Have a small bowl of sugar nearby for coating the candies. Cut the elderberry mixture into 1-inch squares, then place each square in the bowl of sugar, turning it gently to coat with the sugar. Lift it out, shaking off excess sugar, and place on a baking sheet. Let sit for 30 minutes. Store in an airtight container at room temperature for up to 1 week.

for the membrillo

Place the elderberry mixture in an airtight container in the refrigerator. Slice as needed to serve with cheese. The membrillo will keep for up to 3 weeks in the refrigerator.

TIPS AND TECHNIQUES

Try sprinkling a few grains of fleur de sel on the membrillo before serving.

If the sugar dissolves on the candies before serving, simply give the candies another light coating before you serve them.

SUBSTITUTIONS AND VARIATIONS

Substitute huckleberries for the elderberries. Follow the proportion of 2 cups juice to 2 cups sugar.

Elderberry Fool

The weighty cassislike flavor of elderberries is transformed here into a happy, fluffy fool. The whipped cream becomes a thick lilac poof with a rich purple elderberry syrup ribboned around the parfait glass. It looks so creamy you're quite surprised by the fine crunch in every spoonful. The tiny elderberry seeds are a surprising textural counterpoint. Don't strain the seeds out. They're a vital delight in this simple dessert.

[SERVES 6]

for the elderberry syrup
1 pound elderberries, stems removed
¾ cup sugar
1 tablespoon fresh lemon juice
Pinch of kosher salt

Place the elderberries in a large mesh strainer over a bowl or pot. Using a wooden spoon, crush and press the berries, working them back and forth in the strainer, to extract all the juice. You should have ½ to ¾ cup of juice.

Combine the juice, sugar, lemon juice, and salt in a small saucepan over medium-high heat. Bring to a boil, then turn down the heat and simmer for 6 to 8 minutes, or until just thickened. Chill for at least 4 hours or overnight before using.

for the elderberry compote
¼ cup sugar
⅛ teaspoon kosher salt
1 cup elderberries, stems removed
½ teaspoon fresh lemon juice

Place the sugar, ¼ cup water, and the salt in a small saucepan over medium heat. Bring to a boil, whisking occasionally, and cook for 2 minutes. Add the elderberries and bring back to a boil. Cook for 1 minute, then turn off the heat and let the mixture sit for 10 minutes. Strain the mixture through a fine-mesh strainer into a bowl or measuring cup. Save the liquid and set aside the berries.

Place the liquid back in the saucepan over medium-high heat. Bring to a boil, then turn down the heat and simmer until the mixture has reduced to a syrupy consistency, 3 to 5 minutes. Remove from the heat. Add the berries back into the syrup and stir in the lemon juice. Chill for at least 4 hours or overnight before using.

for the fool

1½ cups heavy cream

1 tablespoon sugar

⅛ teaspoon kosher salt

¾ cup elderberry syrup (above)

Reserved elderberry compote (above)

Finely grated zest of 1 lemon

Make sure the elderberry syrup and compote are cold.

Combine the cream, sugar, and salt in the bowl of a standing mixer fitted with the whip attachment. Whip until the cream holds a firm, not stiff, creamy peak.

Using a large rubber spatula, fold the syrup and half the compote into the cream, creating a swirled effect with visible streaks of cream and elderberry. Fold using a minimum of strokes, so as not to lose the loft of the cream.

Divide the fool among 6 dessert glasses or dishes. Just before serving, top with the remaining compote and the lemon zest.

TIPS AND TECHNIQUES

The fools can be assembled several hours ahead of time and refrigerated until ready to serve. In that case, save the final topping of the compote and lemon zest until just before serving.

The compote will keep in an airtight container in the refrigerator for up to 2 weeks. It will keep in the freezer for up to 2 months.

If you have some cream and keep some extra compote and syrup on hand, the fools can be a great last-minute dessert and will come together in a matter of minutes.

SUBSTITUTIONS AND VARIATIONS

Other berries, such as huckleberries, blueberries, mulberries, raspberries, blackberries, and more, can be substituted for the elderberries.

The fool mixture can be made into a trifle by spreading it between layers of crumbled cake or cookies.

Candy Cap Mushrooms

LACTARIUS RUBIDUS

This is cruel, really. I'd wondered whether to include this wonderfully bizarre mushroom in the book at all. Most wild mushroom lovers in the world will pass through life without ever having tasted this intense and haunting maple-flavored mushroom. But then I remembered that I'll probably never see a unicorn-horned narwhal or eat Turkish orchid ice cream, yet my heart's warmed by just knowing such things exist.

This sweet little russet mushroom is found only from the central Oregon coast to the central coast of California. Within this limited territory, this aromatic mushroom has cult status among a few privileged chefs and mushroom geeks. Candy caps are splendid fresh, but their special notoriety resides in their use as a dried mushroom. Just a tablespoon of the small dried mushrooms can fill your kitchen with a maple aroma that lingers for long periods of time. My dry mushroom storage room will probably smell like candy caps for years. The intense smell is remarkable, but it's the long, lingering quality of its haunting fragrance and flavor that's simply astonishing.

Very few people eat substantial amounts of candy cap mushrooms, but if they do, this magical candy cap incense seeps systemically throughout their bodies, only to ooze out of the pores of their skin. Years ago a panicked chef called. After dinner service the previous night he'd eaten multiple servings of a candy cap dessert. The next morning the sleeping wife with whom he'd crawled into bed awoke next to her chef/husband, who smelled like he'd been either rolled in maple syrup or out cavorting with an IHOP waitress. His new, sweet smell persisted for two hours after his shower.

The less concentrated flavor of fresh candy caps is quite suitable for savory things that are used to having a sweet touch added. I love them with duck, pork, and winter squash. During the first couple of years of the French Laundry, I took a young cook out mushroom hunting. He returned with candy caps. This young fellow introduced Thomas Keller to this virtually unknown mushroom.

In this unexpected master-underling role reversal, chef Keller's curious mind opened wide to candy caps. He has often used them powdered as a spice. They have a mysterious Madeira-like quality used this way.

Those of us lucky enough to live within their limited territory can find candy caps growing under pines, Douglas firs, and a few oak trees. Their small size is compensated for by their gregarious habit of appearing in groups around their host tree. These precious patches need routine picking in order for the picker to accumulate a nice stash.

This is not the easiest mushroom to identify. There are look-alike mushrooms all over the country. Members of the *Lactarius* genus that candy caps are a part of have the odd quality of emitting a milky latex of varying colors when their gills are cut. The latex of candy caps is an unchanging watery white. The often hollow stem must snap cleanly. Discard the dirty snapped base of the stem. The one- to three-inch cap and the stem are the same beautiful dark-cinnamon rusty color. A similar-looking but bitter-tasting *Lactarius* occupies the same territory as candy caps. Paw through your field guide or get a veteran to show you the subtleties of the identification. I use a helpful little trick. As I pick, I quickly run the soft part of my pinky finger over the cap. A candy cap's top skin has a unique kitty-tongue roughness, even in the rain, when the latex can be hard to see. The maple aroma is not very strong when candy caps are still fresh. Another little trick is to put a few mushrooms on your dashboard. As you drive with the heater and defroster on, your car will start to smell like pancakes. Don't let the candy caps fall into the vents!

This mushroom has a very short life. You can cook some fresh ones and then dry the rest. Don't dawdle. Dry them quickly. Don't despair if your stash is small. A little goes a very long way.

kitchen notes

CLEANING AND PREPARATION: Try to prepare candy caps the same day that you pick them. Remove any mushrooms with buggy stems or blobs of downy mold. If you're drying the mushrooms, don't worry if they are in pieces. Clean stems are fine. A lower temperature for your dryer is best.

COOKING METHODS: Your imagination is the only limit with candy caps. While I love them served with duck, pork, and winter squash, their normal route is as dessert: custards, cookies, ice cream, pound cakes, steamed puddings, bread puddings, and on and on. Infusing dried candy caps into a cooking liquid or powdering them and/or creaming them into butter are all good ways to release their flavor. Having Candy Cap Hot Bourbon (page 325) is one of my favorite ways to launch a mushroom hunt with my chefs.

STORAGE: Cook or dry them within twenty-four hours. When dried, they will keep for years.

IDEAL CANDY CAPS: Just finding them at all. Dried candy caps are rare and expensive but worth it. If you buy them, make sure they are from a very reputable source. Although harmless, the previously mentioned bitter look-alike mushroom can sneak into the bags of less knowledgeable mushroom tinkers.

Butternut Squash and Candy Cap Mushroom Crème Brûlée

Twenty-five years ago I tried to explore using candy caps' potential beyond just making very good cookies. Making a candy cap crème brûlée way back then seemed near the pinnacle of culinary swankiness. Now, some overly refined gourmands regard crème brûlées as a tad pedestrian. But crème brûlée is as common as cotton because it was delicious back then, and it's still delicious now.

I adore candy caps with butternut squash. Incorporating squash into this crème brûlée makes a complex and heavenly dessert.

Extracting the candy caps' flavor is nicely done here by simmering the dried mushrooms in cream. The same method can also take you to ice cream or custard recipes. Do go to the little extra trouble of making the candy cap sugar for the top of your crème brûlée. Any leftover sugar is a great prize. You'll keep returning to the jar to open it, smell it, and dip little spoonfuls of it into this and that.

[SERVES 8]

---

1 medium butternut squash (2 pounds), peeled, seeded, and cut into 2-inch pieces

3 cups heavy cream

¼ ounce dried candy cap mushrooms

5 large egg yolks

⅔ cup Candy Cap Sugar (page 322), plus ½ to 1 cup more for caramelizing tops

1 teaspoon pure vanilla extract

1 teaspoon fresh lemon juice

⅛ teaspoon kosher salt

Position a rack in the center of the oven. Preheat the oven to 350°F.

Place the butternut squash and ½ cup water in a 9 x 13-inch baking dish. Cover with aluminum foil. Cook for 35 to 40 minutes, or until soft and tender. Place the squash in a fine-mesh strainer over a large bowl or in the sink and let drain for 30 minutes to release excess moisture. Using a wooden spoon, press gently to extract all the liquid. Place the squash in the bowl of a food processor. Puree until very smooth. Discard the liquid. Measure out 1¾ cups of puree, using any remaining in another recipe. Set aside.

Lower the oven to 325°F.

Arrange eight 6-ounce ramekins or baking dishes in a large roasting pan. Bring a large pot of water to a simmer while you finish making the crème brûlée custard.

Place the cream and candy cap mushrooms in a medium saucepan over medium-high heat. Bring just to a boil, then turn off the heat and let sit for 30 minutes. Strain the cream through a fine-mesh strainer into a bowl, pressing on the mushrooms to extract all of the infused cream.

Whisk together the egg yolks, ⅔ cup of the candy cap sugar, the vanilla, the lemon juice, and the salt in a large bowl. Reheat the cream just to

a boil. Remove from the heat and slowly whisk the hot cream into the egg mixture. Whisk in the butternut squash puree. Strain through a fine-mesh strainer into a medium-size bowl. For a creamier texture, strain several times.

Divide the mixture among the 8 ramekins. Pour enough simmering water into the roasting pan to come halfway up the sides of the ramekins.

Bake for 25 minutes, or until just set. The very centers may still appear to be slightly jiggly. Remove the crème brûlées from the water bath and place the ramekins on wire racks to cool to room temperature. Cover and refrigerate for at least 4 hours or overnight.

to finish

Sprinkle 1 to 2 tablespoons candy cap sugar evenly over the tops of each crème brûlée. Brown the tops using a blowtorch or by placing the ramekins under the broiler until the sugar is melted and bubbling. Wait 1 to 2 minutes for the sugar crust to cool and set up before serving.

TIPS AND TECHNIQUES

The drier the butternut squash puree the better. Make sure to cook it until it is very tender, then give it the full time to release all the excess liquid. This can be done a couple of days ahead of time. Refrigerate the puree until ready to use.

SUBSTITUTIONS AND VARIATIONS

You can use regular or vanilla-infused sugar in place of the candy cap sugar.

Other winter squash varieties, such as acorn or kabocha squash, can be substituted for the butternut. Just be sure to precook the squash until very tender and to puree until smooth. Use the same amount of other squash as for the butternut.

If you'd like to add a little spice, try a pinch of cardamom or allspice. Too much, however, will overpower the delicate flavor of the candy cap mushrooms.

Black Walnuts

A black walnut is a mighty fortress. It's best that you understand this before you begin the assault. It will be messy and difficult; so is gold mining. Unlike prospecting, however, at the end of your black walnut campaign, you're guaranteed to have a bag of extremely rich nuggets.

The delicious wild black walnut and the splendid tree it drops from are among the special food treasures of the New World. It may sound peculiar, but the United States is the most richly nut-endowed country in the world. Perhaps this is obvious to many, but I was quite surprised. Our native pecans, hickory nuts, butternuts, piñon nuts, and great black walnuts put us at the summit of the gourmet nut world. Excluding the piñon pine, it's easy to see the kinship of these nut trees in their very similar compound leaves and stately postures. The stunning flavor of all of these is matched by the difficulty of cracking into the vault in which they're hidden. The familiar and easily opened Old World English walnut tastes nice enough, but it's a pale shadow of the Technicolor flavor intensity of our American black walnuts.

The regally straight black walnut trees are found from coast to coast. They're found in the wild, but they can also surprise you by lining old roads or lording over parks and backyards. Because English walnuts are grafted onto tough American black walnut rootstock, untended orchards can be a fine place to find black walnuts. Black walnuts' vigorous shoots often overtake the weaker English grafted tops. In forests, they generally stand as one or two isolated individuals rising from rich soil. They like clearings and can even create their own "space" by exuding juglone, a compound that is a growth retardant to other plants. This makes gathering the nuts, usually in late September, a little easier. When they begin to fall (often after a windy night), put on good gloves and fill your buckets.

The black walnut, the richest of all nuts, is the original "hard nut to crack." You'll need gloves, a hammer, ratty clothes, and a hard surface that you don't care about getting stained. There are three basic steps: removing the hull from the nut, drying the walnuts, and shelling out the nut meat. Piles of pages are written about this process.

Hulling is good for venting anger. The hull of a ripe black walnut will have a green-gold color and a little "give." You have to remove the hull, which seamlessly covers the nut. Wearing strong old boots, step on the nut and roll it around forcefully until the hull starts to come off. *With gloves on,* peel off any remaining hull. Many people toss the nuts on their driveway and drive over them repeatedly. Corralling them in a pothole can keep them from becoming projectiles. Yes, they are that tough.

Drying the nuts is a cakewalk. Put them about three to four nuts deep into trays or boxes. You could hang them in a strong mesh bag also. Hide them somewhere protected from thieving squirrels and from moisture. After three or four weeks, an interior nut meat should be dry enough to snap.

Shelling requires patience and an eye to the tasty prize. You see black walnuts only in pieces because the steely chambers encasing the nut meats make whole nuts impossible. Soak the whole nuts in water for a few hours to soften the shells. My father believed in using a thick board with a one-and-a-half-inch knothole. You can drill a hole too. Put the nut with the point up into the hole. Cover it with a rag and strike the nut with a hammer. This keeps the shards from flying everywhere. After they are broken, put the shattered nuts into a bowl. Open a bottle of wine, get two nutpicks, and charm a friend into settling down to pick the meat out of that bowl of nuts and maybe even the conversation. Better yet, ask a walnut-savvy older relative for help if you're part of the younger generation unfamiliar with this once widely adored American culinary treasure.

kitchen notes

CLEANING AND PREPARATION: Review the methods above or look online for more information on cleaning and preparing these nuts. A final inspection of the cleaned nuts is important. Toss the nuts into a colander to sieve out the duff that could have fine woody shreds, and then look over the nuts for stray larger bits of nutshell.

COOKING METHODS: The great flavor is made even better with light toasting. Black walnuts' intense flavor makes it possible to use smaller amounts in recipes than you would use for English walnuts. Black walnuts are sensational on a cheese plate or just tossed with maple sugar as a postdinner treat.

STORAGE: The high oil content makes black walnuts go rancid quickly. Freeze them and use within a year.

IDEAL BLACK WALNUTS: Heavenly black walnuts appear perfectly hulled and shelled by the forest elves . . . if only. Even the finest will always be in chunks; sadly, they're never whole.

Bourbon Black Walnut Sundae

Hide this from the children. If I'd known about this as a child, I'd have fallen in love with bourbon at ten instead of twenty. Make this sundae and, like me, you'll end up craving this easy dessert of luscious goo and liquored-up nuts far too often. Caramel binds in marriage two of America's greatest taste treasures: our rich, native black walnuts and fine bourbon. This recipe makes plenty of boozy caramel. This is a wise thing because you'll absolutely require another sundae. The caramel holds nicely in your refrigerator for up to two weeks. Don't soak the black walnuts in bourbon for more than fifteen minutes or you'll drown the black walnut flavor. Hickory nuts or English walnuts are a noble substitute.

[SERVES 4 TO 6]

for the bourbon caramel sauce

½ cup light brown sugar

1 cup granulated sugar

½ cup light corn syrup

4 tablespoons (½ stick) unsalted butter,
    cut into 8 pieces

⅛ teaspoon kosher salt

1 cup heavy cream

3 tablespoons bourbon

¼ teaspoon fresh lemon juice

Whisk together the brown sugar, granulated sugar, corn syrup, butter, salt, and cream in a medium heavy-bottomed saucepan. Place over medium-high heat. Bring to a boil, whisking frequently. Be careful as the mixture comes to a boil because it will bubble up to the top of the saucepan. When the mixture is boiling, turn down the heat to medium and continue cooking, stirring frequently, until it is thickened, 7 to 8 minutes. It should be at a constant, energetic simmer. Whisk in the bourbon and lemon juice, then remove from the heat. Serve warm.

Makes 2 cups.

for the sundae

¾ cup coarsely chopped black walnuts

¼ cup bourbon

1 pint French vanilla ice cream

Position a rack in the center of the oven. Preheat the oven to 350°F.

Place the walnuts on a baking sheet and toast in the oven until fragrant and lightly browned, 6 to 7 minutes. Cool to room temperature.

Place the walnuts in a small bowl and stir in the bourbon. Let sit for 2 to 3 minutes before proceeding.

Divide the ice cream among 4 to 6 dessert dishes. Top with a generous spoonful of warm caramel sauce. Spoon the walnuts over the top.

TIPS AND TECHNIQUES

The caramel sauce can be made ahead and kept, covered in an airtight container, in the refrigerator up to 2 weeks. Rewarm over low heat or in a microwave before serving.

Try sprinkling a few grains of fleur de sel on the caramel topping.

winter

Black Trumpets
[Horns of Plenty and Trumpets of Death]

CRATERELLUS CORNUCOPIOIDES;
C. FALLAX; C. CINEREUS

It takes time and faith to learn how to see something that just doesn't seem to be there. Trying to meet this darkly elegant and perfectly disguised mushroom for the first time requires genuine patience. As you do with morels, you need to tune up your "mushroom eye." When you can do this, suddenly the mushroom leaps out in relief from the optical illusion posed by these black craters scattered amid a mix of earth and dark leaves. There are no better descriptions than author David Arora's, calling them "black petunias," or the great mycologist Charles McIlvaine's, describing their color as that of "well-worn velveteen."

My friend the legendarily nearsighted mushroom picker nicknamed Coke Bottle Danny tackled this black-on-black fungal eye challenge from a weird angle. He'd discovered the same strange phenomenon I'd stumbled upon one night when sneaking out of a tent with a flashlight to use the forest facilities: The undersides of black trumpets reflect light like road reflectors. Danny would strap on his headlamp and his backpack and then march out into the black night. His headlamp, pointed up the side of a ravine, would show the trumpet clusters' whereabouts like bunny eyes staring back. He'd pick until the black trumpet–filled baskets covered his backpack frame, then find a soft spot to fall asleep. After waking up, he'd get his bearings in the light of day and stomp back in.

Here in our western territory, Danny and the rest of us primarily hunt *Craterellus cornucopioides*. The distinctions among the three species listed above are nearly meaningless. The horn of plenty, *C. cornucopioides*, dominates in the West, while *C. fallax* is the common black trumpet of the East. The rarer *C. cinereus*, with its crossed spore-bearing veins, is sprinkled throughout most of the world. The odd one or three is found in many baskets of blacks. These black cousins share a similar taste in mycorrhizal (symbiotic) partners. Beech and oaks host black trumpets most often in the East, while tan oaks partner up with trumpets in the coastal West. It's a big world for black trumpets. My chef friend Staffan Terje's Swedish mom picks basketfuls under Swedish oaks, while another friend exports them in quantity from Portugal, Morocco, and Turkey. Here in the New World, they range from coast to coast and from northern Michigan's Upper Peninsula south to Mexico. Whatever their citizenship, they seem to like much the same decor. Watch for them in shale soils covered by lush moss. They like creek edges, cut banks, and the edges of trails.

While autumn is harvesttime in the East, we lucky ones in the West can often gather trumpets from December through March. Memorize these mushrooms' tricky mycorrhizal patches, because they return year after year.

The eating of something the French call trumpets of death may give you pause. Fear not this sexy mushroom. With its rich, woodsy flavor, I think of it as the blue cheese of the mushroom world.

kitchen notes

CLEANING AND PREPARATION: How I wish we could leave black trumpets whole and stuff them like dark ice cream cones, but alas, pieces of the forest fall into these lovely open trumpets. The mushrooms must be split open and cleaned inside. Grit is the enemy. If you harvest them by cutting just above the dirty part of the stem, 80 percent of the cleaning is done. After you pull them apart, holding both sides of the trumpet's cup, run water over the mushroom as you slide your fingers down to the bottom with a little rub. If you have several pounds to clean, put the split mushrooms in a bowl of water. Agitate this brew and skim the forest debris off the top of the water. Drain the water and wash again in clean water. Wash a third time if the mushrooms are very dirty. After either process, place the wet mushrooms on a towel-lined cookie sheet. They dry out quickly. See illustrations on page 327. You can then tear them into thin strips. To create the "poor man's truffles" effect, cut across these strips to form the illusion of little squares of black truffle.

COOKING METHODS: Because they are very thin, black trumpets cook fairly rapidly. They are often cooked separately and added later to a dish to prevent the "blackness" from bleeding throughout. This practice is a particularly good one when cooking them with fish or eggs.

STORAGE: Don't be surprised that they can remain perfect in the refrigerator for two to three weeks. Keep a damp cloth over them to keep them from drying out.

IDEAL BLACK TRUMPETS: They should be black, not gray or brittle from dryness. The tips of the trumpet cup should be the same color as the rest of the mushroom and *not* rubbery. "Rubber lips" are a sign of freezing, drying, or aging of the mushroom. The narrow base should be trimmed and have minimal dirt.

"Poor Man's Truffle" Risotto

God meant risotto to be cooked in the woods over an open fire while you hold a wineglass in one hand and a spoon in the other, while surrounded by dear friends after a long day of mushroom hunting. This is absolutely true. With your butter, cheese, and mushroom stock from home steaming over the fire, plus the mushrooms you've hunted, you're likely to have the best risotto and the best campfire meal of your life. With many hands to stir and friends all around the fire, risotto becomes a communion that would make mushroom-loving Italian peasants of decades past proud. Wild mushrooms like porcini or chanterelles found during other seasons are welcome into this ideal camp risotto. The required flourish of mascarpone makes it clear that this isn't hobo risotto.

If you *have* to make risotto indoors, consider cutting the black trumpets into the small pieces that have been used for a little black truffle fakery. This trick resulted in the pet name "poor man's truffles." To take the charade one step further, you can finish with a little superior-quality truffle oil (see Guidebooks and Sources, page 336).

[SERVES 4 TO 6]

4 tablespoons (½ stick) unsalted butter
½ pound black trumpet mushrooms, cleaned
1½ teaspoons kosher salt, or more to taste
2 garlic cloves, finely minced
4 cups Traditional Mushroom Stock (page 315)
2 shallots, finely minced
1½ cups arborio or carnaroli rice
½ cup dry white wine
¼ cup grated Parmesan
3 tablespoons mascarpone

Place 2 tablespoons of the butter in a large sauté pan over medium-high heat. When the butter is melted and bubbling, add the mushrooms, tossing quickly to coat with the butter. Add ½ teaspoon of the salt. Cook, stirring, as the mushrooms release their liquid. Continue cooking until the liquid has evaporated and the mushrooms are dry. Add the garlic and cook for 1 more minute. Remove from the heat and set aside.

Place the mushroom stock and 1 cup water in a large stockpot and bring to a simmer over medium heat.

Place a medium nonreactive saucepan over medium heat. Add the remaining 2 tablespoons butter. When the butter is melted and bubbling, add the shallots. Cook, stirring frequently, until the shallots are tender, 3 to 4 minutes. Add the rice and stir to coat evenly with the butter and shallots. Cook, stirring frequently, until the rice starts to turn translucent, 3 to 4 minutes. Add the white wine. Cook, stirring constantly, until all the liquid is absorbed. Ladle in 1 cup mushroom stock. Add another ½ teaspoon salt. Cook, stirring continuously, until the liquid is absorbed and the rice mixture starts to feel heavy as you stir it. The more vigorously you stir, the more starches in the rice are released, creating a creamier texture. Ladle in another 3 cups of stock and repeat the stirring after each cup. After the fourth addition of stock, add the mushrooms and the remaining ½ teaspoon salt and continue stirring until most of the liquid is absorbed and the rice is just tender to the bite. The cooking time will be 30 to 35 minutes. Stir in the Parmesan and the mascarpone. Taste for seasoning, adjust as desired, and serve immediately.

TIPS AND TECHNIQUES

If the risotto must sit a few minutes before serving, ladle in a little more of the stock to restore the creamy consistency.

SUBSTITUTIONS AND VARIATIONS

Drizzle the finished risotto with some excellent-quality white truffle oil.

This risotto recipe will work with many mushroom varieties.

You can add chopped fresh herbs to the risotto just before serving: chives, flat-leaf parsley, or thyme, for example.

You can use homemade or canned chicken broth or vegetable broth as a substitute for the mushroom stock.

You can substitute crème fraîche for the mascarpone.

Black Trumpet Mushroom and Yukon Gold Potato Gratin

After a few days teaching in California, the chef at the Ritz in Paris asked Sarah to come to his Parisian kitchen and teach some healthy California cooking. While Sarah was in the Ritz kitchen, this chef taught her this very wicked thing. What evil French genius would teach a nice Georgia girl to simmer potatoes in porcini cream? I'd made black trumpet and potato gratin many a time, but I'd never realized it could be raised to such a level of fungal debauchery. Leaving the black trumpets in wide pieces adds a luscious silky texture to the gratin.

[SERVES 6]

2 cups heavy cream
½ ounce dried porcini mushrooms,
    thoroughly rinsed to remove any dirt
1 bay leaf
1½ teaspoons kosher salt
¼ teaspoon freshly ground black pepper
1 tablespoon pure olive oil
½ pound black trumpet mushrooms, cleaned
1 clove garlic, finely minced
1½ pounds large Yukon Gold potatoes
¼ cup grated Gruyère

Position a rack in the center of the oven. Preheat the oven to 350°F.

Generously butter an 8-inch square baking dish.

Place the cream, porcini mushrooms, and bay leaf in a medium heavy-bottomed saucepan. Bring to a boil, then turn off the heat and let steep for 20 minutes. Place a fine-mesh strainer over a medium bowl. Pour the cream mixture through the strainer, pressing on the porcini to extract all the cream. Discard the bay leaf. Return the cream to the saucepan. Whisk in 1 teaspoon of the salt and the pepper. Set aside. Thinly slice the porcini and set aside.

Heat the oil in a large sauté pan over medium-high heat. When the oil is hot, add the black trumpet mushrooms, tossing quickly to coat with oil. Add the remaining ½ teaspoon salt. Cook, stirring occasionally, as the black trumpets release any liquid. Continue cooking and stirring until the liquid has evaporated. Add the garlic and cook for 1 more minute. Remove from the heat and cool. Stir in the porcini. Set aside.

Peel the potatoes and place in a bowl of water to prevent browning.

Bring the cream back to a simmer. Make sure the heat is low to prevent scorching. Remove the potatoes from the water and pat dry. Slice the potatoes very thin, ⅛ inch thick, on a mandolin or slicer. Add the potatoes to the simmering cream and cook for 5 minutes. The cream will become thick from the starch in the potatoes. Remove from the heat.

Place one-third of the potatoes and cream in the prepared baking dish. Spread them out evenly over the bottom. Sprinkle with 1 tablespoon of the Gruyère. Top with half of the mushroom mixture.

Make another layer using one-third of the potatoes and cream, 1 tablespoon of the Gruyère, and the remaining half of the mushrooms. Add the remaining one-third of the potatoes and top with the remaining 2 tablespoons Gruyère.

Place the baking dish on a baking sheet and cook for 30 minutes, or until the top is golden brown and the cream is bubbly. Remove the gratin from the oven and let sit for 10 minutes before serving.

TIPS AND TECHNIQUES

The baking sheet under the gratin prevents the potatoes from cooking too rapidly on the bottom before the top is done.

SUBSTITUTIONS AND VARIATIONS

While the porcini mushrooms add a delicious flavor and richness to this dish, the gratin can be made without them. You can drizzle on some truffle oil just before serving to add a touch of elegance to the dish.

Leg of Lamb with Black Trumpet Mushroom Tapenade

This dramatic-looking dish is all about the tapenade. The lush black trumpet essence rolled into the heart of this roast is dramatically revealed as you cut slices. The tapenade has endless places in your kitchen beyond this lamb or even pork. Slide it under chicken skin or slather it onto flattened chicken breasts and then roll them up. Thin-pounded beef iced with this intense black tapenade can be rolled and roasted or sliced into beef-and-mushroom spirals and grilled. This beauteous black stuff can go places I've not yet imagined.

[SERVES 6]

One 4½-pound boneless leg of lamb
Kosher salt and freshly ground black pepper
¾ cup Black Trumpet Mushroom Tapenade
    (page 308)
2 tablespoons extra virgin olive oil

Remove lamb from the refrigerator 1 hour before roasting for more even cooking.

Position a rack in the center of the oven. Preheat oven to 425°F.

Place a rack inside a 9 x 13-inch roasting pan.

Remove any butcher's twine or netting from the leg of lamb. Unroll the leg and open it out onto a cutting board, fat side down. Season the meat generously on all sides with salt and pepper. Spread the tapenade evenly over the surface of the meat, leaving a 1-inch margin on all sides. Tuck and roll the leg back into a compact roast and tie with butcher's twine. Place on the rack in the roasting pan. Rub the oil over the surface of the meat.

Roast for 20 minutes, then lower the heat to 350°F. Continue to roast to medium rare, or until the internal temperature is 130°F in the center,

about 1 hour and 10 minutes. After about 30 minutes, baste the meat with the pan juices as they accumulate. Baste at least 3 times as the meat roasts.

When the meat has reached the desired temperature, remove from the oven and cover loosely with aluminum foil. Remove from the roasting pan. Let rest for at least 15 minutes.

Strain the cooking juices from the roasting pan through a fine-mesh strainer into a small saucepan. Let sit for a few minutes, then skim the fat from the top. Reheat and taste for seasoning, adding salt and pepper as needed. Hold in a warm place.

Remove the twine from the leg of lamb and slice. Serve with the warm pan juices.

SUBSTITUTIONS AND VARIATIONS
Freshly chopped herbs, such as chives or flat-leaf parsley or small amounts of rosemary or thyme, can be added to the pan juices just before serving. Be careful; the delicate flavor of the black trumpet tapenade is easily overwhelmed.

Hedgehog Mushrooms

HYDNUM REPANDUM; H. UMBILICATUM

Belly button, sweet tooth, spreader hedgehog, and pied-du-mouton are all pet names for these charming mushrooms. For mushroom hunters in the winter forests of the Pacific Northwest, these jolly-looking mushrooms provide comic relief from the black trumpets and yellow feet usually growing nearby. When you look down on *Hydnum umbilicatum*, it looks for all the world like a pudgy boy's belly with an "in-y" belly button. It is petite (one to two inches) compared to the robust *H. repandum* (two to seven inches), but it makes up for its size by often appearing in large groups. This is the hedgehog you'll see sold in fine markets throughout the winter.

H. repandum, the sweet tooth, is a bulbous fellow, cream to pastel orange in complexion. If a mushroom ever looked drunk, this one does. Its cap is always askew, growing as it does off center from the stem. The cap is often a "blobby" shape and frequently wraps itself around the mushroom next to it, creating a Siamese twin. It earns the name "spreader" this way. All hedgehogs have the spiny teeth of their namesake instead of gills, but the sweet tooth's spines are usually irregular lengths. When broken or cut, a rusty brown stain appears on the mushroom's flesh and teeth. It can be a mess. Luckily it's beautiful on the inside, because this is a delicious mushroom that can be found from Morocco to Alaska and nearly all points in between. In fairness, sweet tooths don't always look like they've been on an all-night bender. I've seen *H. repandum* in Alaska and France that were as pert as tidy little poodle feet. It and the belly button hedgehog can be found beginning in August in the Northeast through March in Oregon and California.

A hedgehog's habitat is impossible to generalize about. It loves tan oaks and huckleberry patches in the West, yet switches to varied conifers and hardwoods across the country. It is mycorrhizal everywhere; thus when you learn from other hunters which is the host tree variety in your area, you can home in on the hedgehog's tendency to grow in gregarious numbers in arcs around trees. This is a great beginner's mushroom because there are no dangerous mushrooms pale in color with stems and teeth like this.

When you finally spy a gang of hedgehogs, no matter how crazed you are to grab all these plump little darlings, slow down. There's no mushroom where tidy harvesting is more important. Your cooking experience actually begins right there in the woods when you're crouched on your knees with a knife in your hand. Snap or cut a hedgehog, turn it over, and look at its teeth. Unless it's in a poststorm splash zone, the teeth will be clean. Cut the dirty base from each mushroom. A little tap to the top of each cap will dislodge the odd dirty bit, then place each tidied hog in your basket. Once dirt starts bouncing around in a mushroom basket, it all seems to find its way between a hedgehog's teeth.

In the kitchen hedgehogs often fill the same role as chanterelles. As the chanterelle season ends, chefs usually use hedgehogs in their place. Some chefs prefer hedgehogs because of their slightly bitter flavor component. This faint touch of bitterness is excellent in Italian dishes. Not all chefs feel that hedgehogs are a proper chanterelle replacement, however. I stopped into the French Laundry kitchen the day after bringing in hedgehogs. The darling young men who always greet me fondly there wore dreadful scowls. Thomas Keller had had them remove every single tooth from each little belly button hedgehog. Detached teeth floating about in any dish at the French Laundry was not going to do at all. This level of perfection is not in the cards for most of us, but if you fear the fungal coconut flake appearance of a few hedgehog teeth, use these mushrooms in more rustic dishes where this is of no concern.

kitchen notes

CLEANING AND PREPARATION: Don't worry about bugs; they don't like hedgehogs. Cleaning will be a snap if you picked them as instructed above. Scraping dirt from the stem and tapping the top of the cap will remove most dirt. If not, you may have to gently wash the mushrooms and place them on a rack or cloth-lined sheet pan to dry out.

COOKING METHODS: Like chanterelles, hedgehogs are great in a wide range of dishes. Be careful stirring them, because they are quite brittle. My pal Patrick loves them with fresh peas. They make fantastic gravy and are very nice pickled as well.

STORAGE: Hedgehogs will keep fabulously for more than a week if covered with a clean cloth in your refrigerator. They freeze quite nicely but don't dry well.

IDEAL HEDGEHOG MUSHROOMS: Clean teeth are most important. Since hedgehog teeth grow longer as they age, look for short teeth as a sign of a more vibrant mushroom.

Hedgehog Mushroom and Turkey Pot Pie

This is a deceptively familiar version of the beloved winter favorite, pot pie. It's just what Mom might make after a walk on the wild side. All the comfy traditional ingredients go through magical flavor amplification from the umami-loaded hedgehog mushrooms, which bake under an extra-rich cream cheese pastry. The many little bits of ingredients to make this excellent pot pie make this appear to be a long recipe, but it's so worth doing. It's perfectly legal to make this in other seasons with mushrooms like chanterelles or meadow mushrooms.

[SERVES 6 TO 8; MAKES ONE 9-INCH DEEP-DISH PIE]

---

for the crust

3 ounces cream cheese, at room temperature

8 tablespoons (1 stick) unsalted butter,
    at room temperature

1 cup unbleached all-purpose flour,
    plus extra for rolling out dough

½ teaspoon kosher salt

1 large egg, beaten

Place the cream cheese and butter in the bowl of a standing mixer fitted with the paddle attachment. Beat on medium-high speed until smooth and creamy. Sift the flour and salt into a small bowl and add to the cream cheese mixture. Beat on medium speed until just combined.

Turn out the dough onto a lightly floured surface and quickly gather it into a ball. Flatten the ball slightly, cover with plastic wrap, and refrigerate for 4 hours or overnight.

Remove the dough from the refrigerator 30 minutes before rolling out.

for the turkey broth

2 turkey wings (about 2 pounds)

1 medium onion, cut into quarters

1 medium carrot, cut into 2-inch pieces

1 celery stalk, cut into 2-inch pieces

4 fresh thyme sprigs

2 flat-leaf parsley sprigs

1 bay leaf

Place the turkey wings, onion, carrot, celery, thyme, parsley, and bay leaf in a large stockpot. Add 3 quarts cold water and bring to a boil. Turn down the heat and simmer for 2 hours.

Strain through a colander into a large bowl, reserving the turkey wings and discarding the vegetables. Remove the meat from the wings. Cut it into ½-inch pieces and set aside. Skim the fat from the broth. You should have about 1½ quarts turkey broth.

for the filling

1½ quarts turkey broth (above) or one
    49.5-ounce can chicken broth

1 pound uncooked turkey breast meat or
    turkey tenders

1 pound hedgehog mushrooms, cleaned,
    trimmings saved from cleaning

3 tablespoons pure olive oil

1 medium onion, cut into ½-inch dice

1 carrot, cut into ½-inch dice

1 celery stalk, cut into ½-inch dice

½ cup green peas, fresh or frozen (thawed)

6 tablespoons unsalted butter

¼ cup plus 2 tablespoons unbleached
    all-purpose flour

¼ cup heavy cream

2 teaspoons kosher salt, or more to taste

½ teaspoon freshly ground black pepper,
    or more to taste

½ teaspoon fresh lemon juice

1 tablespoon finely chopped fresh thyme or
    1 teaspoon dried

1 tablespoon finely chopped flat-leaf parsley

Place the turkey broth in a large stockpot. Bring to a boil. Add the turkey breast meat, turn down the heat, and simmer until cooked through, about 15 minutes. Remove the meat to a bowl with a slotted spoon or strainer and set aside to cool. Add any trimmings from cleaning the mushrooms to the broth. Bring back to a boil, turn down the heat, and simmer until the broth is reduced to 3 cups. Strain through a fine-mesh strainer into a bowl and set aside. Cut the turkey meat into ½-inch cubes and place in a large bowl. Add the reserved wing meat and toss to combine.

Heat 1 tablespoon of the oil in a large sauté pan over medium-high heat. When the oil is hot, add the hedgehog mushrooms, tossing to coat evenly with the oil. Cook, stirring occasionally, until the mushrooms have released any liquid. Continue cooking and stirring until all the liquid has evaporated and the mushrooms are starting to turn brown. Add the mushrooms to the bowl with the turkey meat.

Wipe out the sauté pan, add the remaining 2 tablespoons oil, and place over medium heat. When the oil is hot, add the onion. Cook, stirring occasionally, until the onion is soft and translucent, about 3 minutes. Add the carrot and celery and continue cooking until the vegetables are tender, 6 to 7 minutes. Add the vegetables to the turkey meat and mushrooms in the bowl. Add the peas, stirring gently to mix all the ingredients.

Heat the butter in a large saucepan over medium heat. When the butter is bubbling and just starting to turn brown, whisk in the flour until smooth. Continue whisking for 4 to 5 minutes, or until the mixture turns golden brown. Whisk in the reserved turkey broth. Bring just to a boil, then turn down the heat and continue cooking, whisking frequently, until the sauce is thickened and the raw flour taste is gone, about 6 minutes. Whisk in the cream, salt, pepper, lemon juice, thyme, and parsley. Cook for 1 more minute. Pour the sauce over the turkey and vegetable mixture and gently stir together. Taste for seasoning, adding more salt or pepper as needed. The mixture should be highly seasoned. Cool to room temperature before assembling the pot pie.

for the pot pie

Place a rack in the center of the oven. Preheat the oven to 350°F.

Place the dough on a lightly floured surface. Roll out into a rectangle, about 8 by 6 inches. Fold the dough into thirds over itself (like folding a letter). Give the dough a quarter turn to the right and roll out again, as directed. Repeat the process of folding, rolling, and turning the dough a total of 3 times. Make sure the board is floured enough to prevent sticking as you roll out the dough. After the final turn, roll the dough into a 12-inch circle.

Place the filling in a 9-inch deep-dish pie plate.

Gently cover the top of the filling with the circle of dough. Tuck under the excess dough around the edges, crimping it between your fingers to make a decorative edge. Make sure the dough covers the filling completely and comes to the edges of the pie plate. Brush the dough with the beaten egg. Cut 3 to 4 slits in the top of the pie in a circular pattern. Place the pot pie on a baking sheet.

Bake for 1 hour, or until the crust is golden brown and the filling is bubbling around the edges. Remove the pot pie to a wire rack and let sit for 15 minutes before serving.

SUBSTITUTIONS AND VARIATIONS

Chicken breasts can be substituted for the turkey breast meat. You can also use leftover roast turkey or chicken meat, adding this directly to the cooked vegetables and sauce.

Canned chicken broth can be substituted for the turkey broth. Use less salt in the recipe in this case.

Almost any mushroom, or combination of mushrooms, can be used as a substitute for the hedgehog mushrooms.

Hedgehog Mushroom and Caramelized Onion Tart

Is there any dish more versatile than a tart? A tart can find a home in any season. This savory tart can take its place at the table from breakfast to lunch and straight through to dinner as an appetizer or light supper. This recipe can wheel through the seasons with one mushroom after another taking a spin in this delicious crust.

[SERVES 8; MAKES ONE 9-INCH TART]

for the crust

1 cup unbleached all-purpose flour,
    plus extra for rolling out dough
½ teaspoon kosher salt
8 tablespoons (1 stick) unsalted butter, chilled,
    cut into 16 pieces
1 large egg

Position a rack in the center of the oven. Preheat the oven to 350°F.

Place the flour, salt, and butter in the bowl of a food processor. Pulse until the butter is the size of small peas, 8 to 10 times.

Whisk together the egg and 1 tablespoon chilled water in a small bowl. Add to the food processor and pulse just until the dough starts to come together, 5 to 6 times. Turn out the dough onto a lightly floured surface and quickly gather it into a ball. Flatten the ball slightly into a disk shape. Wrap in plastic wrap and refrigerate for at least 1 hour.

Remove the dough from the refrigerator and let sit for 15 minutes before rolling.

Place the dough on a lightly floured surface and roll out into an 11-inch circle, lifting the dough and dusting the surface of the board with flour as needed to keep the dough from sticking. Roll the dough around the rolling pin and unroll it into a 9-inch tart pan with a removable bottom. Gently press the dough into the bottom and up the sides of the tart pan, trimming any excess dough. Prick the bottom of the crust with a fork. Line the tart shell with aluminum foil and fill with pie weights or dry beans.

Bake for 25 minutes. Remove the aluminum foil and weights or beans. Return the pan to the oven and bake for 10 to 15 more minutes, or until the tart shell is an even, light golden brown. Remove to a wire rack and cool slightly before filling.

for the filling

4 tablespoons pure olive oil
2 medium onions, sliced crosswise into
    ⅛-inch slices
1½ teaspoons kosher salt
⅛ teaspoon freshly ground black pepper
½ pound hedgehog mushrooms, cleaned
1 garlic clove, finely minced
1 large egg
½ cup half-and-half
1 tablespoon chopped fresh thyme
    (or ½ teaspoon dried)
2 tablespoons grated Parmesan

Heat 2 tablespoons of the oil in a large, heavy-bottomed sauté pan or skillet over medium heat. When the oil is hot, add the onions, ½ teaspoon of the salt, and the pepper. Stir to coat the onions evenly with the oil.

Cook, stirring frequently, as the onions start to brown. This will take about 5 minutes. As you stir, scrape up the caramelized bits in the bottom of the pan and incorporate them into the onions. When the onions are evenly browned, turn down the heat to low and continue cooking, stirring occasionally, until the onions are sweet and tender. This will take 20 to 25 more minutes. At this point, turn off the heat and cover the pan. Let sit for 15 minutes. Remove the lid and cool to room temperature.

Heat the remaining 2 tablespoons oil in a large sauté pan over medium-high heat. When the oil is hot, add the hedgehog mushrooms and ½ teaspoon of the salt and cook, tossing the mushrooms to coat evenly with the oil. Cook, stirring occasionally, until the mushrooms release their liquid. Continue cooking until the liquid has evaporated and the mushrooms are dry. Add the garlic and cook for 1 more minute. Remove the mushrooms from the pan, place in a bowl, and cool to room temperature.

for the tart

Place the caramelized onions on a clean cutting board. Chop through the onions at 1-inch intervals in one direction, then repeat, going in the other direction. Place the onions in a medium bowl. Put the mushrooms on the cutting board and chop through in the same fashion. Add to the onions in the bowl.

Whisk together the egg and half-and-half in a small bowl. Stir into the onion-mushroom mixture. Stir in the thyme, the Parmesan, and the remaining ½ teaspoon salt. Pour the filling into the cooled crust, spreading it evenly to the edges.

Place the tart on a baking sheet and bake for 45 minutes, or until golden brown and evenly set. Remove to a wire rack and cool for 10 minutes before serving. The tart can also be served at room temperature.

TIPS AND TECHNIQUES

The tart dough can be rolled out, placed in the tart pan, and frozen, if you want to do it ahead of time. Be sure to wrap it tightly in several layers of plastic wrap. It will keep for up to 2 weeks. To bake, take it directly from the freezer, remove the plastic wrap, and line it with aluminum foil. Fill with pie weights or dry beans and proceed as for the crust prebaking directions in the recipe.

The caramelized onions can be made ahead and kept covered in an airtight container in the refrigerator for up to 1 week.

SUBSTITUTIONS AND VARIATIONS

Other fresh chopped herbs, such as flat-leaf parsley, chives, or tarragon, can be used in the filling.

The grated Parmesan can be replaced by Asiago, Manchego, Gruyère, or dry Jack.

Hedgehog Mushroom, Leek, and Chestnut Stuffing

Most great recipes evolve through much tinkering and adjustment. Not this one. It seemed born whole and perfect, like Athena out of Zeus' head, in this case, Sarah's head. Both hedgehog varieties are great here. The little hedgehog teeth that break off while cooking are an advantage in this recipe because they sprinkle their flavor throughout the stuffing. Hedgehogs' tendency to be brittle and break into tiny pieces is also ideal for this stuffing. You may even be the clever forager who can find your chestnuts on the same day. Chestnuts lie ungathered under many an old tree. You can make the cornbread yourself or buy one of the many mixes that are quite acceptable for this stuffing.

[SERVES 8]

stuffing

2 large leeks, trimmed of root ends and
    dark green leaves
6 tablespoons unsalted butter
3 medium celery stalks, cut into ¼-inch dice
2 teaspoons kosher salt
½ teaspoon freshly ground black pepper
1 tablespoon pure olive oil
1 pound hedgehog mushrooms, cleaned
6 cups crumbled cornbread (recipe follows)
½ pound fresh chestnuts, peeled and cut into
    ¼-inch dice (about 1½ cups)
½ teaspoon dried sage
2 teaspoons chopped fresh thyme
    (or 1 teaspoon dried)
2 tablespoons chopped flat-leaf parsley
4 large eggs
3 cups chicken stock

Position a rack in the center of the oven. Preheat the oven to 350°F.

Lightly oil or butter a 9 x 13-inch baking pan. Set aside.

Slice the leeks in half, then crosswise into ¼-inch slices. Wash thoroughly in lukewarm water. Drain through a colander.

Heat 4 tablespoons of the butter in a large sauté pan over medium heat. When the butter is melted and bubbly, add the leeks. Cook until soft, 4 to 5 minutes, then add the celery. Add ½ teaspoon of the salt and ¼ teaspoon of the pepper. Turn the heat to low and continue cooking until both the leeks and celery are tender, another 5 to 6 minutes. Remove them from the sauté pan to a large bowl.

Wipe out the sauté pan and return it to medium-high heat with the remaining 2 tablespoons butter and the olive oil. When the butter and oil are hot, add the mushrooms, ½ teaspoon salt, and the remaining ¼ teaspoon pepper. Toss quickly to coat with the butter and oil. Cook, stirring occasionally, as the mushrooms release their liquid. Continue cooking and stirring until all the liquid has evaporated and the mushrooms are dry and starting to caramelize, 4 to 5 minutes. Add to the cooked leeks and celery in the bowl.

Add the cornbread and chestnuts to the leek mixture. Add the sage, thyme, and parsley and the remaining 1 teaspoon salt. Stir all the ingredients together.

Beat the eggs well in a small bowl. Add to the cornbread mixture. Add the chicken stock and mix thoroughly.

Spoon the stuffing mixture into the baking dish and bake for 1 hour, or until golden brown and slightly puffed.

cornbread

1 tablespoon pure olive oil

1½ cups yellow cornmeal

½ cup unbleached flour

1 tablespoon baking powder

1 teaspoon kosher salt

2 large eggs, well beaten

1¼ cups milk

3 tablespoons unsalted butter, melted

Preheat the oven to 450°F.

Brush the oil onto the bottom and sides of a 9-inch cast-iron skillet or 9-inch square baking dish. Place the skillet or baking dish in the oven while preparing the batter.

Sift together the cornmeal, flour, baking powder, and salt into a large bowl. In a medium bowl, whisk together the eggs, milk, and melted butter. Add to the cornmeal mixture, stirring just until combined.

Remove the preheated skillet or baking dish from the oven. Carefully pour in the batter. Return to the oven and bake for 20 minutes, or until the top is golden brown and puffed.

Cool on a rack to room temperature. The cornbread can be made a day ahead. Makes 6 cups of crumbled cornbread

TIPS AND TECHNIQUES

To peel the chestnuts: Cut an X in each chestnut, using the tip of a small knife. Bring a large pot of water to a boil. Drop in the chestnuts and cook for 5 to 6 minutes. Turn the water off. Take out a few chestnuts at a time to work with. The warmer they are, the easier they are to peel. Peel off the outer husk, using a small knife, if needed. Peel off the inner skin, cutting into the lobes to get out any hidden pieces. These will be bitter and tough if not removed.

SUBSTITUTIONS AND VARIATIONS

Frozen chestnuts can be used. They come already peeled and ready to use.

Cornbread stuffing mix (sold in a bag) can be substituted for the homemade cornbread.

Melted bacon fat can be substituted for the olive oil used to grease the cornbread baking pan. It can also be substituted for the melted butter in the cornbread recipe.

Canned chicken broth can be used instead of homemade. Use less salt in the recipe if using the canned broth.

Yellow Feet
[Winter Chanterelles, Funnel Chanterelles]

CRATERELLUS TUBAEFORMIS; C. XANTHOPUS; C. LUTESCENS

Proselytizer alert! I'm on what seems at times to be a one-woman mission to praise the virtues of this poor Rodney Dangerfield of mushrooms. These delicious little mushrooms are adored in Europe, yet in North America they go largely ignored or are scoffed at. They are common in the woods, inexpensive in the stores, yet sadly still travel under the radar of most cooks.

These small camel-colored mushrooms can grow in such abundance that they seem to almost insult the sensibilities of foragers expecting more challenging prey. The chefs I take mushroom hunting for the first time often stop leaning over to pick them after about five minutes in the forest. With shmoolike generosity, yellow foot mushrooms generally occur in plentiful arcs. Often armies of them are standing together, making harvesting quite easy. Commercial hunters just pull out scissors and cut them down. The drab caps show off their pretty yellow "feet" when pulled from the ground. When you snip off the dirty part of this yellow stem, you'll see that it's hollow. In fact, the funnellike hole usually found at the top of the mushroom goes all the way down the stem like a soda straw. These very moist mushrooms seem to almost suck the water out of the ground.

Yellow feet thrive in damp, mossy areas near rotting wood, most often in conifer forests. I've picked them in the same dark creek for twenty years. These hollow-stemmed yellow feet can be found in the coastal West, the Midwest, and the East in similar habitats. In colder climates, they are up in late autumn. Out West, where huge quantities grow, they flourish from December through mid-March.

Though mycologists insist that they are mycorrhizal (locked in a symbiotic marriage with a host tree), yellow foot mushrooms also seem to behave like saprophytes (independent fungus living on decaying organic matter). This confusing plain-Jane stepsister to the celebrated golden chanterelle runway model appears not to be a chanterelle sister at all. Current DNA work finds my little, misunderstood yellow foot to be closest to the more exotic black trumpets' genus *Craterellus*. This makes sense when you look closely at *C. lutescens*. *C. lutescens* looks just like the common yellow foot except that the spore-bearing underside is as wrinkle free as a black trumpet's.

Yellow foot's culinary ancestry is the appetizing thing. The French, Finns, Swedes, and Spanish can't seem to get enough of this mushroom. The melting stew of mushroom goodness that the yellow foot becomes after cooking is embraced by European chefs. In North America, however, the thin walls of the yellow foot don't provide the chewiness that most of our chefs expect. But their silky texture, different from the chunkier chanterelle, is to be relished. These rich-flavored mushrooms ooze umami and add their deep, woodsy aroma to the lucky foods to which they're introduced.

kitchen notes

CLEANING AND PREPARATION: It all begins with clean picking. This has extra importance with these dainty mushrooms. They benefit from a little sun or drying slightly with a fan because they're usually quite wet when fresh from the boggy ground they grow in. With the larger mushrooms, hold both sides of the cap and pull apart. They'll split down the hollow stem, revealing any dirt or fir needles that are hiding there. If the yellow feet are dirty, run water on them; if not, place them with the clean mushrooms. Little ones may not need splitting.

COOKING METHODS: Yellow feet are heaven when braised with meats. In general, they are better cooked slowly. This gives the slightly fibrous stems the thorough cooking they need.

STORAGE: These mushrooms don't have a very long shelf life. They can keep for five days uncovered in your crisper, but monitor them for possible "meltdown." Unlike golden chanterelles, these dry wonderfully. One of my favorite flavorings is dried yellow foot powder. The mushrooms pickle and freeze surprisingly well too.

IDEAL YELLOW FEET: Though they're always moist, they should be "bouncy" when patted. The stalk should be a golden yellow. The parasol-shaped caps should be at least one inch across and without tattered edges.

Milk-Braised Pork Shoulder with Yellow Foot Mushrooms

Staffan Terje, chef/owner of Perbacco in San Francisco, is a great friend, a great chef, an intrepid foraging companion, and most important here, a man who loves and understands yellow foot mushrooms. He was raised in coastal Sweden by a mushroom-hunting mom. Choosing between his and his mother's many yellow foot dishes was tough, but this pork dish from a pork master won. The braising melts the mushrooms into a sumptuous sauce. Alongside the pork, pureed potatoes, polenta, or pasta would wear this sauce like the fine robe that it is.

[SERVES 4 TO 6]

3 pounds yellow foot mushrooms, cleaned

One 4-pound boneless pork shoulder roast, tied

2 teaspoons kosher salt, plus more to taste

½ teaspoon freshly ground black pepper,
    plus more to taste

2 tablespoons pure olive oil

1 medium onion, cut into ½-inch dice

1 fennel bulb, cleaned and cut into ½-inch dice

5 medium garlic cloves, coarsely chopped

2 bay leaves

1 quart milk

1 cup dry white wine

2 tablespoons unsalted butter

1 large shallot, finely minced

2 tablespoons finely chopped flat-leaf parsley

Position a rack in the center of the oven. Preheat the oven to 325°F.

Set aside 1 pound of the mushrooms.

Season the pork shoulder generously all over with salt and pepper. Heat the oil in a 6-quart braising pot over medium heat. Add the pork shoulder and brown evenly, 1 to 2 minutes per side. Remove the pork from the pot and set aside.

Add the onion, fennel, and garlic to the pot and cook for 2 to 3 minutes, stirring frequently. Add the remaining 2 pounds mushrooms, the salt, and the pepper and stir to combine. Turn the heat to high and cook until any liquid has evaporated and the vegetables are starting to brown, 10 to 12 minutes. Add the bay leaves. Turn down the heat to low and place the pork shoulder on top of the vegetables in the pot. Pour the milk and white wine around the vegetables. Turn the heat back up to high and bring the liquids just to a boil. Cover the pot and place in the oven. Cook for 2½ to 3 hours, or until the meat is very tender.

Carefully remove the pork shoulder from the pot and hold in a warm place.

Strain the vegetables and the braising liquid through a colander into a large pot or bowl. Reserve the braising liquid. Puree the vegetables using a food mill or food processor. Whisk the pureed vegetables back into the braising liquid. Taste for seasoning, adding salt and pepper as needed. Hold in a warm place.

Heat the butter in a large sauté pan over medium-high heat. When the butter begins to brown, add the shallot and cook, stirring frequently, for 1 minute. Add the reserved 1 pound mushrooms, stirring to coat them evenly with the butter and shallot.

Cook until the mushrooms have released their liquid. Continue cooking, stirring occasionally, until all the liquid has evaporated and the mushrooms are starting to brown.

to serve

Remove the string or netting from the pork. Slice and arrange on a platter. Nap the pork slices with the sauce and scatter the sautéed mushrooms over the top. Sprinkle with parsley.

TIPS AND TECHNIQUES

Seasoning the pork shoulder roast with the salt and pepper a day ahead is recommended. Season the meat, place it on a rack in a shallow pan, cover lightly with parchment paper, and refrigerate overnight. Remove from the refrigerator 1 hour before cooking.

SUBSTITUTIONS AND VARIATIONS

Chanterelles or hedgehog mushrooms can be substituted for the yellow foot mushrooms.

Dandelions and Curly Dock Weed

TARAXACUM OFFICINALE; RUMEX CRISPUS

What wild food could be more common than dandelions? We all know what they are. Even children in New York high-rises have probably picked and blown on the feathery white globe of seeds, as children everywhere do. Those ethereal floating seeds land then grow into the tasty and nutritious plant that all gardeners wish a speedy death. It wasn't always so. European settlers brought dandelions to the New World as a necessity for medicine and food. The young leaves emerge in late winter, providing large doses of vitamins A and C just when they are needed after a winter diet. Traveling with us, dandelions have been brilliant in colonizing every state. Where's their habitat? Anywhere we are.

Now, I can almost hear you saying, "Come now, I've picked and tasted lawn dandelions, and they were awful!" No doubt you have, but I bet you picked them in mid- to late spring or summer. You saw the famous bright yellow flower, recognized the dandelion, and tasted it with a resulting "Yuck." You were too late. Its delicious season was already over. As the plant's energy turned to producing its perky canary-colored flowers, milky latex began to flow in the plant, making the mature dandelion greenery impossibly bitter.

Before the flowers form, look for the distinctive jagged "tooth of the lion" leaves, growing in a low rosette, with no hairy fibers on the leaves. Like lions' teeth, the points along the leaves' sides aim backward toward the mouth or crown of the dandelion. Watch for the first dandelions on the south face of grassy pesticide-free areas. For fresh salads, the short leaves, less than four inches, are what you want. The pale chartreuse leaves are best. These are often found in shady areas. Larger leaves are ideal for a wilted salad or as cooked greens, as in the recipe that follows. Take no more than half the plant's leaves. The leaves grow back vigorously from the large roots' storehouse of energy. You can prolong this tender season by the old European blanching method. Put a clay pot or bucket over the dandelion plants for six to seven days. (Good luck explaining the buckets all over your lawn.) The leaves under it will grow long, tender, and pale.

I prefer the leaves, but other folks use the roots, crowns, and flowers as well. The root, dug in the winter or springtime, has been used as a coffee substitute. The crown, the growing zone at the top of the root and very base of the leaves, is used as a vegetable. The flowers are used for traditional treats like fritters, but if you are going to cook them, always twist off the bitter green base first. You can make dandelion flower wine, but you'll probably wonder why you did after you taste it. Be extremely conscious of the environment you're gathering in. There's a lively chemical industry aimed right at dandelions.

CURLY DOCK WEED: Starting earlier than the dandelion, dock weed emerges from a sturdy underground root, which sends out its excellent leaves from midwinter on in much of the country. Dock weed is fantastically widespread. I'd likely win the lion's share of any bets placed that there are dock plants within four hundred yards of most houses. The plants emerge in the same area each year and will become excellent neighbors for you after you taste them. You'll see the family resemblance in this cousin of rhubarb; however, unlike rhubarb leaves, docks' leaves are safe, lemony, succulent, and one of my very favorites. Dock weed is best cooked. It shrinks less than any green I know. Dock also combines well with other wild and domesticated greens, adding its lemon flavor and complexity to any pot. For a proper identification, search online under *Rumex crispus*.

If you're a bit insecure about early-season identification of these greens, don't worry. Look upon the time as the courting stage of a long relationship. Refer to your field guide and watch dandelions, dock, and even chicory grow their unique flowers and flower stalks. Remember them, and you'll be ready for all the late winters and early springs to come.

kitchen notes

CLEANING AND PREPARATION: A good soaking bath is wise for these low-growing greens. This leaches away some of the bitterness. Lift the leaves out of the water, leaving behind any dirt that settles at the bottom. Dock weed can benefit from deribbing the larger stems.

COOKING METHODS: There is a small but wonderful window for using these greens fresh. Beyond this, wilted salads and cooking are ideal. Touches of bacon, vinegar, onion, or lemon all can have their place.

STORAGE: The greens will keep for four to five days wrapped in a moist paper towel in the refrigerator.

IDEAL DANDELIONS AND DOCK WEED: Look for the tender, short, paler leaves for fresh salad. Larger leaves are suitable for cooking.

Stir-fried Dandelion Greens with Duck Fat and Garlic

If you've cooked with duck fat before, you can jump into this simple recipe with gusto because you've experienced duck fat as the culinary gem that it is. Its unctuous and rich flavor is worth going that little bit out of your way for. Believe it or not, it's close to olive oil on the health meter. You can buy containers of duck fat at fine grocers, or you can buy a duck, render the trimmed fat, and have a lovely duck ready to roast another night.

[SERVES 4]

for the duck-fat–roasted garlic
1 cup rendered duck fat
12 garlic cloves, tough stem ends removed

Place the duck fat and garlic in a small heavy-bottomed sauté pan over low heat. Slowly bring the mixture to a simmer. The garlic will burn quickly, so keep an eye on it. If it cooks too much, it will taste bitter and unpleasant. Cook until the garlic is just turning light golden brown. Turn off the heat and let the garlic cool in the duck fat, about 30 minutes. The cloves will continue to brown as they sit in the fat.

Remove the garlic cloves from the duck fat. Store the garlic and duck fat separately in the refrigerator in covered containers for up to 1 week. Let stand at room temperature about 1 hour before using.

2 bunches dandelion greens (about 1 pound)
2 tablespoons rendered duck fat
½ teaspoon kosher salt
¼ teaspoon freshly ground black pepper
12 cloves duck-fat–roasted garlic (above)

Trim the tough ends from the dandelion greens and discard. Wash the greens thoroughly and drain.

Bring a large pot of salted water to a boil. Drop the greens into the boiling water and cook for 1 minute. Drain in a colander. When the greens are cool enough to handle, place them on a cutting board and cut into 2-inch ribbons.

Heat the duck fat in a large sauté pan or cast-iron skillet over medium-high heat. When the fat is hot, add the greens, stirring to coat with the fat. Add the salt, pepper, and garlic cloves. Cook, stirring frequently, until the greens are just tender, 2 to 3 minutes.

Serve immediately.

TIPS AND TECHNIQUES
Curly dock weed and younger dandelion greens don't need to be blanched before sautéing.

SUBSTITUTIONS AND VARIATIONS
Olive oil can be substituted for the duck fat for cooking the garlic cloves. Store the oil and garlic separately in the refrigerator. The garlic-flavored olive oil is delicious for sautéing potatoes, vegetables, fish, and meats or using in a hearty vinaigrette.

Persimmons

DIOSPYROS VIRGINIANA (AND D. KAKI)

Some things in life are so luscious, so desirable, that you just can't help but cross the line and lose a little of your religion for them. The lines can get a bit blurry around diets, budgets, lovers, or, in this case, geography and the definition of *wild*. Those of you in the East blessed with lovely wild persimmon trees can feel justly superior to the western states, which are without native persimmons. Although not "wild," Asian Hachiya persimmon trees pepper most western states, planted, then often ignored, in farmsteads and backyards far and wide. If we cheat a bit and call all these trees foragable, then persimmons can be gathered in all but the most northern states.

Native American persimmons range from Pennsylvania to Texas to north Florida. Conveniently for foragers, these pretty trees with the nearly black, checked bark are partial to growing on roadsides and at the fringes of the woods. While my mom's favorite Florida trees were just eight feet tall, I've eyed giants in Indiana and Ohio that were more than seventy feet tall. The leaves of these trees are large, lovely, glossy ovals. These efficient trees leaf out late and drop their colorful autumn leaves early, leaving their beautiful fruit hanging like apricot orange Christmas ornaments on their bare branches. The best time to find this tree is when these orange globes are bobbing on branches so obviously. The native Eastern persimmon is, at most, a dainty two inches in diameter. Its color is a muted orange. The planted Hachiya persimmon is a brilliant, shiny orange ball more than three inches across. You just can't miss them.

There are some surprising arcane sides to this homey American fruit. It is a myth that it takes a frost to ripen persimmons. Their exotic flavor reflects their long-season tropical ancestry. As a far-flung part of the equatorial ebony family, persimmons simply ripen very late—usually after frost occurs in North America. In southern Texas there's a wild black persimmon of spectacular flavor called the sapote. Then farther yet to the south is the treasured zapote fruit of tropical Mexico. Even its gorgeous wood reminds one of its ancestry. I once brought persimmons home and was very confused when my dad put the luminous wood part of a fine golf club in the hand not holding a ripe persimmon and said, "They're the same." Both the sweet custardy persimmon and the jewel hardwood come from this extraordinary American tree.

When harvesting persimmons, ripeness is everything. To say that our native persimmons and our "cheater" Hachiya persimmons are both astringent when unripe is a nice way of saying that if someone tricks you (and they always will) into tasting one before it's dead ripe, even your hair will pucker up. But my how they do change. Ripe persimmons are as soft as pudding inside. Their sweetness and complexity are things of wonder. Picking them ripe off the tree is ideal, although the lower branches may be the picking zone to which you have to resign yourself. Trying to knock ripe fruit from high branches usually results in unfortunate splatting. When the fruit gets ripe, a persimmon tree is a twenty-four-hour party. By day, we stretch for the low branches while birds peck away up high. When the night shift takes over, raccoons and possoms scramble up where we can't reach. There's enough for critters and humans alike.

kitchen notes

CLEANING AND PREPARATION: There's little to worry about here. Many wild persimmons will have a few flat black seeds inside. You can run all the little persimmons through a food mill and have perfect pulp easily.

COOKING METHODS: Although they're fit for royals just plain and fresh, persimmons are cooked because of their abundance when they're ripe. Most people bake with the prepared pulp. Like the great persimmon pudding included here, cookies, cakes, and breads made from persimmons turn brown when baked. Unbaked options like our trifle will hold the lovely orange color. Adapt our mulberry ice cream (see page 128), or even make a daiquiri with your stashed bright orange persimmon puree.

STORAGE: My favorite way to store persimmons is just putting the whole *completely ripe* persimmon in the freezer. I love to see them when I peek into the freezer, plus their skin prevents freezer burn. When you want to use them, thaw and run them through a food mill. You can also freeze the pulp in airtight containers or in resealable plastic freezer bags for six months.

Korea is a persimmon-preservation-crazy country. Tons of persimmons are dried each year as traditional New Year presents. Korean Gamsikcho, a drinkable persimmon vinegar, is greatly prized as a tonic and for flavoring.

IDEAL PERSIMMONS: The ripeness required for great persimmons makes them very uncommon in farmers' markets. Find your own and wait until they're soft as mousse inside. Most will ripen off the tree.

Persimmon Praline Trifle

Sarah and I sat in her backyard at a table covered with persimmons and began to imagine a dessert that would hold on to the brilliant orange color and gooey greatness of their perfect ripeness. The recipe began as the PPP, the persimmon praline parfait. After a touch of rum for complexity, a creamy white stripe, and the crunch of praline, we found it was actually too luscious, as impossible as that seems. Sarah added pound cake for structure, and this trifle was born. You can make your own pound cake and pralines or simply buy these two ingredients and make this magnificent dessert very easily. If you freeze whole soft, ripe persimmons, you can thaw them and make this throughout the cold winter months. Make sure the persimmons are at Jell-O-like dead ripeness. I just adore this dessert.

[SERVES 8]

for the praline

½ cup firmly packed light brown sugar

½ cup granulated sugar

¼ cup half-and-half

1 tablespoon unsalted butter

½ teaspoon pure vanilla extract

⅛ teaspoon kosher salt

4 ounces pecan halves, about 1 cup

Line a baking sheet with a silicone mat or use a nonstick baking sheet. Spray either surface with nonstick vegetable cooking spray. Set aside.

Combine the brown sugar, granulated sugar, and half-and-half in a medium heavy-bottomed saucepan. Bring to a boil, then turn down the heat to low, and cook for 5 minutes, stirring constantly. Stir in the butter, vanilla, and salt and continue cooking until the mixture registers 260°F on a candy thermometer. Working quickly, remove the pan from the heat, stir in the pecans, then pour out the mixture onto the prepared baking sheet, spreading it as thin as possible. The mixture will start to harden quickly. Let the praline cool completely, then chop it into ¼-inch pieces. Store in an airtight container at room temperature.

Makes about 1½ cups.

for the trifle

8 ounces mascarpone

1 pint heavy cream

⅓ cup granulated sugar

6 tablespoons Myers's rum or dark rum

⅛ teaspoon kosher salt

6 medium wild or Hachiya persimmons, very ripe

2 cups cubed pound cake (½-inch cubes)

Place the mascarpone, cream, sugar, 2 tablespoons of the rum, and the salt in the bowl of a standing mixer fitted with the whip attachment. Starting the mixer on low and gradually increasing the speed to medium high, whip the mixture just until it holds a firm, creamy peak.

Place a medium-mesh strainer over a large bowl. Remove the stem ends from the persimmons. Squeeze the soft pulp out of the skins. If some skin gets mixed in, it will be strained out. Using a rubber spatula, press the pulp through the strainer. Scrape off any pulp on the bottom of the strainer and add it to the rest. You should have about 1½ cups of puree.

to serve

To serve in individual glasses, place 2 tablespoons of the mascarpone cream in the bottom of each of 8 glasses. Top each with 1 tablespoon of the persimmon puree, spreading it out to the sides. Set aside half of the pound cake cubes and divide the remaining half among the 8 glasses. Brush the cake cubes with 2 tablespoons of the rum (¾ teaspoon per glass). Top each glass with ½ tablespoon of the praline. Repeat with the remaining ingredients, finishing with the mascarpone cream on top, a final drizzle of persimmon puree, and a sprinkling of pralines.

Cover with plastic wrap and chill for at least 2 hours or overnight.

To serve in a trifle dish, place one-third of the mascarpone cream in the bottom of the dish, spreading it out to the sides. Top with one-third of the persimmon puree. Sprinkle with half the cake cubes. Brush the cake cubes with 2 tablespoons of the rum. Sprinkle with ½ cup of the praline. Repeat the layers, ending with the mascarpone cream on top, a final drizzle of persimmon puree, and a sprinkling of pralines. Cover with plastic wrap and chill for at least 4 hours or overnight.

TIPS AND TECHNIQUES

A silicone mat is used in baking and cooking to provide a nonstick surface. It can withstand high temperatures.

SUBSTITUTIONS AND VARIATIONS

Purchased pralines can be substituted for homemade.

Ladyfingers can be substituted for the pound cake cubes.

Persimmon Praline Trifle [PAGE 290]

Connie's Favorite Persimmon Pudding with Brandy Hard Sauce

Chef Tim Nugent, when he was the pastry chef at Campton Place in San Francisco, gave me this recipe. It's one of the best presents I've ever received. I'll make it until I'm too old to wrestle a pudding mold out of a pan. When persimmons are soft and ripe, I either freeze them whole or peel them, measure the exact amount of pulp required for this recipe, place the pulp in resealable plastic freezer bags, and freeze. The flavor of the pudding is elevated considerably by using black walnuts or hickory nuts if you have them. There's considerable booze in both the pudding and the hard sauce. I'm a bourbon girl, but brandy or even rum adds backbone as well. This is true not only *in* the pudding but in a pretty little glass to be sipped right alongside.

[SERVES 10 TO 12]

for the pudding

5 medium wild or Hachiya persimmons, very ripe
8 tablespoons (1 stick) unsalted butter,
    plus extra for the mold,
    at room temperature
2 large eggs
1¼ cups granulated sugar
3 tablespoons brandy or bourbon
2 teaspoons baking soda
1 tablespoon fresh lemon juice
1¼ cups unbleached all-purpose flour
¼ teaspoon kosher salt
1 teaspoon ground cinnamon
⅔ cup raisins
¾ cup coarsely chopped walnuts

Fill a large stockpot with enough water to come halfway up the sides of an 8-cup pudding mold. Place a small rack in the bottom of the pot. Bring the water to a simmer while you prepare the pudding. Have a tight-fitting lid nearby.

Place a medium-mesh strainer over a large bowl. Remove the stem ends from the persimmons. Squeeze the soft pulp out of the skins. If some skin gets mixed in, it will be strained out. Using a rubber spatula, press the pulp through the strainer. Scrape off any pulp on the bottom of the strainer and add it to the rest. You should have about 1¼ cups of puree.

Grease the pudding mold, using 2 tablespoons of the butter.

Melt the remaining 8 tablespoons butter and let cool for 5 minutes.

Combine the eggs and sugar in the bowl of a standing mixer fitted with the paddle attachment and beat for 3 minutes on high speed, until thickened and pale. Lower the speed and beat in the melted butter, persimmon puree, and brandy.

Dissolve the baking soda in 2 tablespoons boiling water in a small bowl. Beat into the persimmon mixture. Beat in the lemon juice.

Sift the flour, salt, and cinnamon into a medium bowl. Add to the persimmon mixture, beating on low speed until smooth. Remove the bowl from the stand and stir in the raisins and walnuts.

Pour the pudding into the prepared pudding mold. Cover the mold and place on the rack inside the pot of simmering water. Cover the pot tightly with aluminum foil, then cover with the lid. Steam the pudding for 2 hours.

Remove the pudding from the pot and place it on a wire rack. Remove the lid from the pudding mold. Let the pudding cool for 10 minutes, then unmold it onto the wire rack. Serve warm or at room temperature with the hard sauce.

for the brandy hard sauce

2 cups confectioners' sugar

⅛ teaspoon kosher salt

8 tablespoons (1 stick) unsalted butter,
      at room temperature

1 tablespoon brandy or bourbon

1 teaspoon freshly grated lemon zest

½ teaspoon fresh lemon juice

1 tablespoon heavy cream

Sift together the confectioners' sugar and salt in a small bowl.

Cream the butter in the bowl of a standing mixer fitted with the paddle attachment. Add the confectioners' sugar mixture and beat until smooth. Add the brandy, lemon zest, lemon juice, and cream and beat until smooth, about 1 minute.

Makes about 1½ cups.

TIPS AND TECHNIQUES

The persimmon puree will keep in an airtight container in the refrigerator for up to 1 week. It can also be frozen for up to 2 months.

The hard sauce can be made ahead and kept in an airtight container in the refrigerator for 1 week. Remove from the refrigerator at least 30 minutes before serving.

Tunas, or Prickly Pear Fruit

*OPUNTIA FICUS-INDICA; O. ENGLEMANNII;
O. MEGACANTHA; O. VARIOUS HYBRIDS*

Most Americans are still strangers to the well-armed fruit, called a tuna, sitting jauntily atop the thorny green nopales paddles. This is such a pity, because the prickly pear cactus is one of the New World's greatest contributions to hungry humankind. Since the New World's conquest, many species of *Opuntia* have quickly spread their thorny, paddled arms around the world. From Europe to Africa to the Middle East, it is now easier to list where the cacti don't grow than where they do. The prickly pear cactus hitched a ride to the Old World by virtue of the fact that its fruit protected the seamen who ate it from scurvy. After its first service to Europeans, the "Indian fig," as many in the Mediterranean call it, became ensconced for centuries. Arid Sicily, Israel, and Malta, in particular, have a torrid love affair with this fruit, which has spawned excellent native liquors and foods.

In Mexico, the land that loves tunas best, members of the *Opuntia* genus are both wild and cultivated. The egg-shaped fruit born from spring's flashy flowers can be yellow, red, purple, green, and even white. Mexicans prize the panorama of color and flavor. Americans and the rest of the world primarily know the tuna variety with a fuchsia interior and a flavor reminiscent of watermelon and raspberries. When you penetrate the armed exterior of the fruit, you find a thin layer of flesh with the juicy inside sprinkled with round seeds too big to chew yet small enough to swallow. Mexicans savor it, seeds and all, with just a little squeeze of lime.

The various species of prickly pear cactus grow as far north as British Columbia and well into the northeastern United States. Wherever land is dry, sandy, and poor, these cacti thrive, whether it is in a desert, seashore, or vacant lot or, increasingly, when planted on someone's property. You might spot a stand of these while driving past an eroded ravine, growing as a fence between fields, or a hedgelike stand of them near a shopping center. They're one of several foods in this book that straddle wild and semicivilized life. Other than private-property issues, there are few restrictions on the harvest of the fruit. The plant remains intact to bloom and fruit next year. The increasing popularity of tunas means that the ripe fruit you keep meaning to stop and pick has a way of disappearing in the night.

This amazing plant's ability to provide nutritious tuna fruits and nopales paddles from barren land has been a blessing to Native Americans and to other cultures worldwide. As with stinging nettles, it's that pleasure and pain thing. Both are such treasure troves of nutrients that evolution has armed them to the teeth, preventing pesky creatures like us from eating them to the ground.

We've snuck prickly pear fruit harvest into the winter chapter by cheating a little. You can pick the fruit into December and January, but in many areas, harvest is in autumn. Your first step for harvest is grabbing gloves, tongs, and a sharp knife. Tunas look safe compared with the cactus's spiky paddles, but they're covered with insidious glochids. These tiny barbed hairs seem to almost leap at your skin. To see if the tunas are ripe, try twisting one with a gloved hand. If it is soft to the touch and twists off easily, it's ripe. You may want to continue to pick with tongs to reach the tunas more safely. Techniques for freeing the tunas of their nasty glochids range from rolling the fruit rigorously in sand with a broom to washing them vigorously with gloved hands and a brush to peeling them. To peel them, simply cut the tips off both ends, run a slit from top to bottom, and remove the leathery skin in one piece. At this point, you can eat the tunas immediately or run them through a food mill.

kitchen notes

CLEANING AND PREPARATION: See above. If the tuna bites you with its tiny teeth despite the precautions, pour or dip some warm wax on the spot of your flesh impaled with the thorns, or pour a little white glue on it. Let it cool or dry and pull it off.

COOKING METHODS: Tunas are lovely in vinaigrettes, sorbet, agua fresca (a sweetened fruit water found in most Mexican restaurants and markets), and endless cocktails.

STORAGE: They keep uncovered for about four days in the refrigerator. In Mexico tunas are preserved in degrees of concentration from syrup all the way to sweet disks of dried tuna fruit called *queso de tuna*.

IDEAL TUNAS: In heaven tunas have no thorns. Here, however, the declawed tunas, when gently squeezed, should feel as soft as a ripe peach.

Prickly Pear Pavlova

The elegance of this classic dessert named for the famous Russian ballerina contrasted with the spiny little barrel-shaped fruit from the desert is just hysterical. Moscow meets Mesoamerica. The fruit is tastier than a kiwi and, lord knows, no tutu is a more stunning color. Our too-often-neglected native tunas deserve culinary fates beyond the standard margaritas or simply being peeled and eaten fresh. Once you master defanging your tunas and make your first prickly pear puree, you'll get very excited about stalking this easily found fruit.

[SERVES 8]

for prickly pear curd

1½ pounds prickly pear fruit (approximately 6)

1 cup granulated sugar

4 large egg yolks (reserve egg whites
    for meringues)

2 large eggs

⅛ teaspoon kosher salt

1 teaspoon finely grated lime zest

2 tablespoons fresh lime juice

1 tablespoon unsalted butter, cut into 2 pieces

Cut the prickly pears in half. Using a spoon, scoop out the flesh and seeds into a medium nonreactive saucepan. Stir in ½ cup of the granulated sugar. Place over low heat. As the sugar starts to dissolve, press the fruit with a potato masher to release its juices. Cook until the mixture begins to simmer and the sugar is completely dissolved, about 5 minutes. Strain through a fine-mesh strainer, pressing gently on the solids to extract all the juices. Discard the solids. You should have ¾ to 1 cup juice.

    Fill a medium saucepan with 2 inches of water and place over low heat. Bring to a simmer.

    Whisk together the egg yolks, whole eggs, remaining ½ cup granulated sugar, and salt in a bowl large enough to rest inside the saucepan without touching the water. Whisk in the prickly pear liquid, lime zest, and lime juice. Stir in the butter with a wooden spoon. Place the bowl over the simmering water. Cook, stirring frequently, until the mixture is thickened and smooth, about 10 minutes.

    Strain the prickly pear curd through a fine-mesh strainer into a medium bowl. Press plastic wrap directly onto the surface of the curd and refrigerate until completely chilled, 4 hours or overnight.

for the meringues

2 teaspoons cornstarch

¾ cup superfine sugar

Reserved 4 large egg whites,
    at room temperature

1 teaspoon white vinegar

1 teaspoon pure vanilla extract

Position a rack in the center of the oven. Preheat the oven to 200°F.

    Line a large baking sheet with parchment paper or a silicone mat and spray with nonstick vegetable cooking spray.

Combine the cornstarch with 2 teaspoons of the superfine sugar in a small bowl. Set aside.

Place the egg whites in the bowl of a standing mixer fitted with the whip attachment. Beat the egg whites on high until they become frothy.

Begin adding the remaining superfine sugar, 2 tablespoons at a time, beating for 45 seconds between additions. The last addition will be the cornstarch-sugar mixture. Turn the mixer to low and beat in the vinegar and vanilla. Raise the mixer speed to high and beat for 1 more minute. The mixture should hold a very stiff peak.

Divide the meringue mixture into 8 mounds, spaced evenly apart, on the prepared baking sheet. Spread each mound into a 4-inch circle with a slight indentation in the center. The back of a soup spoon works well for this.

Bake for 1½ to 2 hours, or until the meringues are dry to the touch. Place on a wire rack to cool. They will crisp up further as they cool. Use immediately or store in an airtight container at room temperature for up to 4 days.

for the pavlova

1 cup heavy cream
1 tablespoon granulated sugar
⅛ teaspoon kosher salt
4 blood oranges, peeled and segments separated
Zest from 2 limes

Combine the cream, sugar, and salt in the bowl of a standing mixer fitted with the whisk attachment. Whip the mixture just until it forms soft peaks.

Divide the whipped cream among the meringues, spreading just to the edges. Divide the prickly pear curd among the meringues. Arrange the blood orange segments over the curd and sprinkle with the lime zest. Serve immediately.

TIPS AND TECHNIQUES

Use a wooden spoon rather than a whisk to stir the curd. A whisk will prevent it from thickening properly.

If you have a gas oven, the meringues can be kept inside overnight with the heat turned off after baking. They will continue to dry out.

A silicone mat is used in baking and cooking to provide a nonstick surface. It can withstand high temperature.

SUBSTITUTIONS AND VARIATIONS

Other fruit can be substituted for the blood oranges: mango or papaya slices, navel orange segments, pineapple segments, or pomegranate seeds.

The pavlova can be made as one large meringue rather than as individual portions.

wild
pantry

OPPOSITE: *Jelly bag with cooked elderberries*

FROM LEFT TO RIGHT: *Black trumpets, morels, porcini, candy caps*

When hunger dogs winter's heels, old traditions point your feet straight at the pantry, cellar, or whatever little hiding place you may have carved out. It's time to go in and spend your culinary savings account lavishly. You'll feel mighty clever.

The words *fresh*, *seasonal*, and *local* smack their noses up against the closed door of a landscape covered in snow or fallow fields. Preserving food is our old way of dealing with this fact of life. It is the natural course of things for food to be abundant for a little window in time. Blackberries will be lusciously ripe for just a couple of weeks. Rich porcini flush quickly as the rain comes. They won't wait for your schedule. Be it pickling or jelly making, rally yourself for gathering and deal yourself into the working game in your kitchen. Better yet, deal in some friends or family too; have a working party. Putting up food together links you with thousands of years of human tradition. And it's a blast.

My grandmother's larder had sassafras-smoked wild pig bacon, hickory nuts, sassafras roots, blocks of ice with bass frozen inside, and tupelo honey from the swamp across the road. As her proud granddaughter, I look around here at a veritable food zoo. Jars of pickled sea beans and ramps imprisoned in their jars are flanked by bottles of vodka with huckleberries settling at the bottom. The wild things keep civil company with all their tame distant cousins. In my barn, over a thousand pounds of dried mushrooms load the racks over the freezers packed with thousands of pounds of wild berries and frozen porcini.

Putting up food can be done on a tiny scale too. Most all of these ideas are quite easy, requiring modest efforts and resulting in glorious treats. A pantry may sound like a great luxury of space available to very few of us. This just isn't true. Underneath a king-size bed you can actually fit eighty cases of half-pint jars and have room left over for some bottles of infused vodka. Freezer space may be limited but you can get fifteen pounds of frozen berries into an 8 x 10 x 12-inch space. Whether you live in a farmhouse or an urban apartment, these treasures are completely doable.

Pour yourself a chanterelle vodka martini after a rough day or spread elderberry jelly on toast with your mom. Either way, you've made the wild world part of your home and brought it to those you share it with.

Savory Spreads and Condiments

Ramp Pesto

[MAKES ½ CUP]

½ pound ramps with greens, washed and patted dry,
    root ends trimmed
3 tablespoons extra virgin olive oil
¾ teaspoon kosher salt, or more to taste
Pinch of freshly ground black pepper
1 tablespoon pine nuts, toasted
1 tablespoon grated Parmesan
½ teaspoon fresh lemon juice, or more to taste

Cut the greens off of the ramps. Dice the bulbs into
¼-inch pieces.

    Bring a medium pot of salted water to a boil. Have
a bowl of ice water next to the stove. Drop the greens
into the boiling water and cook for 2 minutes. Lift the
greens out of the water with a strainer and plunge them
immediately into the ice water. Drain and squeeze dry.
If they are still moist, roll them up in a kitchen towel and
twist the ends tightly to squeeze out all the excess
moisture. Coarsely chop the greens and set aside.

    Heat 1 tablespoon of the oil in a small sauté pan
over medium heat. Add the ramp bulbs, ¼ teaspoon of
the salt, and the pepper. Stir together and cook until the
bulbs are tender, about 5 minutes. Remove from heat.
Cool to room temperature.

    Place the ramp greens and bulbs in the bowl of a
food processor. Pulse a few times to chop them together,
then process continuously for 1 minute. Stop the machine
and scrape down the sides of the bowl. Process for
1 more minute, or until the ramp mixture is very finely
chopped. Add the pine nuts, Parmesan, remaining
2 tablespoons oil, remaining ½ teaspoon salt, and lemon
juice and process until smooth. Taste for seasoning,
adding more salt and/or lemon juice as needed.

    Store in an airtight container in the refrigerator
for up to 10 days or in the freezer for up to 1 month.

Black Trumpet Mushroom Tapenade

[MAKES ¾ CUP]

4 tablespoons extra virgin olive oil
½ pound black trumpet mushrooms, cleaned
1 teaspoon kosher salt
¼ teaspoon freshly ground black pepper
2 garlic cloves, finely minced
1 small anchovy, rinsed
1 teaspoon capers, rinsed and drained
½ teaspoon finely grated lemon zest
¼ teaspoon fresh lemon juice, or more to taste

Heat 1 tablespoon of the oil in a large sauté pan
over medium-high heat. When the oil is hot, add the
mushrooms, tossing to coat evenly with the oil. Add
½ teaspoon of the salt and the pepper. Cook, stirring
occasionally, until the mushrooms have released their
liquid. Continue cooking until the liquid has evaporated
and the mushrooms are dry. Add the garlic and cook for
1 more minute. Remove from the heat and cool to room
temperature.

    Place the mushrooms, anchovy, and capers in
the bowl of a food processor. Process until very finely
chopped, stopping the machine to scrape down the sides
of the bowl as you go. Add the lemon zest, lemon juice,
and remaining ½ teaspoon salt. Process for 1 more
minute. Scrape down the sides. With the machine running,
drizzle in the remaining 3 tablespoons oil. Taste for
seasoning, adding more salt and/or lemon juice as needed.

to make with dried black trumpet mushrooms

1½ ounces dried black trumpet mushrooms

Rehydrate the mushrooms in a large bowl of warm water
for 15 minutes. When they are softened, plunge and rinse
them in multiple changes of water to remove any sandy
grit, leaves, or fir needles. They will need at least 3 to
4 washings to get them clean. Pat the mushrooms dry
before proceeding with the recipe.

Johnny's Marinated Mushroom Relish

[MAKES 2 CUPS]

⅓ cup pure olive oil
4 medium shallots, thinly sliced
3 garlic cloves, thinly sliced
1 pound mushrooms, such as chanterelles, cremini,
    or porcini, cut into ¼-inch dice
¼ cup chopped flat-leaf parsley
⅓ cup dry vermouth
1 tablespoon Dijon mustard
1 tablespoon light brown sugar
1½ teaspoons kosher salt, or more to taste
¼ teaspoon freshly ground black pepper,
    or more to taste
1 bay leaf
¼ teaspoon crushed red pepper flakes
1 teaspoon chopped fresh thyme
1 teaspoon chopped fresh oregano

Heat the oil in a large sauté pan or skillet over medium
heat. When the oil is hot, add the shallots and garlic
and cook slowly until soft and translucent, 4 to 5 minutes.
Add the mushrooms and cook until they begin to release
their liquid, 2 to 3 minutes. Add the parsley, vermouth,
mustard, brown sugar, salt, and pepper. Turn up the
heat and bring the mixture just to a boil, then turn down
the heat and simmer for 6 to 8 minutes, or until the
mushrooms are fully cooked. Add the bay leaf, red pepper
flakes, thyme, and oregano. Taste for seasoning, adding
more salt and/or pepper as needed. Remove the bay
leaf before serving. Serve warm, at room temperature,
or chilled.

The relish will keep in an airtight container in the
refrigerator for up to 2 weeks.

ABOVE RIGHT: *Ramps*

Pickles

Basic Pickling Brine

[MAKES ABOUT 3 CUPS]

1 cup white wine vinegar
½ cup sugar
1½ tablespoons kosher salt
2 quarter-size slices peeled fresh ginger
¾ teaspoon coriander seeds
½ teaspoon black peppercorns
1 small bay leaf

Place the vinegar, sugar, salt, ginger, coriander seeds, peppercorns, bay leaf, and 2 cups water in a medium saucepan and bring to a boil over medium-high heat, whisking to dissolve the sugar and salt. When the mixture comes to a boil, turn down the heat and let simmer for 2 minutes. Remove the bay leaf before serving.

Pickled Ramps

[MAKES ½ POUND]

1 recipe Basic Pickling Brine (above)
½ pound ramp bulbs, cleaned

Prepare a batch of pickling brine. When the mixture comes to a boil, add the ramp bulbs. Bring back to a boil, then turn down the heat and simmer for 10 minutes. Remove from the heat and let the ramps cool in the pickling liquid to room temperature.

Place in a nonreactive container with a lid and store in the refrigerator for up to 3 months.

Pickled Sea Beans

[MAKES ¼ POUND]

1 recipe Basic Pickling Brine (left), omitting the salt
¼ pound cleaned sea beans

Prepare a batch of pickling brine, omitting the salt. (The sea beans are naturally salty.) When the brine comes to a boil, turn down the heat and simmer for 2 minutes.

Place the sea beans in a nonreactive lidded container large enough to hold them and the brining liquid. Pour the hot liquid over the beans and give them a stir to make sure that they are completely covered. Cool to room temperature.

Cover with the lid and refrigerate for up to 2 months.

Pickled Chanterelles

[MAKES 1 POUND]

2 recipes Basic Pickling Brine (above left)
1 pound cleaned chanterelles, turn or cut into
    medium-size pieces (leave whole if small)

Prepare the pickling brine. When the mixture comes to a boil, turn down the heat and let simmer for 2 minutes. Add the mushrooms and bring the mixture back to a boil. For small mushrooms, cook 1 minute more, then remove from the heat. For larger mushrooms or pieces, cook 2 minutes more, then remove from the heat. Cool the mushrooms in the pickling liquid to room temperature. Place in a nonreactive container with a lid and store in the refrigerator for up to 2 months.

OPPOSITE: *Pickled ramps, pickled chanterelles*

Mushroom Powders

Rubs and Flavored Salts

Mushroom powders can be made easily with just a few simple tools: a spice or coffee grinder, a regular-mesh strainer, and a fine-mesh strainer. Make sure the mushrooms you've dried yourself or purchased are clean and grit free. Although dried porcini makes the best known, puffballs, yellow feet, and other fungi make excellent mushroom powders.

Porcini Powder

[MAKES ½ CUP]

½ ounce dried porcini mushrooms, grit free

Break up any large pieces of dried mushrooms into pieces that will fit into the grinder easily.

Grind the mushrooms to a fine powder. Place the regular-mesh strainer over a bowl and add the ground mushrooms. Sift. Regrind any pieces that don't pass through the strainer the first time. When all the mushrooms have been ground and sifted through the first strainer, place the powder in the fine-mesh strainer and sift again. Regrind any pieces left in the strainer and sift again to achieve the finest powder possible. Discard any bits that don't pass through the strainer.

Store in an airtight container in a cool, dark place. The powder will keep for up to 3 months.

Wine Forest Mushroom Rub

[MAKES ¾ CUP]

½ ounce dried porcini mushrooms
¼ ounce dried shiitake mushrooms
⅛ ounce dried fairy ring mushrooms
¼ ounce dried morel mushrooms
1 small bay leaf
1 tablespoon kosher salt
¼ teaspoon black peppercorns
¼ teaspoon granulated garlic
¼ teaspoon dried ground lemon peel

Combine the porcini, shiitakes, fairy rings, morels, bay leaf, salt, peppercorns, garlic, and lemon peel in a medium bowl and toss together. Break up any large pieces of dried mushrooms. In batches, place the mixture in a spice or coffee grinder and grind to a fine powder.

Sift through a fine-mesh strainer placed over a bowl. Regrind any pieces that are left in the strainer.

Store the rub in an airtight container in a cool, dark place. It will keep for up to 2 months.

Juniper Berry Rub for Meat and Game

[MAKES ½ CUP]

¼ cup juniper berries
2 tablespoons kosher salt
½ teaspoon black peppercorns
1 teaspoon dried orange peel
½ teaspoon whole allspice

Combine the juniper berries, salt, peppercorns, orange peel, and allspice in a spice or coffee grinder. Grind to a fine powder.

Store the rub in an airtight container in a cool, dark place. It will keep for up to 2 months.

OPPOSITE: *Flavored salts* [PAGE 314]

Fennel Pollen Rub
for Fish and Poultry

[MAKES ABOUT ⅓ CUP]

1 tablespoon fennel pollen
3 tablespoons fennel seeds, toasted
1 tablespoon kosher salt
1 teaspoon coriander seeds
¼ teaspoon dried ground lemon peel
¼ teaspoon dried orange peel
½ teaspoon celery seeds
½ teaspoon white peppercorns
¼ teaspoon granulated onion

Combine the fennel pollen, fennel seeds, salt, coriander seeds, lemon peel, orange peel, celery seeds, peppercorns, and onion in a small bowl. Place in a spice or coffee grinder and grind to a fine powder.

Store the rub in an airtight container in a cool, dark place. It will keep for up to 1 month.

FLAVORED SALTS

These flavored salts are delicious as a finishing touch on grilled foods, salads, soups, pastas, or vegetables. Sprinkle them on just before serving.

Porcini Salt

[MAKES ½ CUP]

½ cup kosher salt
1 tablespoon Porcini Powder (page 312)

Combine the salt and porcini powder in the bowl of a food processor. Pulse 3 to 4 times to incorporate.

Store the salt in an airtight container in a cool, dark place. It will keep for up to 2 months.

Fennel Salt

[MAKES ½ CUP]

1 tablespoon fennel seeds, toasted and ground
    to a powder in a spice or coffee grinder
2 teaspoons fennel pollen
½ cup kosher salt

Combine the ground fennel, fennel pollen, and salt in the bowl of a food processor. Pulse 3 to 4 times to incorporate.

Store the salt in an airtight container in a cool, dark place. It will keep for up to 2 months.

Douglas Fir or Spruce Tip Salt

[MAKES ½ CUP]

½ cup kosher salt
Heaping 3 tablespoons Douglas fir or spruce
    tip needles

Place the salt and needles in the bowl of a food processor. Process until the needles are finely chopped.

Store the salt in an airtight container in a cool, dark place. It will keep for up to 1 month. The moisture in the fir tip needles may cause the salt to form some clumps—just break them up before using.

Mushroom Stocks

Traditional Mushroom Stock

[MAKES 1 QUART]

2 tablespoons pure olive oil
1 pound button mushrooms, cleaned and
    cut into quarters
½ teaspoon kosher salt
1 medium onion, coarsely chopped
1 small celery stalk, coarsely chopped
1 large garlic clove, coarsely chopped
2 fresh thyme sprigs
3 flat-leaf parsley sprigs
½ ounce dried porcini mushrooms, rinsed

Heat the oil in a large stockpot over medium-high heat.
When the oil is hot, add the button mushrooms and salt.
Stir to coat evenly with the oil. Cook until the mushrooms
release their liquid. Continue cooking until the liquid has
evaporated and the mushrooms are just starting to brown,
5 to 6 minutes. Add the onion, celery, and garlic and cook
for 2 minutes. Add the thyme, parsley, and porcini
mushrooms and 2 quarts cold water.

  Bring the mixture to a boil, then turn down the heat
to a bubbling simmer and cook for 45 minutes. Turn off
the heat and let sit for 30 minutes. Strain the stock
through a fine-mesh strainer. Discard the solids.

  Store in an airtight container in the refrigerator for
up to 1 week. Freeze for up to 4 months.

Fish-Friendly Mushroom Stock

[MAKES 5 CUPS]

1 tablespoon pure olive oil
1 pound button mushrooms, cleaned and
    cut into quarters
½ teaspoon kosher salt
2 medium leeks, white part plus 1 inch green left on,
    cleaned and sliced ¼ inch thick
1 small fennel bulb, cut into ½-inch dice
1 small celery stalk, coarsely chopped
¼ cup dry white wine
2 fresh thyme sprigs
4 flat-leaf parsley stems
1 bay leaf

Heat the oil in a large stockpot over medium-high heat.
When the oil is hot, add the mushrooms and salt, stirring
to coat evenly with the oil. Cook until the mushrooms
release their liquid. Continue cooking until the liquid has
evaporated and the mushrooms are just starting to brown.
Add the leeks, fennel, and celery and cook for 2 minutes.
Add the white wine, thyme, parsley stems, and bay leaf
and 2 quarts cold water.

  Bring the mixture to a boil, then turn down the heat
to a bubbling simmer and cook for 45 minutes. Turn off
the heat and let sit for 30 minutes. Strain the stock
through a fine-mesh strainer. Discard the solids.

  Store in an airtight container in the refrigerator for
up to 1 week. Freeze for up to 4 months.

Infused Vinegars

BASIC INFUSED VINEGARS

Choose a good-quality white wine vinegar with at least
6 percent acidity.

Extract the juice from the fruits by crushing or gently
cooking the fruit. Combine the juice and fruit pulp with the
vinegar and let steep for 4 to 5 days in a cool, dark place.

Strain the mixture through a jelly bag, which is a cloth
bag with a stand, available where canning supplies are
sold. for 4 to 6 hours, discarding any sediment remaining
in the bag.

Store the vinegar in a clean glass container with a lid
in a cool, dark place. It will keep up to 2 years.

Mulberry Vinegar
[MAKES 1½ TO 2 CUPS]

¾ pound fresh mulberries, rinsed
1 cup white wine vinegar

Place the mulberries in a nonreactive bowl. Crush with a
potato masher or the back of a wooden spoon until juicy.
Stir in the vinegar. Cover with plastic wrap and let sit for
4 to 5 days in a cool, dark place.

Strain the mixture through a jelly bag for 4 to 6 hours,
discarding any sediment remaining in the bag.

Store the vinegar in a clean glass container with a lid
in a cool, dark place. It will keep up to 2 years.

Elderberry Vinegar
[MAKES 1½ CUPS]

½ pound elderberries (about 1 cup)
2 tablespoons sugar
1 cup white wine vinegar

Place the elderberries and sugar in a small saucepan over
medium heat. Crush the elderberries with a wooden spoon
and stir to dissolve the sugar. Bring the mixture just to a
boil, remove from the heat, and cool to room temperature.

Combine the elderberry mixture and vinegar in a
nonreactive bowl. Cover with plastic wrap and let sit for
4 to 5 days in a cool, dark place.

Strain the elderberry mixture through a jelly bag for 4
to 6 hours, discarding any sediment remaining in the bag.

Store the vinegar in a clean glass container with a lid
in a cool, dark place. It will keep up to 2 years.

Rose Hip Vinegar
[MAKES 1½ CUPS]

½ pound fresh rose hips, cleaned
2 tablespoons sugar
1½ cups white wine vinegar

Place the rose hips in the bowl of a food processor.
Pulse until very finely chopped.

Place the rose hips, 2 tablespoons water, and the
sugar in a small saucepan over medium heat. Heat,
stirring to dissolve the sugar, just until the mixture comes
to a boil. Remove from the heat and cool to room
temperature.

Combine the rose hip mixture and the vinegar in a
nonreactive bowl. Cover with plastic wrap and let sit for
4 to 7 days in a cool, dark place.

Strain the rose hip mixture through a jelly bag for 4
to 6 hours, discarding any sediment remaining in the bag.

Store the vinegar in a clean glass container with a lid
in a cool, dark place. It will keep up to 2 years.

Compound Butters

Persimmon Vinegar

[MAKES 1½ CUPS]

3 large or 4 to 5 medium very ripe Hachiya persimmons
(about 1¼ pounds)
1 cup white wine vinegar

Remove the stem ends of the persimmons and squeeze the pulp into a regular-mesh strainer set over a nonreactive bowl. Using a rubber spatula, push the pulp of the persimmons through the strainer. Add the vinegar and whisk to combine. Cover with plastic wrap and let sit for 4 to 5 days in the refrigerator.

Strain the persimmon mixture through a jelly bag for 4 to 6 hours, discarding any sediment remaining in the bag.

Store the vinegar in a clean glass container with a lid in the refrigerator. When it settles, there will be some sediment on the bottom, which is normal. It will keep up to 2 years.

BASIC COMPOUND BUTTERS

Use room-temperature unsalted butter as a base for the compound butters.

Finely chop, puree, or mince the ingredients to mix into the butter. They will blend in more evenly and, when melted, add just the right amount of seasoning and texture to the dish.

Beat or process the butter first to make it soft and creamy before adding the rest of the ingredients.

A little bit of fresh lemon juice and/or grated lemon zest provides a bright note to any flavored compound butter.

The butter can be rolled into a tight log, wrapped in plastic wrap, and either refrigerated or frozen. It can also be packed into a storage container with a lid and either refrigerated or frozen.

Bring the butter to room temperature before using, so it will melt easily onto the hot food.

Porcini Butter

[MAKES ABOUT 1 CUP]

1 ounce dried porcini mushrooms, rinsed to remove
    any fine sand or grit
½ pound (2 sticks) plus 2 tablespoons unsalted butter,
    at room temperature
3 garlic cloves, finely minced
1 teaspoon Porcini Powder (page 312)
½ teaspoon kosher salt, or more to taste
⅛ teaspoon freshly ground black pepper
½ teaspoon fresh lemon juice, or more to taste

Place the porcini mushrooms and 1 cup cold water in a
small saucepan over medium-high heat. Bring to a boil,
then turn off the heat and let sit for 15 minutes. Drain the
mushrooms, saving the liquid. Press on the porcini to
extract all the liquid. Set aside the mushrooms. Return
the porcini liquid to the saucepan and place over medium-
high heat. Cook to reduce the liquid to 1 tablespoon.
Remove from the heat and set aside.

Finely mince the rehydrated mushrooms.

Place 2 tablespoons of the butter in a medium sauté
pan over medium heat. Add the mushrooms and cook for
1 to 2 minutes. Add the garlic and cook for 2 to 3 more
minutes, or until the garlic is softened. Stir in the reserved
mushroom liquid and cool to room temperature.

Place the mushrooms in the bowl of a food
processor. Process until they are very finely chopped,
stopping and scraping down the sides of the bowl as
needed. Cut the remaining 2 sticks butter into 8 pieces.
Add to the food processor along with the porcini powder,
salt, pepper, and lemon juice. Pulse together until the
butter is creamy and the mushrooms are evenly
incorporated. Taste for seasoning, adding more salt and/
or lemon juice as needed.

Roll the butter into a log and wrap in plastic wrap or
place in an airtight storage container. The butter will keep
in the refrigerator for up to 10 days. It can also be frozen
for up to 1 month.

Ramp Butter

[MAKES ABOUT 1 CUP]

¼ pound cleaned ramps (greens and bulbs)
2 tablespoons pure olive oil
½ pound (2 sticks) unsalted butter, at room temperature
½ teaspoon fresh lemon juice, or more to taste
½ teaspoon kosher salt, or more to taste
¼ teaspoon freshly ground black pepper,
    or more to taste

Cut the greens off the ramps and chop finely. Finely mince
the bulbs.

Heat the oil in a medium sauté pan over medium-
high heat. Add the ramp bulbs and cook until tender,
3 to 4 minutes. Add the greens and cook for 3 to 4 more
minutes, or until they are wilted and tender. Cool to room
temperature.

Place the butter in the bowl of a food processor or a
standing mixer fitted with the paddle attachment. Process
or beat to soften for about 30 seconds. Stop the machine
and add the ramps, lemon juice, salt, and pepper. Process
or mix until well incorporated. Taste for seasoning, adding
more salt, pepper, and/or lemon juice as needed.

Roll the butter into a log and wrap in plastic wrap or
place in an airtight storage container. The butter will keep
refrigerated for up to 1 week. It can also be frozen for up
to 1 month.

Jams and Jellies

Huckleberry Jam

[MAKES ABOUT SIX ½-PINT JARS]

4 cups huckleberries (about 1½ pounds), cleaned
4 cups sugar
¼ cup fresh lemon juice
½ teaspoon unsalted butter
One 3-ounce packet liquid pectin

Sterilize and prepare the jars for canning, and have them ready while you make the jam.

Place the huckleberries, sugar, lemon juice, and butter in a large saucepan over medium-high heat. Stir frequently to dissolve the sugar and release the juices from the berries. Bring to a full rolling boil, then quickly stir in the pectin. Bring back to a full rolling boil and boil hard for 1 minute.

Pour the jam immediately into the prepared jars, leaving ¼ inch of headspace, and seal in a water bath for 5 minutes. (See www.uga.edu/nchfp/ for complete preserving information.)

Elderberry Jelly

[MAKES ABOUT SIX ½-PINT JARS]

3½ pounds elderberries, cleaned
¼ cup fresh lemon juice
One 1¾-ounce packet powdered pectin
4½ cups sugar
½ teaspoon unsalted butter

Place the elderberries in a large saucepan over medium heat. Crush the berries with a potato masher or wooden spoon to release the juices as the mixture comes up to a boil. When it reaches a boil, turn down the heat and simmer for 10 minutes. Remove from the heat and cool slightly.

Drain the elderberries through a jelly bag for 4 to 6 hours. Discard the elderberries. Measure the juice. You should have 3 cups. Add water if you don't.

Sterilize and prepare the jars for canning, and have them ready while you make the jelly.

Place the elderberry juice and lemon juice in a large saucepan over medium-high heat. Whisk in the pectin. Bring the mixture to a boil, stirring to dissolve the pectin. When the mixture comes to a full rolling boil, stir in the sugar and butter with a wooden spoon or spatula. Bring back to a full rolling boil, one that cannot be diminished by stirring, and boil hard for 1 minute.

Pour the jelly immediately into the prepared jars, leaving ¼ inch of headspace, and seal in a water bath for 5 minutes. (See www.uga.edu/nchfp/ for complete preserving information.)

Rose Hip Syrup

[MAKES ABOUT 1½ CUPS]

5 ounces fresh rose hips, about 1 cup, cleaned
1 cup sugar

Place the rose hips in the bowl of a food processor. Pulse until the rose hips are finely chopped.

Place 1 cup water in a small saucepan and bring to a boil over medium-high heat. Add the rose hips, stir, and bring back to a boil. Cover with a lid and remove from the heat. Let sit for 15 minutes. Pour the rose hips and liquid through a clean jelly bag set over a container and let drain for 1 hour. Refrigerate the liquid and save the rose hips. Clean the jelly bag to reuse.

Bring another 1 cup water to a boil in a small saucepan over medium-high heat. Add the rose hips and bring back to a boil. Again, cover, remove from the heat, and let sit for 15 minutes. Drain through the jelly bag for at least 4 hours or overnight. Discard the rose hips.

Combine the infused liquids and measure. Add water, if needed, to measure 1½ cups. Place the liquid and the sugar in a small saucepan. Bring to a boil over medium-high heat, whisking to dissolve the sugar. Boil for 3 minutes, or until the mixture is the consistency of a thin syrup. Remove from the heat to cool.

Store the syrup in an airtight container in the refrigerator for up to 2 months.

to make with dried rose hips

8 ounces dried rose hips
1 cup sugar

Crush the rose hips by placing them in a plastic bag and pounding them with a mallet or the bottom of a small saucepan. You can also use a food processor, pulsing to break them up.

Place the crushed rose hips and 4 cups water in a medium saucepan. Bring to a boil over medium-high heat, then turn down the heat and simmer for 15 minutes. Remove from the heat and let sit for 10 minutes. Drain through a clean jelly bag into a container for at least 4 hours, or overnight. Discard the rose hips.

Measure the liquid. Add more water, if needed, to measure 1½ cups.

Place the rose hip liquid and the sugar in a small saucepan. Bring to a boil over medium-high heat, whisking to dissolve the sugar. Boil for 3 minutes, or until the mixture is the consistency of a thin syrup. Remove from the heat to cool.

Store the syrup in an airtight container in the refrigerator for up to 2 months.

Spruce or Douglas Fir Tip Syrup

[MAKES 1 CUP]

1 cup spruce or Douglas fir tips
1 cup sugar
2 tablespoons light corn syrup
Pinch of kosher salt

Place the spruce tips in the bowl of a food processor. Pulse until the tips are finely chopped, stopping halfway through to scrape down the sides of the bowl. Set aside.

Place ⅓ cup plus 2 tablespoons water, the sugar, the corn syrup, and the salt in a small saucepan over medium heat. Whisk together as the mixture comes up to a boil. Boil, without stirring, for 1 minute, then remove from the heat. Stir in the spruce tips and let the syrup steep at room temperature for 2 to 3 hours. Strain through a fine-mesh strainer. Discard the solids.

Store in an airtight container in the refrigerator for up to 1 month.

Wild Booze and Cocktails

Candy Cap Sugar

[MAKES 4 CUPS]

½ ounce dried candy cap mushrooms
4 cups sugar

Wrap the candy cap mushrooms in a piece of cheesecloth and tie. Place the sugar in a container with a lid. Bury the bundle in the middle of the sugar. Let sit for 2 to 3 days before using, giving the mushrooms time to infuse the sugar. As you use the sugar, add more to the container to keep infusing.

The sugar will keep in an airtight container at room temperature for up to 6 months.

INFUSED BOOZE

Chanterelle Vodka

Using dried chanterelles leaves the vodka clear. Fresh chanterelles make murky vodka.

[MAKES ONE 750-MILLILITER BOTTLE]

⅔ cup dried chanterelles, lightly packed
One 750-milliliter bottle fine-quality vodka

Place the chanterelles and vodka in a large clean jar. Cover and place in a dark place for 1 week, swirling the jar every couple of days.

Strain through a fine-mesh strainer and discard the chanterelles. Pour the infused vodka into a clean bottle and store indefinitely in the freezer.

cocktail suggestions

Drink straight up in a martini glass or, à la chefs' forays, from any container available before heading into the woods.

Wild Fruit Vodka

[MAKES ONE 750-MILLILITER BOTTLE]

⅔ cup fresh fruit, such as huckleberries,
    mulberries, or peeled prickly pear
One 750-milliliter bottle fine-quality vodka

Place the fruit in a small bowl and mash lightly with a potato masher to release the juices. Combine the fruit and juices with the vodka in a large clean jar. Cover and place in a dark place for 2 to 3 weeks.

Strain through a fine-mesh strainer and discard the fruits. Pour the vodka into a clean bottle and store indefinitely in the freezer.

OPPOSITE: *Douglas Fir Needle Vodka*   [PAGE 324]

Spruce or Douglas Fir Needle Vodka

[MAKES ONE 750-MILLILITER BOTTLE]

1 cup spruce or Douglas fir needles,
    stripped from the branches
One 750-milliliter bottle fine-quality vodka

Place the spruce or Douglas fir needles and one-third of the bottle of vodka in a blender. Blend at high speed for 2 minutes. Pour into a large clean jar. Pour the remaining two-thirds vodka into the blender and swirl it around to gather any green residue on the sides and bottom of the blender. Pour into the jar and stir to combine. Cover and store in the refrigerator for 1 week.

Strain the mixture through a fine-mesh strainer and discard the green puree. Strain again through a coffee filter. Pour the vodka into a clean bottle and store indefinitely in the freezer.

cocktail suggestion

Simply pour this frozen green vodka into a chilled martini glass and float a tender fir tip on top.

Elderberry Shrub

"Shrub" is an old colonial term for an acidic fruit-based drink. A wild array of fruits can be used to make delicious shrubs. The concentrated flavor of the shrub holds its own in the following shrub cocktail or you can skip the alcohol and make a very refreshing soft drink by adding sparkling water. Strange as it may sound, this shrub mixed with olive oil and vinegar makes an extraordinary salad dressing.

[MAKES 1 QUART]

4 cups elderberries (about 2 pounds), cleaned
2 cups sugar
2 cups good-quality red wine vinegar

Place the elderberries, ½ cup water, and the sugar in a large saucepan over medium-high heat. Bring to a boil, stirring to dissolve the sugar. When the mixture reaches a boil, turn down the heat and simmer for 10 minutes. Stir in the vinegar and turn up the heat. Bring back to a boil, then turn down the heat and simmer for 20 more minutes. Remove from the heat. Cool to room temperature.

Strain the mixture through a fine-mesh strainer into a large measuring cup, pressing on the berries to extract all the liquid. Discard the solids. Pour the liquid into clean glass bottles or jars. Cover tightly and refrigerate.

The shrub will keep in the refrigerator for up to 1 year.

Elderberry Shrub Cocktail

[MAKES 1]

1 ounce Elderberry Shrub (above)
1½ ounces bourbon or vodka
Ice
Soda water
Fresh mint sprig (optional)

Combine the elderberry shrub and bourbon in a 10-ounce glass. Fill the glass with ice and pour soda water to fill. Stir and garnish with a mint sprig, if using.

Candy Cap Hot Bourbon
[MAKES 1]

2 teaspoons Candy Cap Sugar (page 322)
1½ ounces bourbon
Dime-size piece of lemon peel

Combine the sugar and bourbon in an 8-ounce mug.
Pour in ¾ cup boiling water and stir to dissolve the sugar.
Add the lemon peel and serve.

Elderflower Liqueur
[MAKES APPROXIMATELY 1 QUART]

1½ cups elderflower blossoms
750 milliliters Everclear grain alcohol (151 proof)
¾ cup water
¾ cup simple syrup (see below)

Combine the elderflower blossoms and the Everclear
in a clean glass bottle with a stopper or lid.
    Place in a cool, dark place for 3½ weeks to infuse.
    Strain the blossoms and liquid through a coffee filter
or jelly bag to obtain a clear liquid. Discard the blossoms.
    Combine the infusion with the water and simple
syrup and mix well.
    Store in a closed container in a cool, dark place.

for simple syrup
Combine ⅔ cup water and ⅔ cup sugar in a small
saucepan. Bring to a boil while whisking to dissolve
the sugar. Boil for 30 seconds, then remove from the
heat. Cool to room temperature before using.

Elderflower Fizz
[SERVES 1]

1½ ounces Elderflower Liqueur (left)
1½ ounces half-and-half or cream
1 teaspoon sugar
1½ teaspoons lemon juice
1 egg white

Place the elderflower liqueur, half-and-half, sugar,
lemon juice, and egg white in a blender. Blend on
high for 1 minute. A cocktail shaker works great too.
    Pour into a chilled 6-ounce glass to serve.

cocktail suggestions

• Use tuna (prickly pear) juice with tequila or rum over ice.

• Put a couple of slices of fresh matsutake in the pot
  as you heat sake to make matsutake sake.

• Use a fresh ramp in place of celery as a swizzle stick
  in a bloody Mary.

Techniques for Wild Mushrooms

CLEANING

1. The ever-useful potato peeler is ideal for cleaning the base. ⌃

porcini

2. Porcini and many other mushrooms can be cleaned with just a wet washcloth. ⌄

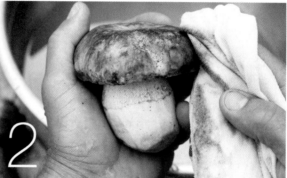

chanterelles and similar mushrooms

Start cleaning your mushrooms hours before you use them and you'll have clean, dry mushrooms when you're ready to cook. You can do this even the day before.

Clean chanterelles require just a little brushing, but from some habitats they're dirty and must be washed. Forget all that nonsense about never washing mushrooms because the flavor will wash away. The chanterelle in your hand probably took 1 to 3 weeks to grow and has already gone through plenty of rain baths.

1. Turn cool to lukewarm water from your faucet to a low flow.

2. Hold the mushroom briefly under the water and brush lightly with a clean brush. Also rinse the dirt from the brush itself under the flowing water. This way you can keep lifting the dirt from the mushroom while minimizing water the mushroom soaks up. Repeat this until clean.

3. First place the washed mushrooms in a colander to drip. Then put these cleaned mushrooms on a towel-lined pan or anything flat with drainage holes. Put the mushrooms by a fan or a sunny window. *The goal here is to be rid of the excess moisture and have nice dry sautéable mushrooms.* After they're clean and dry, put them in the refrigerator. See the "Kitchen Notes" section for each mushroom variety for more storage information.

Restaurants cleaning many pounds of mushrooms often dunk them in a sinkful of water. This isn't ideal. If you must do this, the plunging should be quick and vigorous to avoid excess soaking. Have a skimming ladle to remove floating particles from the water you're cleaning them in or you'll just be coating them again in the debris as you lift them out.

In the home kitchen, you can also use your sink's handled sprayer for a fast spray wash.

black trumpets, yellow feet, and hollow varieties

1. Trim off the dirty bottom tip of the mushroom and then split open the vase-shaped mushroom. Rinse and rub the inside and outside of the mushroom to clean away the inevitable forest debris and dirt. ⌃

2. Place the damp, cleaned mushroom on a towel-lined pan to drain and dry out again. ❯

Mushroom Cooking Techniques

SAUTÉING

1. Tear or cut cleaned mushrooms into medium-size pieces. ❯

2. Heat a thin layer of oil in a large sauté pan over medium-high heat and add the mushrooms when the oil is hot. ❮

3. Continue cooking the mushrooms as they release their liquid. The excess liquid will cook off and concentrate the flavor of the mushrooms. ⌃

4. The mushrooms are finished when they are dry and starting to caramelize. ❯

ROASTING

1. Toss the cleaned mushrooms in a large bowl with melted butter or olive oil, salt, pepper, chopped garlic, and fresh thyme leaves. Place in a single layer on a baking sheet. ❮

2. Roast the mushrooms in a hot oven (425°F) until golden brown and crisped. ❯

BUTTER POACHING

Bring 4 tablespoons of water to a boil in a medium saucepan. Whisk in 16 tablespoons (2 sticks) of butter, 1 tablespoon at a time, to form an emulsion. Simmer ½ pound of the cleaned mushrooms in the emulsion until tender, about 15 to 20 minutes, depending on the size. Small whole mushrooms are ideal, or chunks if larger. Use the remaining butter for potatoes, risotto, vegetables, pasta, etc. Chef Todd Humphries taught us this nifty trick. ❮

GRILLING

1. Brush the mushrooms on both sides with olive oil and season with salt, pepper, and chopped fresh thyme leaves. ‹

2. Grill over a medium fire until the mushrooms are well marked and golden brown on one side, then turn and continue grilling them until tender and cooked through. ›

Basket-Grilled Morels: See page 11. ‹

COOKING FROZEN MUSHROOMS

As you'd expect, sauces, soups, and many other finished mushroom dishes can freeze quite nicely, but only a few mushrooms freeze well raw. Raw porcini and matsutake are two of the best. *To freeze:* Slice or cut the cleaned mushrooms in half, vacuum seal or bag them as airtight as possible, then freeze. *To cook:* Cooking these frozen mushrooms requires unusual treatment: They need to be cooked before they completely thaw or they turn into mushroom Jell-O.

1. The day before you cook them, take the frozen mushrooms out of the freezer and place them in the refrigerator. The next day they should be in an even semifrozen state.
2. Cut them however you wish, toss them in oil, and immediately sear them in a very hot sauté pan or put them into a preheated roasting pan and into a very hot (475°F) oven. Cook until soft and slightly browned. They'll be ready for pasta, steak, or whatever.

REHYDRATING DRIED MUSHROOMS

Dried mushrooms are fabulous and underused in American kitchens. In Europe and much of Asia, they are immensely popular and are common in pantries. Dried porcini, morels, black trumpets, fairy rings, and yellow feet are fantastic. At least two of these should be in every pantry. Skip dried chanterelles, which resemble shoe leather even after hours of soaking. A pound of dried mushrooms began as 8 to 10 pounds of fresh. Roughly 3 ounces of dried mushrooms replace a pound of fresh.

To rehydrate:

1. Put the dried mushrooms in tepid water for at least 15 minutes, depending on how thick the dried mushrooms are. I like a narrow tall bowl to soak them in. This concentrates the debris, which falls to the bottom in a small area, leaving plenty of clean water for the floating mushrooms above.
2. Vigorous swishing after 5 minutes of soaking allows the frequently present sand to loosen, fall, and settle to the bottom.
3. When the mushrooms are soft and pliable, gently lift them out of the water. Strain this water through a fine sieve and use in cooking. A coffee filter in a funnel works well also. Black trumpets and dried fairy rings can be extra gritty and may need more than one soaking.

Wild Calendar

	Jan	Feb	Mar	Apr	May	Jun	Jul	Aug	Sep	Oct	Nov	Dec
Blackberries							■	■				
Black Trumpets [Horns of Plenty and Trumpets of Death] (East)								■	– –	– –	– –	– –
(West)	■	■	■									■
Black Walnuts										■	■	
Blewits (East)								■	■	■	■	■
(West)	■										■	■
Candy Cap Mushrooms (East)	■										■	■
Cauliflower Mushrooms (East)						■			■	■	■	■
(West)									■	■	■	■
Chanterelles (East)					– –	– –	– –	– –	– –	– –		
(West)	■								■	■		
Chickweed			■	■								
Cuitlacoche (Huitlacoche)								■	■	■	■	
Curly Dock Weed	■	■	■	■								
Dandelions (East)			■	■								
(West)		■	■									
Elderberries (East)								■	■			
(West)									■	■		
Elderflowers					■	■	■					
Fairy Rings (Mousseron) (East)				– –	– –	– –	■	■				
(West)			■	■	■	■	■	■				
Fennel, Wild				■	■	■	■	■	■	■	■	
Fiddleheads				■	■	■						
Hedgehog Mushrooms (East)									– –	– –	– –	– –
(West)	■	■									■	
Huckleberries							■	■	■	■		
Juniper Berries (East)										■	■	■
(West)	■										■	■
Lobster Mushrooms							■	■	■	■		

■ East of the Mississippi   ■ West of the Mississippi   – – European Imports

	Jan	Feb	Mar	Apr	May	Jun	Jul	Aug	Sep	Oct	Nov	Dec
Maitake, or Hen of the Woods									X	X	X	
Matsutake Mushrooms									X	X	X	X
Meadow Mushrooms								X	X	X	X	X
Miner's Lettuce/ Spring Greens			X	X								
Morels				X	X	X						
Morels, Gray						X	X	X				
Mulberries							X	X				
Nettles, Stinging			X	X	X	X	X	X				
Nopales			X	X	X	X	X	X				
Persimmons										X	X	X
Porcini (King Boletes)					X	X		X	X	X	X	X
Puffballs					X	X	X	X	X			
Purslane					X	X	X	X				
Ramps				X	X							
Raspberries							X	X				
Rose Hips	X								X	X	X	X
Sea Beans					X	X	X	X				
Spruce and Douglas Fir Tips				X	X	X						
Tuna or Prickly Pear Fruit			X	X	X							
Yellow Foot Mushrooms	X	X						X	X	--	--	--

Acknowledgments

Nearly every book I've ever held contains a little song of gratitude for that strange figure "my literary agent." I now know that this title is quite a lot more than a flashy introduction at a party. Katherine Cowles—a wise, good-hearted, and patient woman—has not only made this book happen, but has also earned a spot as one of the five people I'd be ready to be stranded with in a wild place. No matter that she's a sophisticated urbanite—you just know she'll find a way to make good things happen. I even thank her for the living hell of having to sit still indoors and write.

Sarah Scott's reputation as a supremely talented chef with an extraordinary palate is exceeded only by her good-heartedness. We worked in truly blessed harmony throughout the creation of this book. Her good judgment combined with a deep silly streak made it possible to face the mountain of work. You'll come to know her special gift for creating deliciousness yourself as these well-tested and polished recipes come to life in your own kitchen.

Sarah and I thank Sara Remington. Her extraordinary talent as a photographer lights up these pages. Less visible is her dedication to this book, sense of adventure, and love of wild foods. She gave us mountains of her time and put her whole heart into this work. With Sara came the magnificent stylists Ethel Brennan and Erin Quon. Our food shoots were blasts filled with beauty, bawdy humor, and delicious food.

We thank Viking Studio for its enthusiasm for this book. Lucia Watson and Miriam Rich provided us a fertile combination of freedom and nimble shepherding. We are immensely grateful for the very long leash we were on to realize our vision of this book. They also allowed us to select the immensely talented Janet Mumford, whose design so beautifully weaves the elements of this book together. She captured the spirit of our book.

Our thanks to Steve Sando (Rancho Gordo), who not only introduced Kitty Cowles and contributed both nopales recipes, but also listened to endless whining and got to whine right back.

My thanks to the generous and darling chefs: Todd Humphries (Martini House/St. Helena, California), Sean O'Toole (Bardessono/Yountville, California), Staffan Terje (Perbacco, Barbacco/San Francisco), Donald Link (Herbsaint, Cochon/New Orleans), Hiro Sone (Ame, Terra/San Francisco), John Gerber, Stuart Brioza, Mateo Granados, John Desmond, Nicole Plue (Redd/Yountville, California), and Stephen Durphee (Culinary Institute/St. Helena, California). Most of these chefs are not only pals, but have also hiked on many a trail with me, yelping with joy in the woods. Special thanks to Todd Humphries, the greatest wild foods chef I know. I look forward to the great cookbook he will create.

Thanks are hardly enough to Thomas Keller for his kind words and long years of support. His profound understanding of the symbiosis between a chef and a forager has made rattling through his door and making him smile one of my greatest rewards.

Thanks to the large tribe of mushroom pickers and friends without whom my life and business simply could not exist. Rolly, Doris, Don, Joan, Charlie, Guy, and a long list of remarkable people who lead wild lives of a challenging freedom that is incomprehensible to the average American. I love and thank them all. My local gang of Toni, Ashby, Kathy, Tom, Gretchen, Sean, Cindy, John, Robin, the Humphries, and beloved brother Patrick Hamilton are fungal family and provided morel, moral, and immoral support for this book.

Immeasurable thanks for the limitless dedication and friendship of Robin Hannah, Kim Daniels, Marge Caldwell, and Inocensia Fregoso. Without them my business would have crumbled and this book wouldn't be in your hands.

Kisses forever for my loving and trusting mom, who'd open the door and let me out knowing the snakes and gators would never get me.

—Connie Green

Thanks to Kitty Cowles—dear friend and fabulous agent—who has the gift of seeing potential and nurturing it into reality with intuition, patience, and tenacity. She wields the whip of motivation deftly and lovingly and made this book come to life.

Thanks to Connie Green—coauthor and raison d'être for this book. My life is so much the bigger for walking with Connie along trails and through the woods, learning to see with new eyes the abundance of wild foods that surround us and giving me the opportunity to work with a whole new world of ingredients and flavors. Her keen eye for the hidden treasures in nature and ability to write about them with love and expertise are evident in this book.

Thanks to Sam Gittings—my best friend and champion—who tirelessly tasted everything along the way, offering, with courage and humor, suggestions that inevitably made things better. I really did listen.

Thanks to the members of the Robert Mondavi family, who have been my mentors for more than twenty-five years, providing the opportunity to work with the best chefs and finest wines in the world. I continue to be inspired by their example, to constantly reach for excellence and to live life with passion and pleasure.

Thanks to Thomas Keller, who has been a guiding light and provided invaluable encouragement through the years.

Thanks to Susie Heller, who generously gave of her expertise, who always picked up the phone, and who provided a willing, discerning palate.

Thanks to Bobbie Lee Jackson, a natural cook and my first teacher, who patiently let me stand beside her in the kitchen when I was barely tall enough to reach the counter and who first showed me the pleasure and love that food holds, for both the cook and those she feeds.

Thanks to my family for being a solid foundation in my life—for your laughter, infectious enthusiasm, and unconditional love.

Thanks to my friends, fellow cooks, and all who tasted, prepped, cleaned up, and kept me going along the way: Janet, Barbara, Dan, Tessa, Bonnie, Doug, Ed, Lisa, Nancy, Eldon, Prentice, Jeff, Cameron, Scott, Gilles, Fred, Frank, Matt, Jaci, Jeff, Polly, Neil, Karen, Marvin, Sheryl, Lori, Michelle, and TIAPOS.

—Sarah Scott

Guidebooks and Sources

general wild foods
A more extensive list of books can be found at www.wineforest.com.
Brill, Steve. *Identifying and Harvesting Edible and Medicinal Plants*. New York: Hearst Books, 1994.
Elias, Thomas S., and Peter D. Dykeman. *Edible Wild Plants*. New York: Sterling, 2009.
Gibbons, Euell. *Stalking the Wild Asparagus*. New York: Alan C. Hood & Co., 1962.
Marrone, Teresa. *Abundantly Wild*. Cambridge, MA: Adventure Publications, 2004.
Medsger, Oliver Perry. *Edible Wild Plants*. New York: Macmillan, 1939.
Phillips, Roger. *Wild Food*. London: Macmillan, 1983.
Thayer, Samuel. *The Forager's Harvest*. Ogema, WI: Forager's Harvest, 2006.
Tilford, Gregory L. *Edible and Medicinal Plants of the West*. Missoula, MT: Mountain Press Publishing, 1997.
Welsch, Roger. *Wild 'Em and Reap*. Guilford, CT: Globe Pequot, 2006.
www.foraging.com
www.uga.edu/nchfp/—National Center for Home Food Preservation; great information on food preservation: jam, pickles, etc.
www.wildfoodadventures.com
www.wildmanstevebrill.com

wild mushrooms
Mycological societies exist all over the country and are great sources of knowledgeable people to hunt with.
www.mykoweb.com—a great mushroom information Web site and includes a listing of mushroom clubs throughout North America
www.namyco.org—the site of the North American Mycological Society and also lists clubs and activities

east of the mississippi
Barron, George. *Mushrooms of Northeast North America: Midwest to New England*. Auburn. WA: Lone Pine, 1999.
Lincoff, Gary H. *The National Audubon Society Field Guide to North American Mushrooms*. New York: Alfred A. Knopf, 1981.
Roody, William C. *Mushrooms of West Virginia and the Central Appalachians*. Lexington: University Press of Kentucky, 2003.

west of the mississippi
Arora, David. *All That the Rain Promises and More*. Berkeley, CA: Ten Speed Press, 1991.
———. *Mushrooms Demystified*. Berkeley, CA: Ten Speed Press, 1986.

wild food sources (forage for yourself first!)
www.earthy.com—many wild and gourmet foods
www.kalustyans.com—spices, cuitlacoche, white soy sauce, and a vast array of other foods
www.ranchogordo.com—cuitlacoche, tequisquite, and great heirloom beans
www.wineforest.com—wild mushrooms, cuitlacoche, foods, rubs, seasonings, dried mushrooms, elderberry shrub, truffle oil, etc.

Index of Vegetarian Recipes

Index of General Recipes

mushrooms, cooking (cont'd)
  roasting, 329
  sautéing, 328
mushroom stocks (Traditional
    Mushroom Stock, Fish-Friendly
    Mushroom Stock) 315
mussel and fiddlehead soup, Todd
    Humphries's, 33–34

N

nettle malfatti with brown butter,
    lemon, and Parmesan, 47–49
nopales:
  "grilled cheese" paddles with salsa
    fresca, 110–11
  and heirloom tomato salad with
    epazote, Steve Sando's, 108

O

onions, caramelized:
  Gerber's porcini panini with teleme
    and, 186–88
  and hedgehog mushroom tart,
    270–71
oxtail broth, cauliflower mushrooms
    in, 212–13

P

panini, porcini, with teleme and
    caramelized onions, Gerber's,
    186–88
panna cotta, elderflower, with
    elderflower syrup, 68–69
pappardelle with blewits, pearl onions,
    and celery root, 160–61
Parmesan, nettle malfatti with brown
    butter, lemon and, 47–49
persimmon(s):
  -infused vinegar, 318
  praline trifle, 290–91
  pudding with brandy hard sauce,
    Connie's favorite, 294–95
pesto, ramp, 308
pickles, pickling, 311
pistachio and rose hip baklava,
    167–69

pizzetta, maitake, 196–97
polenta, soft, 140
porcini, 326
  butter, 319
  -dusted rib eye with porcini butter
    and grilled porcini, 189
  panini with teleme and caramelized
    onions, 186–88
  powder, 312
  salt, 314
pork:
  loin, juniper-rubbed, with prunes
    and savoy cabbage, 222–24
  shoulder, milk-braised, with yellow
    foot mushrooms, 277–79
potato(es):
  and sea bean salad, Auntie
    Nemo's, 119
  Yukon Gold, and black trumpet
    mushroom gratin, 258–59
pot pie, turkey and hedgehog
    mushroom, 267–69
poultry:
  bacon-wrapped duck-stuffed
    morels, 93–94
  fennel pollen rub for fish and, 314
  grilled quail with chanterelles,
    pancetta, and soft polenta,
    138–41
  hedgehog mushroom and turkey
    pot pie, 267–69
  juniper-and-maple-glazed duck,
    220–21
praline persimmon trifle, 290–91
prickly pear Pavlova, 301–2
prunes, juniper-rubbed pork loin with
    savoy cabbage and, 222–24
pudding, Connie's favorite
    persimmon, with brandy hard
    sauce, 294–95
puffball steaks, chicken-fried, with
    creamy mushroom gravy,
    148–49
purslane salad with hot bacon
    vinaigrette and garlic croutons,
    60–61

Q

quail, grilled, with chanterelles,
    pancetta, and soft polenta,
    138–41
quesadilla, cuitlacoche and squash
    blossom, 153–55

R

ramp(s):
  butter, 319
  fiddleheads, and asparagus fritto
    misto with Meyer lemon aioli,
    35–37
  and goat cheese soufflés, twice-
    baked, 24–25
  pesto, 308
  pickled, 311
  and shrimp grits, 22–23
  -up Sunday brunch scrambled
    eggs, 27
relish, Johnny's marinated mushroom,
    309
rib-eye, porcini-dusted, with porcini
    butter and grilled porcini, 189
risotto, "poor man's truffle," 256–57
rose hip(s):
  -infused vinegar, 317
  and pistachio baklava, 167–69
  syrup, 321
rubs, (Wine Forest Mushroom Rub,
    Juniper Berry Rub for Meat and
    Game, Fennel Pollen Rub for Fish
    and Poultry), 312, 314

S

salads:
  Auntie Nemo's sea bean and
    potato, 119
  purslane, with hot bacon vinaigrette
    and garlic croutons, 60–61
  Sarah's seaside sea bean and
    seared tuna, 115–16
  Steve Sando's nopales and
    heirloom tomato, with epazote,
    108

wild spring greens, with creamy chive dressing, 59

salmon, pan-roasted wild, with morels and fava beans, 12–13

salts, flavored (Porcini Salt, Fennel Salt, Douglas Fir or Spruce Tip Salt), 314

sauces:
  bourbon caramel, 246
  brandy hard, Connie's favorite persimmon pudding with, 294–95
  elderberry port, spice-roasted venison with, 230–31
  hollandaise, lobster mushroom and rock shrimp eggs Benedict with, 75–77
  Meyer lemon aioli, fritto misto of fiddleheads, ramps, and asparagus with, 35–37
  morel and cacao, Mateo's roasted veal chop with, 16–17
  salsa fresca, nopales "grilled cheese" paddles with, 110–11

savory spreads and condiments, 308–9
  black trumpet mushroom tapenade, 308
  Johnny's marinated mushroom relish, 309
  ramp pesto, 308

savoy cabbage, juniper-rubbed pork loin with prunes and, 222–24

sea bean(s):
  pickled, 311
  and potato salad, Auntie Nemo's, 119
  and seared tuna salad, Sarah's seaside, 115–16

seafood:
  fennel-dusted halibut with wild fennel broth, 102–3
  pan-roasted wild salmon with morels and fava beans, 12–13
  ramp and shrimp grits, 22–23

rock shrimp and lobster mushroom eggs Benedict with dazzling hollandaise, 75–77

Sarah's seaside sea bean and seared tuna salad, 115–16

Todd Humphries's fiddlehead and mussel soup, 33–34

short rib-stuffed morels, braised, Sean O'Toole's, 90–92

shrimp:
  and ramp grits, 22–23
  rock, and lobster mushroom eggs Benedict with dazzling hollandaise, 75–76

shrub, elderberry, 324

soufflés, twice-baked ramp and goat cheese, 24–25

soups:
  classic meadow mushroom, with wild mushroom and herbed ricotta tartines, 82–83
  cuitlacoche, with crema mexicana spiral, 156–57
  luscious chanterelle and corn chowder, 137
  morel and toasted rye bread, 8–9
  Todd Humphries's fiddlehead and mussel, 33–34
  see also broths; mushroom stocks

spring rolls, cauliflower mushroom and king trumpet, 214–15

spruce tip(s):
  salt, 314
  syrup, 321
  syrup, buckwheat waffles with, 42
  vodka, 324

squash blossom and cuitlacoche quesadilla, 153–55

stocks. See mushroom stocks

stuffing, hedgehog mushroom, leek, and chestnut, 272–73

sugar, candy cap, 322

sundae, bourbon black walnut, 246

syrups:
  elderberry, 234

elderflower, elderflower panna cotta with, 68–69

rose hip, 321

spruce or Douglas fir tip, 321

T

tapenade, black trumpet mushroom, 308

tart, hedgehog mushroom and caramelized onion, 270–71

tartines, wild mushroom and herbed ricotta, 83

teleme, Gerber's porcini panini with caramelized onions and, 186–88

trifle, persimmon praline, 290–91

tuna, seared, and sea bean salad, Sarah's seaside, 115–16

turkey and hedgehog mushroom pot pie, 267–69

V

veal chop with morel and cacao sauce, Mateo's roasted, 16–17

vegetarian recipe index, 337

venison, spice-roasted, with elderberry port sauce, 230–31

vinaigrette. See dressings

vinegars, infused, 317, 318

vodka:
  chanterelle, 322
  spruce or Douglas fir needle, 324
  wild fruit, 322

W

waffles, buckwheat, with spruce tip syrup, 42

white chocolate and huckleberry blondies, Nicole Plue's, 177

white soy, foil-wrapped matsutake with ginger and, 205

Y

yellow foot mushrooms, milk-braised pork shoulder with, 277–79

Index